If you had
planned
to irritate and
frustrate this
reader with your
"new" layout,
be assured that
you have done
so beyond
your wildest
expectations.

The Atlantic 1981

RECEIVED MY AUGUST
15 COPY OF *TIME* ▪
I HATE YOUR NEW
FORMAT ▪ THE LINES
ARE REMINISCENT
OF CHEAP TABLOIDS ▪
SITTING OF YOUR
COVER SUBJECT ▪
WHO GAVE YOU SUCH
A LOUSY IDEA ▪
WHOEVER IT WAS
MUST HAVE FLUNKED
ART CLASSES IN
HIGH SCHOOL ▪ IT
ALMOST MAKES ME
WANT TO CANCEL
MY SUBSCRIPTION ▪
ITS ICKY LOOKING

Time 1977

Just
received
the April
issue.
Why, why
did you
do it?

The Atlantic 1981

The new format
caused me
considerable
distress. Gone
is that sleek
and yet relaxing
magazine. You
now resemble
one of those
magazines like
Newsweek or
U.S. News.

Fortune 1983

New York magazine, 1974

FIFTY YEARS OF MAKING MAGAZINES

MAG

WALTER BERNARD & MILTON GLASER

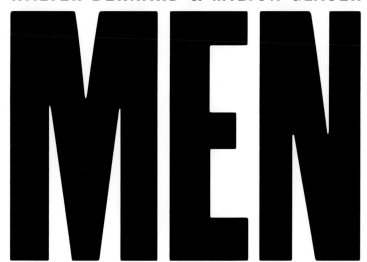

MEN

FOREWORD BY GLORIA STEINEM

Columbia University Press

New York

Staff for this book

Anne Quito
WRITER / EDITOR

Fausta Kingué
DESIGN

Natalia Olbinski
DESIGN

Bina Bernard
CONTRIBUTING EDITOR

Richard Litell
CONTRIBUTING EDITOR

Tina Buckman
PICTURE RESEARCH

Aimee Pong
Ivana Vasic
DESIGN ASSISTANTS

For Clay Felker

Columbia University Press
Publishers Since 1893
New York   Chichester, West Sussex
cup.columbia.edu

Library of Congress Cataloging-in-Publication Data
Names: Bernard, Walter, 1937- author. | Glaser, Milton, author.
Title: Mag men / Walter Bernard, Milton Glaser.
Description: [New York, New York] : Columbia University Press,
  [2019] | Includes index.
Identifiers: LCCN 2019025483 (print) | LCCN 2019025484 (ebook)
  ISBN 9780231191807 (cloth) | ISBN 9780231549530 (ebook)
Subjects: LCSH: Bernard, Walter, 1937- | Glaser, Milton.
  Graphic artists –United States –Biography.
  Magazine design –United States –History.
  Graphic design (Typography) –United States –History.
Classification: LCC Z246.5.M34 B47 2019 (print)
  LCC Z246.5.M34 (ebook)
  DDC 741.6/520922 [B] –dc23
LC record available at https://lccn.loc.gov/2019025483
LC ebook record available at https://lccn.loc.gov/2019025484

Columbia University Press books are printed
on permanent and durable acid-free paper.
Printed in Canada

Page 1 photo by Cosmos Sarchiapone

In the fall of 1938, when I was thirteen and living in a small pension in Versailles with my family (who were refugees from Nazi-occupied Austria), my father's bachelor uncle came to visit from London. He had brought with him the current issue of *Esquire* magazine and forgot it in his room when he left. I found it later and carried it with me through France, Morocco, and to New York. I loved the feel of the glossy paper, the smell of the printed pages, the girls, the serious writing. On bad days I opened that magazine and a promise of a wonderful sort of life emanated from its pages like a seductive perfume.

—Henry Wolf

Henry Wolf (1925–2005) was one of the twentieth century's great art directors. He brought elegance and wit to his brilliant designs for *Esquire, Harper's Bazaar,* and *Show* magazines.

207 East Thirty-Second Street,
New York City

CHAPTERS

Foreword

If, tomorrow, I had to choose just one medium, it would be magazines. They have more depth and visual pleasure than newspapers, more availability on the street than books, and less expense and more fact-checking than the Internet. I definitely would opt for the joys of magazines.

Also, if I had to name the kind of group that gave me the most learning, fun, and new ideas, it would be an editorial meeting of a magazine. There is something about word and visual people sitting together in a room, riffing off each other's ideas like jazz musicians, arguing and coming up with a result that no one of us would have imagined on our own. It's as much a proof of freedom as laughter, which is also a mark of edtorial meetings.

I learned most of this thanks to Clay Felker, Milton Glaser, Walter Bernard, and the creation of *New York* magazine. There we had the excitement and challenge of trying to capture on our pages the spirit of this city we love. We also had the added challenge of being the first of the city magazines and of raising enough money to start this new venture.

That was good for us, too. Because we had to endlessly explain what we wanted to do, this caused us to discover and plan what we really did want to do.

From the beginning, Milton and Walter were the creative ones who cared about both words and images. We, the word people, might have sacrificed images to get more words, but these two understood the importance of both. They even attended to the subtleties of typefaces right along with photography and illustration.

I'm grateful to both of them for this book that passes on the excitement and learning at magazines—errors, victories, and everything in between. I know that *Mag Men* will inspire future word-and-image creations that we can't even imagine right now.

And when that happens, we will all be in an editorial meeting together.

—Gloria Steinem

Introduction
An Interview by Anne Quito

A magazine is designed to arrive in our hands as a perfect package. Whether a school publication or a major newsstand periodical, a magazine offers a lively assortment of items that seem to come together seamlessly. Of course, this is an illusion, as Walter Bernard and Milton Glaser will quickly tell you. The award-winning graphic designers, who have worked on over 100 publications, know that each issue involves an enormous amount of teamwork, logistics, and luck. What follows is my interview with Walter and Milton about their five decades in the business.

When did you first become interested in designing magazines?

Walter Bernard: After a long day's work as a carpenter, my father relaxed by reading the *Saturday Evening Post* and *Life* magazine after dinner. I remember snatching them up as soon as he was done. We had no TV until I was a teenager, so those magazines showed me the world beyond New Jersey. What thrilled me the most were the famous illustrators of the period: Norman Rockwell, Stevan Dohanos, Albert Dorne, Edwin Georgi, Constantin Alajalov, and many others.

Milton Glaser: My introduction to magazines came via comic books. A lot of kids got interested in design and illustration because of comic books. You might say they were once a big educational force. I learned to draw by copying comics like *Smokey Stover* and *Superman*. Growing up, I also read *Liberty*, the *Saturday Evening Post*, *Reader's Digest,* and all the things that fueled America through those years. I didn't specifically pursue magazine design, but the first professional job I held was at Condé Nast. Figuring out the dynamic between words and images has always been fascinating, but I knew early on that my interests went beyond designing publications.

How did the two of you meet?

WB: As a student, I knew of Milton from his many illustrations on paperback book covers. We first met when I took a night class at the School of Visual Arts that he and Henry Wolf taught. They were both very good teachers, but Milton was more articulate, with the capacity to explain things more fully.

Why begin this book with a quote from Henry Wolf?

WB: I think it explains how someone falls in love with magazines. Henry Wolf was the greatest magazine art director of that time. His work was clever, whimsical, and extremely elegant. As a regular *Esquire* reader, I dreamt of working for him. I never got that chance, but Henry did help me get a job at *Esquire* with Sam Antupit, who succeeded him.

MG: Henry and I were very good friends, but it's almost funny that we ended up teaching a design class together because our aesthetic was very different. We often argued about how things should be done, though to some degree he mentored me, too. He loved the magazine business and did beautiful layouts. I learned a lot from him.

How did you get to work together at *New York* magazine?

MG: I was running Push Pin Studios with Seymour Chwast at the time and *New York* was one among many projects. As a weekly, it needed ongoing attention every day, and there was a problem of producing the ideas that we had. I knew Walter and knew that he could produce magazines of a professional quality that few people could achieve. I believed that we could work successfully together. I hired him to assist me in executing the magazine in the beginning, but eventually we shared that responsibility.

WB: I was in my fourth year at *Esquire* magazine in 1968 when the call came. I was hoping I would hear from Henry Wolf. To my surprise it was Milton, asking if I'd be interested in working with him at *New York*—an offer I couldn't refuse. I came on board and began our nine-year adventure. Those fruitful years working together gave us the idea of forming a publication design studio in 1982. We called it WBMG (our initials), which in retrospect sounded like a radio station.

Before desktop publishing, how did it all get done on time?

WB: Magazines were certainly produced by hand. We specified type, pasted up layouts, and corrected mistakes by inserting missing characters with glue and tweezers. I remember one closing night, Gloria Steinem was with us editing her George McGovern story to fit. With no time to reset the manuscript, we made the corrections by hand, letter by letter. In those pre-computer days, producing an issue involved complex logistics. For example, at *New York* magazine, our close was early enough on Thursday so someone could make a train to our printer in Philadelphia. At *Time* magazine, our couriers took a flight to Chicago twice a week to hand-carry the mechanicals to our printers. In fact, we prepared a duplicate packet of the entire issue in case anything went wrong in transit.

You have helped shape magazines about politics, advertising, literature, business, sports, fashion, even pregnancy. How did you find a way into such a diverse range of topics?

WB: In all cases, you learn about any subject from a strong editor. True, some art directors have a flair for particular topics because of their personal interest. Designing a sports magazine might have bored Milton, but it was exciting for me. But a knowledgeable editor with a strong point of view can guide you to developing an appropriate design. *New York* magazine, being the eclectic publication that it was, also served as a great training ground. In addition to covering politics and culture, there were articles about food, shopping, real estate, and crime that made it into the main well. We worked in an open space like a newsroom. Editors, writers, and designers mingled and learned from each other.

As consultants to magazines, how did you navigate the internal politics of established publications?

MG: Our personal friendships with clients helped. Sir James Goldsmith, a dear friend of mine, owned *L'Express* and *Lire*. He introduced us to the staff, which made things smoother. The same goes for Katherine Graham, whom I met through Clay Felker. Knowing that we had her support gave us confidence when working on the redesign of *The Washington Post*.

WB: We always emphasized that we were there to help. Occasionally we were asked to evaluate the design staff, but we always tried to convey that we were there to support them. We were in and out of projects fairly quickly, so we did not get involved in office politics. *The Washington Post* was an exception. Our involvement lasted for over a year. Ben Bradlee, the executive editor, and Donald Graham, the publisher, asked me to spend several months listening to every editor in each department. Shelby Coffey III, the deputy managing editor, arranged for me to meet with the typesetters, sales people, pressmen, and delivery truck drivers. Bradlee and Graham wanted me to know everyone and for everyone to know me. It really did help to smooth the way.

Collaboration is a major theme of this book. Why?

WB: Because it is an essential part of magazine work. The art department is like a kitchen, where all the ingredients and the cooks come together. This is often where decisions are made, negotiations take place, arguments are resolved, and ideas are exchanged. If you wanted to see how an issue was progressing, you would go into the art department. At *New York* magazine, for example, our large flat filing cabinets—like a big kitchen table—served as an informal gathering place where discussions flourished.

MG: At *New York* especially, it was a sense of collaboration that bound us and made the experience so satisfying. In some ways, we retain a relationship to all of those who ever worked there. We shared that moment in time; the sense of purpose and affection made us a community.

WBMG's managing editor, Killian Jordan, says your greatest strength was that you took: "a full-bore approach to every project." Was that always appreciated by editors?

WB: We were a small studio and we only took a few magazine projects at a time. We usually had one major project and several minor ones. This means we could really pay attention to each, and work closely with the editors. For every magazine project we took on, we can honestly say that we designed it and didn't simply pass all responsibility to our staff. Our clients expected that when they hired WBMG they were really working with W. B. and M. G.

What other projects did you work on at WBMG?

WB: Aside from magazines, we have designed five major newspapers: *The Washington Post*, *Barron's*, *La Vanguardia* (Barcelona), *ABC* (Madrid), and *O Globo* (Rio de Janeiro). We also designed several books. The most ambitious one was *Our Times: An Illustrated History of the 20th Century*, edited by Lorraine Glennon and Daniel Okrent. Our former *New York* magazine colleague Nora Ephron got us to venture into designing film titles. We enjoyed working on the title sequence for five of her films, including *Sleepless in Seattle* and *You've Got Mail*. There is a common thread through all these projects. They all deal with the news and storytelling.

How do you handle criticism?

MG: I'm interested in solving a problem and communicating information clearly. If you can orient the conversation to be about ideas, then you can avoid reducing everything to an ego issue. Sometimes you meet people who are forceful, intelligent, and respectful. They can lead you to do better work.

WB: I think criticism is informative. I still have a thick folder of reader mail—handwritten notes, faxes, telegrams—reacting to the 1977 redesign of *Time* magazine. It's amusing to read them now, but I remember management made sure that I saw every piece of feedback that arrived because they were nervous about all the changes we had made. One time, a reader actually got through the switchboard. I picked up the phone and heard an irate subscriber complain that he couldn't find a thing in the "confusing" new format. I suggested we go through the issue together. In the course of doing so, he decided the magazine was slowly improving and wished me luck. You are never happy to hear anything bad about your work, but there's always another issue to prepare and you have to move on.

How do you design for the short attention span of readers?

MG: When we were working at *New York* magazine in the 1970s, we learned that the attention span for uninterrupted reading of most people then hovered around seven minutes. This coincided with the length of two commercial breaks in most TV programs. We designed features to be read by somebody with the temperament of the so-called "TV generation." The design of *New York* had constant interruptions—headlines, subheads, drawings, jokes— all to prevent reader fatigue and loss of attentiveness. There's a psychic load in the mere act of turning a page. I'm familiar with the anxiety that piles of beautiful, unread magazines bring to people. Magazines tend to accumulate in my own house. I always resolve to thumb through them. The truth is, I rarely do. It's a matter of discretionary time.

Do you think it's essential for graphic designers to be good readers?

MG: Absolutely. Reading inspires a respect for language. That balance between narrative and visualization is critical. It's true you can be a gifted artist without ever reading. There's no exact correlation. But for magazine designers, you have to at least get the gist of the article to know what you're dealing with. In art school, they very rarely ask you to read books, but these are a few I recommend to my students: *Art and Illusion: A Study in the Psychology of Pictorial Representation* by E. H. Gombrich, *Ways of Seeing* by John Berger, and *The Gift: Creativity and the Artist in the Modern World* by Lewis Hyde. I believe you have to read the stuff that ultimately nourishes you.

Are print magazines still important today?

WB: Yes, but in a different way. Magazine and newspaper reporting still drives the culture and provides source material for the online media and television. But huge audiences are no longer reading the same issue at the same time like they did in the 1950s or 1960s. These days, magazines need their own online presence to gain readership and attract advertisers.

MG: Advertising in magazines has diminished because print doesn't offer the interactive dimension that electronic channels do. But the reason print remains interesting is you respond to it differently. First of all, its permanence gives you a sense that it's more important and that it is retainable. This is the element that keeps print alive. Sometimes, the material you read is so satisfying that you want to hold on to it. Of course, this is not always the case because there's a lot of trivia in magazines today. The role of magazines shifted from providing understanding to entertainment. That's a big change. Almost everything in our culture today is about entertainment—the presidency is about entertainment. We shouldn't misunderstand what that means.

So do you hold on to old magazines?

MG: I've been increasingly throwing away more stuff. It's a process that feels both sad and exhilarating at the same time. It's great to get rid of all the stuff that no longer means anything to you. In doing so, you get to examine your understanding of "meaning." That reinforces some idea you have about your own historical past that you want to retain. Outside of that, there's almost no reason for keeping anything.

It's an attitude I now have about books. They're going into the landfills and they will bury us all. What you have to do is to find books that sustain your interest, the way a painting does. A great painting is always interesting, no matter how many times you pass it. This is what I'd like to try to do with books; to make a book that always has available something new to say each time you open it. That makes the book mutable—a live object.

What do you hope the reader takes away from this book?

WB & MG: This book chronicles our experience working with the many talented people who make magazines happen. We celebrate over ninety artists, writers, photographers, and editors who worked with us over the years. The work in this volume includes selections from our nine years at *New York* magazine, our time working separately, and the many years working together as "magazine doctors" at WBMG. Occasionally, we have each written a separate text, with individual initial bylines, but most of the book is in our collective voice.

We have tried to include successes and failures—some hits but also swings and misses. Along with an emphasis on graphics, we recount stories and observations from our many colleagues who contributed to the material in this book. Magazines are not created in a vacuum. External forces affect editors, writers, and readers. "In the News" items found throughout this book recall contemporary events, large and small, to help place the magazine story in a historical context. On its most fundamental level, a magazine is a collection of energy and information. We hope the reader will take away an appreciation for the complexity, invention, and joy it takes to produce a good one.

We began working together on July 1, 1968. The pace was hectic from the start, but we quickly found our stride as art director and design director. With lean budgets and a brilliant staff, we managed to produce a weekly magazine that, if far from perfect, had a real impact on the city and beyond. What follows is a close look into the inner workings at *New York*: the thinking behind most graphic decisions, including some clever ideas and some stupid mistakes.

***New York* Magazine**

CHAPTER

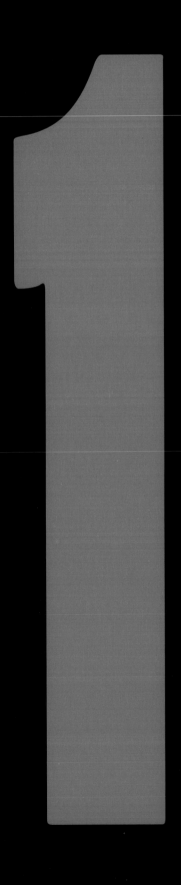

"Shall We Start a New Magazine?"

My wife, Shirley, reminded me that one night, at our home, Clay Felker and I were talking about our plans to start a magazine based on the *New York* Sunday supplement that had folded a few weeks earlier, along with the rest of *The World Journal Tribune.*

"Why don't you ask the *I Ching* for advice?" Shirley asked. (It was the sixties, after all.) We had gotten into the habit of asking the Chinese *Book of Changes* for guidance every time we had a deep question. I still have the book, carefully wrapped in a silk scarf. I unwrapped it recently and found a slip of paper inside. I had written, "Clay and Milton: shall we start a new magazine?"

We threw coins, which led us to hexagram number 48: The Well. The judgment read: *The Well. The town may be changed, but the well cannot be changed. It neither decreases nor increases. They come and go and draw from the well. If one gets down almost to the water and the rope does not go all the way or the jug breaks, it brings misfortune.*

And then, following this elliptical message, the symbolic image: water over wood, the image of the well. *Thus, the superior man encourages the people at their work and exhorts them to help one another.*

For whatever reason, that sounded encouraging to us, and we resolved to push forward.

The first year was the best and the worst. We were in a building I owned on East Thirty-Second Street. It was a four-story walk-up and we, of course, were on the top floor. When I think of Ruth Gilbert, our "Around Town" editor, walking up the stairs, in her late sixties, and weighing over 310 pounds, struggling to arrive at her desk each day, it brings tears to my eyes.

There were forty men and women desperately crowded on that floor with a single, non-gender-specific bathroom. The skylight leaked when it rained and in cold weather, everyone worked in overcoats and gloves, which may account, in part, for the number of spelling errors that turned up in every issue. Clay had the only office, as befits an editor-in-chief, that was the size of a broom closet with a decrepit brown leather couch he'd brought from home. The room had a door, but no ceiling, so any private conversation was heard by the entire staff.

We were an unlikely partnership. I was born in the Bronx, the son of immigrants from Hungary. Clay was from St. Louis, obsessed with sports and journalism. My feet take size 15 shoes and are as flat as a tabletop. Clay's feet were tiny with the highest arch imaginable. Between the two of us, we represented almost the entire range of human possibilities in regard to the male foot.

Inevitably, we had different views of the city. I loved the Lower East Side—cheap food and left-wing politics. Clay, with his outsider curiosity, was obsessed with the city's power establishment and the lives of the rich, the talented, and the perverse. Although, truthfully, I can't think of anything Clay wasn't interested in, except perhaps introspection.

Clay was a man of action who experienced the world viscerally, through his gut. His intuition led him to identify writing talent. Like few other editors in our time, I never heard him actually say, "I'll make you a star" to anyone, but that was a promise he could actually deliver on.

Clay's operating theory was constant disequilibrium. You might be working on a piece for a month and when you thought it was done, Clay would cut it in half, change the point of view, or abandon it entirely. He would create a new cover story three hours before deadline. He created an atmosphere of excitement and anxiety that attracted an extraordinary community of talent. As someone said about Picasso, "An idea wasn't safe when Clay was in the room." Clay's enthusiasm for a sound piece of work—whether it was a photograph, a drawing, or a piece of writing—brought out the best in people. He would shout with pleasure on such occasions, often frightening a new staff member. On the other hand, Clay and I would often have shouting matches in the middle of the office. (There were no doors to close.) This was not a good business practice, but everyone got used to it.

In retrospect, I realized that the arguments were always about the same thing. "Make it bigger" was Clay's most frequently recurring phrase. No matter what it was—a photograph, the text type, the headline, the pull quotes—Clay's reaction to any layout was always the same, "Make it bigger." My standard response, before I lapsed into profanity, was always, "When everything is big, nothing is big," a clever response that did me no good.

Clay always wanted everything to be bigger—big headlines, big events, big changes, and big ideas. He made our city more interesting to all of us who live here, which is not the same as making it glamorous for visitors. Paradoxically, those of us who were born here need others, drawn to this magic city from outside, to help us see it. Clay did this for us, and all of us within his circle of work and friendship were changed by the experience and have led bigger lives because of it.—MG

COFOUNDERS
Milton Glaser and Clay
Felker confer in Clay's
office in the early 1970s.
Photo by Cosmos Sarchiapone

CLAY FELKER (1925–2008)
is widely credited with
inventing the template
for the modern magazine.
The son of editors from
Webster Groves, Missouri,
Clay dedicated his entire
career to the printed word.
Aside from cofounding
New York in 1968, he
helped shape numerous
publications such as *Life*,
Sports Illustrated, *Esquire*,
the *Village Voice*, and
Adweek. He was an ardent
champion of "New Journal-
ism," a compelling style
of news writing that borrows
from literary techniques.

IN THE NEWS items found throughout this book recall contemporary events, large and small, to help place the accompanying story in the proper time frame.

Martin Luther King, Jr. Assassinated
On April 4, 1968, while standing on the balcony outside room 306 of the Lorraine Motel in Memphis, Tennessee, talking to Jesse Jackson in the courtyard below, Martin Luther King, Jr., was shot on the right side of his neck by James Earl Ray. King was taken to St. Joseph Hospital, where he was pronounced dead at 7:05 p.m. CST.

Kubrick's Film Released
2001: A Space Odyssey was released on April 3, 1968. It became the biggest money maker of the year.

Revealing the Heart of the City

How a beloved Sunday newspaper supplement evolved into a stand-alone magazine

A TYPICAL COVER of *New York* when it was a Sunday supplement (left). The "scenes of the city" theme worked brilliantly in the newspaper and influenced the cover look of the first issue of *New York* magazine (opposite). However, "scenes" did not work well on the cover of a stand-alone weekly.

Having lived in New York all my life, I totally identified with all the aspects of the city, especially with its working people. *New York* magazine was originally a Sunday supplement in the *New York Herald Tribune*. In our version, Clay and I tried to compensate for what we thought was missing from the *Trib*'s coverage, which was a more local feeling. There were whole sections of New York that were left undiscovered. Clay, on the other hand, was looking at the power players in politics, business, entertainment, fashion, etc. Together we covered a lot of ground.

The magazine was really about the heart of the city and the people you wouldn't think about because they weren't in the spotlight.

At the *Tribune*, *New York*'s covers didn't have to work so hard. They often used artful photographs of the city with hardly any cover lines. We admired many aspects of Peter Palazzo's design, so we thought to continue this tradition. After much discussion, our first issue launched with a view of the city as photographed by Jay Maisel on the cover. In retrospect, it looks weak, in both how thinly the logo is drawn and the rather distant view of the New York skyline. It wasn't exactly a dramatic first issue that would knock people off their feet. We learned our lessons quickly and would do better in future issues.—MG

PETER PALAZZO (1926–2005) was the design editor of the *Herald Tribune*'s Sunday magazine from 1963 until the *Tribune*'s demise in 1966. Palazzo traded traditional grids for electrifying, reader-friendly layouts. Louis Silverstein, the art director of *The New York Times*, said his work helped "fuel the revolution in newspaper design of the 1960s and 1970s." Peter also had a hand in refreshing the *Chicago Daily News*, *The Providence Journal*, the *Winnipeg Tribune*, and the *Edmonton Journal*.

APRIL 8, 1968

40 CENTS

**Jimmy Breslin on
The Voices of
A City in Trouble**

**Tom Wolfe
Tells If You're
Honk or Wonk**

**Gloria Steinem on
Ho Chi Minh
In New York**

**Clare Boothe Luce on
Kenneth Galbraith's
State Dept. Novel**

Photograph by Jay Maisel

Fifty Years of Tweaking an Icon

We tried to create continuity with the *Herald Tribune*. Though the logo changed slightly over the years, its essential character endures. Does it encapsulate the essence of New York City? We don't think so, but then again, no single thing could.

1963

PETER PALAZZO designed the original logo for the *Herald Tribune*'s New York Sunday supplement. His version was based on Caslon Italic, and he used the Caslon typeface throughout the design of the magazine. He believed in Caslon because of "the instant impression of integrity it gives to the news."

New York magazine logo, 1963

April 8, 1968

MILTON GLASER: "Because the old *New York* logo was contained within the newspaper, it didn't have to sell on the newsstand. When we went from being a newspaper to a magazine, we needed something that was more assertive, more colorful, more visible. For the launch we switched from Caslon to Bookman Swash Italic and thinned out the letterforms. In retrospect, we made a mistake in terms of the impact of the logo. It's really ineffectual as a masthead. After a few issues, we decided to make the letterforms thicker. This was a real functional requirement. It has to be visible on the newsstand at a certain distance, and the old lettering was just too thin."

Three versions of the *New York* magazine logo from 1968 to 1994

1965

18

October 10, 1994

MICHAEL BIERUT, graphic designer: "When Kurt Andersen became editor of *New York* in 1994, he asked me to redesign the logo. I found Bookman Swash Italic unimaginatively ugly back then. Kurt had a copy of the *Herald Tribune* Sunday supplement in his office, and I said we should return to something based on Peter Palazzo's Caslon Italic. I just loved that 'y'! At the time, I distinctly remember saying, 'Bookman Swash Italic is always going to look ugly.' A couple of years ago I saw a book cover that really caught my eye. The title was set in Bookman Swash Italic and it looked just great. Ugly, but great."

New York magazine logo from 1994 to 2004

November 8, 2004

ADAM MOSS, editor-in-chief of *New York* magazine (2004-2019): "I had a visceral reaction to the 'y' letterform in the logo we inherited. I hated it everywhere—including on the roof of our building! I never knew why my allergy was so intense. I loved the original logo, and our project was all about 'restoration,' so it seemed obvious to revisit some version of the original logo. Luke Hayman [Design Director from 2004 to 2006] iterated the logo design, updating its forms and deliberating on its weight and size. The new logo was never meant to have one size. It was meant to be flexible enough to accommodate different cover designs, though it's true that the bleed off the edges has become the default." Before Luke came on board, Paula Scher made the original suggestion to bleed the logo. Ed Benguiat drew the new skinny version. After a few issues it was decided—because of the scale—to go even skinnier.

New York magazine logo from 2004 to present day

A Note About This Typeface

At the launch in April 1968 the magazine used Times Roman for both text and headlines. Typesetting was done at Curtis Publishing in Philadelphia, whose menu of styles was distinctly limited. After unsatisfying experiments with various sans-serif headlines, we finally chose Egyptian Bold Condensed as the only bold face left on the list with some character. As of February 1970, it became a popular signature typeface for the magazine and is still used in its pages today.

2019

Pierre Trudeau Elected
At forty-eight, Pierre Trudeau, Canada's most eligible bachelor, succeeded Conservative Lester B. Pearson to become the country's youngest prime minister, on April 20, 1968. A karate expert, Trudeau liked fast cars, was a flamboyant dresser, and caused Trudeau-mania in his country and in tabloids around the world. He opposed independence for Québec.

***Hair* on Broadway**
Originally performed at the Public Theater, *Hair*—the rock musical that personified the hippie counterculture—opened on Broadway at the Biltmore Theater, on April 29, 1968. No nudity was allowed at the Public Theater, but it was a part of the show on Broadway. The songs, with lyrics by Gerome Ragni and James Rado and music by Galt MacDermot, became the anthem of the antiwar movement.

Our Fourth Issue Nearly Killed the Magazine

A revealing portrait of Andy Warhol's muse by Barbara Goldsmith and Diane Arbus startled readers and scattered advertisers.

Born Janet Susan Mary Hoffmann, Viva is an actress who starred in several of Andy Warhol's "porno chic" films, such as *Blue Movie*, *Tub Girls*, and *The Nude Restaurant*. Barbara Goldsmith's revealing profile of the underground superstar, made vivid by the shocking Diane Arbus photographs, angered Viva so much that she threatened to sue.

Viva was particularly shaken by the photographs because they were apparently taken under false pretenses. She claimed that Arbus told her not to bother getting dressed because she was just shooting above the shoulders.

There was a lot of apprehension about publishing this piece because it was so revealing. The nude that Arbus submitted wasn't really a nude; it was a naked person. A formal nude recalls other nudes in art history, starting with the Renaissance. This was something else. It was a morbid picture of a woman destroying herself.

Many readers canceled their subscriptions. Several advertisers dropped us, and the board threatened to fire Clay. We were in a rather depressed mood during the first few months of the magazine and it took some time to recover. Without knowing the dynamic between Viva and Arbus, I have to say that I was in favor of publishing it. We had to do something that people would talk about. Rather than being invisible and not make a ripple, we chose to make mischief. I still believe that you have to get through the passivity of daily life.—MG

BARBARA GOLDSMITH (1931–2016) was a founding editor of *New York*. She wrote about the city's lively art scene and its colorful personalities. Barbara wrote several well-received books, including *Little Gloria . . . Happy at Last*, a vivid account of the dramatic custody battle for Gloria Vanderbilt. She was a contributor to the New York Public Library's preservation efforts and funded a "PEN/Freedom to Write Award" from 1987 to 2015. In many ways, *New York* could not have launched without her generosity. She lent Clay $6,500 (equivalent to $48,705 in 2019) to obtain the rights to *New York* from the *Herald Tribune* when it closed in 1967.

Photo by Frank Perry

VIVA as a fashion model. Photograph by Lee Kraft

**Gail Sheehy on Why
Commuters Crack Up**

**Barbara Goldsmith on
The Life of a Superstar**

**Cleveland Amory on
A Nation of Hawks**

New York

STICKBALL IN THE SPRING We were still following the *Herald Tribune* style on our covers. Photograph by Richard Kelly

DIANE ARBUS (1923–1971) began her career in 1946 working in partnership with her husband, Allan, as commercial photographers. In 1956 she began working on her own. She gained recognition as a prominent photographer in 1960. Diane turned her sympathetic lens to the city's "freaks" and produced some of the most indelible portraits of people living on the edge of society. Diane suffered from depression throughout her life. Art historians argue that her suicide in 1971 tainted her legacy. However, *The New York Times* published an obituary in its "Overlooked" series honoring Arbus in 2018, forty-six years after she passed away.

est. People hesitate, a girl covers up her breasts because she is embarrassed to show them to you. In Andy's movies people are honest and frank and open. Most people aren't like that at all. Like my parents, everything in their lives is structured by their religion and their politics and their social relationships and anything that doesn't agree with what they think is wrong. Anyway, this whole Puritan atmosphere has one advantage . . . it makes everything seem more exciting when you break away from it.

". . . 'The whole Puritan thing at home has one advantage: it makes everything seem exciting when you break away' . . ."

"I don't put my parents down, though. They had nine kids and the kids are all against everything my parents stand for so they couldn't have done everything wrong. If they had, the kids would just be carbon copies of them."

Viva stood up, tripped over a cup, kicked at it and said angrily, "I can't stand this place. You'd think I'd move to the country, right? Right. But I don't. Who am I going to talk to? Almost all my friends are around The Factory. It's just easier to live here and I'm away on college lecture tours with Andy a lot of the time. We pick up a lot of kids on those college tours. That's where we got Tom Hompertz. We show part of our 25-hour movie and we speak to the kids. We tell them we don't believe in goals, no goals, no purpose. We don't believe in art. Everything is art. The only point is to make a movie to entertain.

"I'm nude because Andy says seeing me nude sells tickets. It's hard to believe. I think I look like a parody, a satire on a nude, a plucked chicken. Since I got an I.U.D. (intrauterine device) and stopped taking birth control pills, I don't even have any breasts. But lately I've gotten a lot of attention and publicity. Some dumb reporter said 'Viva has dropped out of the rat race.' A lot she knows. I've just entered the rat race, I want money and I guess a career. Trying to plan ahead puts me in a terrible state. I can tell you what I'm doing at the moment, but if I think about the future I get all neurotic.

"I have Andy now to think ahead and make the decisions. I just do what he tells me to do. Andy has a certain mystique that makes you want to do things for him." Viva looked up, her eyes blank. Then she said slowly "Sometimes though when I think about Andy, I think he is just like Satan. He just gets you and you can't get away. I used to go everywhere by myself. Now I can't seem to go anywhere or make the simplest decision without Andy. He has such a hold on all of us. But I love it when they talk about Andy and Viva."

The names coupled that way made me think of a time when it was Andy and Edie, so I asked "What happened to 'Superstar' Edie Sedgwick?" "Oh," said Viva, circling her lips with the point of her tongue in a nervous mannerism, "Edie looks fabulous. I visited her in the hospital. She's been there for a long time. I brought her a cactus plant because of its shape. They kept a nurse in the room with us the whole time because before I visited somebody gave her an amphetamine."

Viva stood up and took off her slacks. She kneeled before me, naked from the waist down, and began searching through the pile of clothes on the floor. "I've got to go as soon as I find something to wear," she said. "*Eye* magazine is making an official group photograph and they need me."

At Max's Kansas City, after the photography session, Viva, Warhol and Ingrid Superstar and Brigid Polk, both of whom are featured in Warhol movies, sat at a large round table in the corner. The restaurant accords them celebrity status; Viva sent back her fish, then a steak, meanwhile sniffing methedrine off a spoon. "*I* take it every three hours," Brigid said. "Don't let anybody tell you speed kills. I've been on it for years."

"I just got out of the hospital," Ingrid Superstar said, "and I'm all set for action." She held up a packet of condoms.

Brigid said, "Excuse me for a minute, it's time to wake myself up," and she headed for the ladies' room.

Viva put her head on the table. "I'm so tired and this place is depressing me." She picked up her bag and left.

Later, Viva returned to The Factory, a loft in a business building. The downstairs door was locked. Viva looked for a telephone to summon someone to open the door. The first five booths had been vandalized and were inoperative. From the sixth she grated "Listen you bastard, this is Viva. Get down here fast and open that goddamned door." Incredulous, she stared at the phone. "He hung up," she said. Viva then dialed Warhol's home number and got the answering service. The voice asked if she would like to leave a message. "Yes," she said and proceeded to express it. The answering service hung up.

Viva flung the phone across the booth and walked back to the locked door to wait for somebody to come in or go out. "I'll show them," she raged. "They locked me out, and I'm going to lock them in." With a dime and a bobby pin she attempted to remove the doorknob.

During this operation Warhol arrived. "Why don't I have a key to this place?" Viva shouted. "I'm not treated with any respect around here." Warhol regarded her, bland as farina, whereupon she flung her handbag at him catching him across the side of the face. "You're crazy, Viva" he said dispassionately. "What do you think you're doing?" ▬

Photograph by Diane Arbus

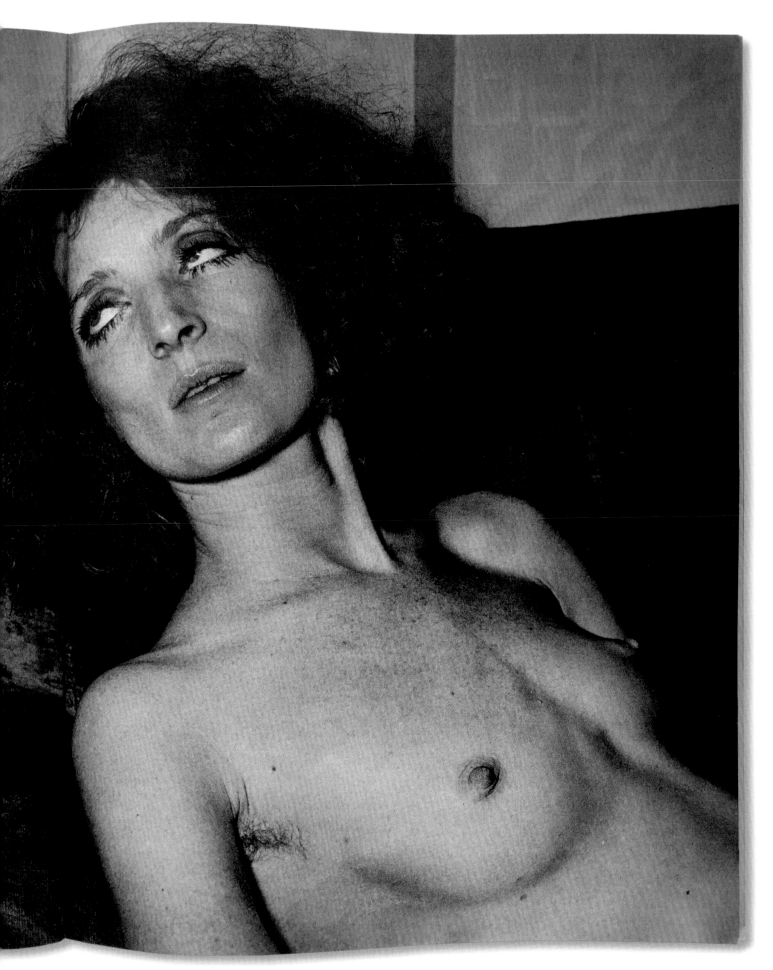

WALTER AND MILTON
in the *New York* magazine
office circa 1972.
Photo by Cosmos Sarchiapone

Secrets in Plain Sight

THE LIGHTS of the San Gennaro Festival on the cover (left). Scenes from the Mulberry Street neighborhood (left and opposite) observed by Robert Weaver.

Nicholas Pileggi's reporting and Robert Weaver's drawings combined to produce an incisive portrait of Little Italy.

Journalist Nicholas Pileggi opened the doors to Manhattan's confounding and secretive Little Italy district. A self-described amateur sociologist à la Margaret Mead on Samoa, he liked to roam New York's streets on foot, which gave him an unrivaled intimacy with various ethnic neighborhoods.

Nick's portrayal of the inner politics of the so-called Italian ghetto was particularly vivid. He wrote: "To a stranger, the neigh-borhood might appear overcrowded, its inhabitants unnecessarily loud, its children overtly rude, its sidewalks and gutters littered with garbage, partially burnt mattresses, broken toys and occa-sional bodies. To the local Italians, however, these streets, with all their confusion and color serve as a vast baroque tapestry against which the players can find both comfort and privacy to act out their traditional medieval roles."

"They used to call the neighborhood 'the artichoke,'" he told *The Guardian* in 2012. "They kept it very tight. Everything inside the artichoke was home base, everything outside was prey. Be-cause I knew some of them and I would talk to them, they would tell you things about the other crew, and then I would talk to the other crew. I became early on a transmitter of gossip."

Knowing that it would be difficult to take photographs in Little Italy, we asked Robert Weaver to sketch scenes from around the neighborhood. He and Nick shared that love of the "pedestrian view." An astute reportage artist, Robert captured the spirit of the vibrant community, filled with drama, color, and noise.

Happily, his colored-pencil illustrations were able to be repro-duced accurately, in contrast to our usual poor printing quality during those years.

NICHOLAS PILEGGI
As the son of a musician from Calabria, Nick found that the neighbor-hood seemed to open up to him. He described the Mafia as "perfectly respectable gentlemen." This essay, along with others he wrote about the Italian mob, became the basis for Nick's award-winning screen-play, *Goodfellas*.
Photo: Nicholas Pileggi

Little Italy:
Study of an Italian Ghetto

By Nicholas Pileggi

"... Mulberry Street has successfully fought against improved public housing, overhead expressways, indoor pushcart markets, compulsory education, American food and the English language..."

"Ghetto! Wha ghetto? This ain't no ghetto, this is our home and we got no riots and we got no crime on the streets and we got no Cleveland here!"

In New York today there is a pocket of such social stability that it has confounded urbanologists, city planners and politicians. Its residents have been unmoved by avaricious realtors; they seem fearless of crime in the streets and resistant to the lure of the suburbs.

For almost 100 years New York's Mulberry Street has been a synonym for "Little Italy," and the symbolic street for a theatrical arena roughly seven blocks long and three blocks wide on Manhattan's Lower East Side. To a stranger the neighborhood might appear overcrowded, its inhabitants unnecessarily loud, its children overtly rude, its sidewalks and gutters littered with garbage, partially burnt mattresses, broken toys and occasional bodies. To the local Italians, however, these streets, with all their confusion and color serve as a vast baroque tapestry against which the players can find both comfort and privacy to act out their traditional medieval roles. As if

in a community besieged by Saracens, the inhabitants of Mulberry Street have remained, after three generations, frozen in the same cliquish conspiracy, poised against the same outsiders as their ancestors before them, seeing in every Irish cop a Moorish bandit. In Little Italy, the roles are acted with style. The gestures are broad, the voices loud, the commitments for keeps and the action is for all to see. An Italian drawing room drama, because of the nature of its characters, must always take place out of doors. The women in brightly colored housecoats decorate and guard almost every window. Like the wilting flowers of Mulberry Street, their elbows planted heavily in pillows, their heads drooping downward toward the street, they watch and are watched in turn. Without such a stage how could one fully savor a revenge, Simonize a car, kiss a hand, cuff a child or maintain one's self respect publicly? With its streets quiet; its dramas indoors, its soups creamed and its women thin, a delightful foreign colony would become just another social glob dissolving in New York's melting pot. Little Italy, how-

ever, more than any other immigrant colony, has remained vendetta-true in its battle against the great American mix-master. At one time or another, it has successfully fought improved public housing, overhead expressways, indoor pushcart markets, compulsory education, American food and the English language. It has also, as a result of this battle, assumed responsibility for a number of characteristics, as well as characters, that the great majority of Italian-Americans would rather forget.

Existing as it does today, a small, rather remote 19th-century southern Italian village, within walking distance of Wall Street or City Hall, and continuing to follow the same customs and rituals that Pietro Germi and Vittorio DeSica have found so profitable and funny, Little Italy manages to cast a shadow of the stereotype Italian far out of proportion to its size. Due primarily to its most deportable product—the Mafia racketeer—attention has been focused on a tiny, though certainly colorful, percentage of the United States' nearly six million Italian-Americans.

Illustrated by Robert Weaver

"Mulberry Street is a neighborhood of grim men who pass on their sombre inheritance through a tradition of sour tales."

"Slouching, laughing, cursing, looking sullen, acting their role, the young stags pose for each other, postureless, alien and bold."

"All seated around, the waiters playing cards with the murderers, they feel comfort and safety with each other."

"Soothing bruised spirits, puffing vain bellows,
calming the hysterical and chilling the implacable,
the men hold court in ritualistic style."

WEAVER ON TEACHING ILLUSTRATION
"On the simplest level it is an incredible oversight on the part of the artist that he neglects to use his eyes. . . . In my own teaching I am trying to remedy this deficiency by ordering students out onto the streets with sketchpads. Once the initial shock of life wears off, the student can begin to discover the magnitude of the world."
—Interview in *American Artist* magazine, 1959

Steinem in the Spotlight

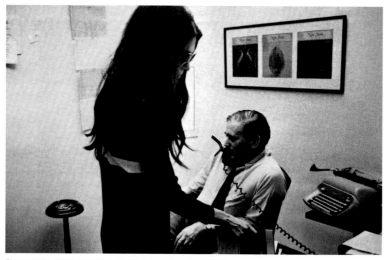

Photograph by Jill Krementz at *New York* magazine, circa 1968

Gloria Steinem made it possible for female journalists to write about everything.

An article about Ho Chi Minh's formative years in the first issue signaled a new focus for Gloria. Prior to becoming one of the magazine's founding writers and a new columnist, she recalls being limited to writing only about "nonpolitical subjects" as a freelance writer. "The low point was actually a very long piece about the history of textured stockings for the Sunday *New York Times Magazine*," she says.

When he was an editor at *Esquire*, Clay gave Gloria her first serious commission: an article about the development and social implications of the then new contraceptive pill. Because of this opportunity, she accepted Clay's invitation to be part of his magazine start-up and join a group of writers for a new weekly called *New York* magazine. "It was then I discovered that editorial meetings could be like great jazz improvisations, with each person playing off ideas, and a better result than any one of us could have created on our own," Gloria says. While Gloria was helping name the departments of *New York*, she gave herself a weekly column called "The City Politic."

Among the early highlights of her tenure at *New York* was an insightful first-person account of Richard Nixon in the throes of his second presidential bid. Clay's assignment was essentially, "Get on Nixon's campaign plane and write about everything I saw," Gloria recalls.

The cover presented a conundrum. We asked photographer Carl Fischer to build a large box, covered with photographs of Nixon. We were hoping to persuade Gloria to pose inside the box, but she hated the idea. "It seemed to me that serious writers didn't do that," she explains. In the end, we met halfway. "As you can see, the result was a compromise," says Gloria. "I was there amid Nixon photos, but with my back to the camera."

GLORIA STEINEM and Clay Felker (left) working together in the early days of *New York* magazine. A reluctant Gloria poses on the cover (opposite), photographed by Carl Fischer.

CARL FISCHER is among the most successful commercial and editorial photographers of the last century. Working with George Lois, he photographed some of *Esquire*'s most memorable covers. Carl was one of our go-to photographers during *New York* magazine's early days. He generously worked for our measly $250 cover fee. His expertise and ability to quickly respond to our ideas (building sets, casting models) enabled us to produce cover images far above our pay grade.
Photo: Carl Fischer

OCTOBER 28, 1968

40 CENTS

New York

Gloria Steinem on Learning to Live with Nixon

A Caricature Comes to Life

Four noted satirical cartoonists explain, in their own words and handwriting, how they drew Nixon. We ran their notations throughout Gloria Steinem's article.

ED SOREL:
"Mouth: He has recovered from his foot-in-mouth attack in 1960. Mouth may thus be drawn smaller than previously."

Photo by Tobey Sanford

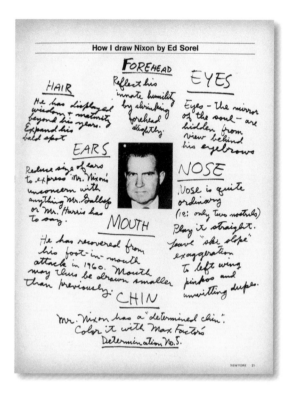

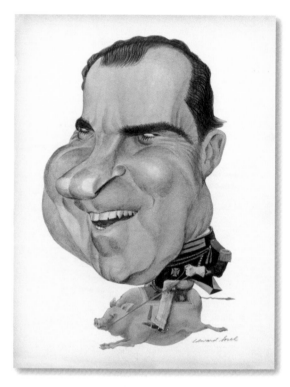

DAVID LEVINE:
"Get those Twiggy lashes."

Photo by Walter Bernard

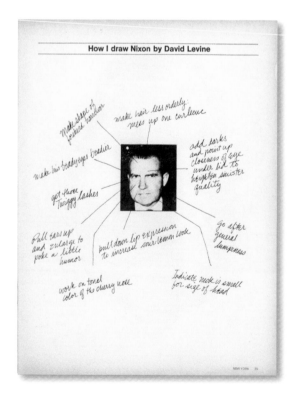

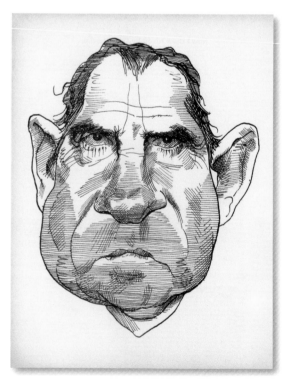

How I draw Nixon by Jack Davis

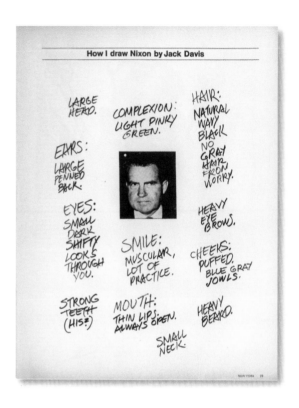

LARGE HEAD.

COMPLEXION: LIGHT PINKY GREEN.

HAIR: NATURAL WAVY BLACK NO GRAY HAIR FROM WORRY.

EARS: LARGE PENNED BACK.

EYES: SMALL DARK SHIFTY LOOKS THROUGH YOU.

HEAVY EYE BROWS.

SMILE: MUSCULAR, LOT OF PRACTICE.

CHEEKS: PUFFED. BLUE GRAY JOWLS.

STRONG TEETH (HIS?)

MOUTH: THIN LIPS. ALWAYS OPEN.

HEAVY BEARD.

SMALL NECK.

JACK DAVIS:
"Complexion: pinky-green. Hair: natural wavy black. No gray hair from worry. Strong teeth (his?)."
Photo: The Davis family

How I draw Nixon by Gerald Scarfe

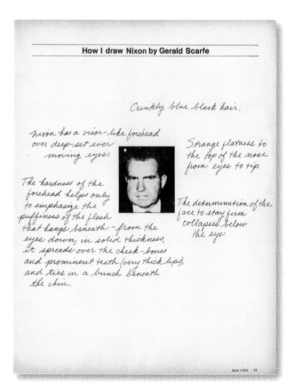

Crinkly blue black hair.

Nixon has a visor-like forehead over deep-set ever moving eyes.

Strange flatness to the top of the nose from eyes to tip.

The hardness of the forehead helps only to emphasise the puffiness of the flesh that hangs beneath – from the eyes down, in solid thickness, it spreads over the cheek-bones and prominent teeth (very thick lips), and ties in a bunch beneath the chin.

The determination of the face to stay firm collapses below the eye.

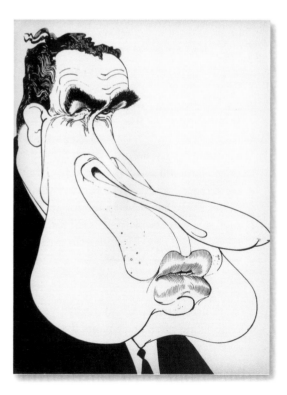

GERALD SCARFE:
"The determination of the face to stay firm collapses below the eye."
Photo: Gerald Scarfe

The Little Column That Could

"The Underground Gourmet" zeroed in on the one thing all New Yorkers crave: a really good, cheap restaurant.

The first of a three-part series "introducing Jewish culinary to non-believers." Photographs by Sol Mednick

New York City's food scene was very different when Jerome Snyder and I started writing this column in the *Tribune* in 1965. One didn't usually seek out cheap restaurants that were not in your neighborhood. Back then, these types of eateries were associated with crime, bad food, and the possibility of getting some disease.

Jerome and I would walk the streets and go to three or four restaurants in the course of a week. We weren't exactly trained to be food critics, but we were willing to try bizarre things. You could say, we learned on the job. It was Jerome's task to steal the menu so we had a record of items and prices, and I made an ink drawing to accompany each review.

A typical story about "The Underground Gourmet": There was a guy who went to Sheepshead Bay every morning to fish for things to serve at his deli. He had a counter with maybe six or seven stools. We ran a column about him and his fishing expeditions; one day 200 or 300 people showed up. That's the kind of response you would get if you wrote about something interesting.

As the column became more popular, we decided to do bigger pieces that dealt with ethnic food and its relation to the social fabric of the city. We concocted features like "A Gentile's Guide to Jewish Food," which tells you how to navigate a Jewish delicatessen and its menu. It gave people who hadn't tasted a real knish a way to evaluate it.

"The Underground Gourmet" exemplified *New York* magazine's brand of service journalism. It was a service to both patrons and under-the-radar establishments that often didn't have the inclination or the budget to advertise in a magazine. The result was that the prohibition against eating strange, cheap food was broken. At some point, it even became fashionable.—MG

JEROME SNYDER (1916–1976) was the first art director of *Sports Illustrated*. In 1962, he moved to *Scientific American* and illuminated complex scientific information for a broad audience for over a decade. His gourmet-literary partnership with Milton emerged as a result of their friendly one-upmanship contests as to who knew more underground eateries in the city. Jerome died in 1976 after suffering a heart attack in the midst of playing touch football in Central Park, which was one of his favorite activities. He was awarded the AIGA medal that same year in recognition of "his unrelenting demand for excellence as an eloquent writer, designer, and illustrator."

Photo: Milton Glaser

JULY 22,1968

40 CENTS

Introducing the Dog of the Year
Dick Goodwin: Incredible Leaping Politician

NEW YORK

A Gentile's Guide
To Jewish Food
By the Underground Gourmet

Illustration by Milton Glaser

MILTON AND JEROME AT WORK. "Although our credentials were better known in graphic rather than culinary arts, we were not entirely without some of the qualities or capabilities necessary for the task. We both were amateur cooks; we are native New Yorkers traumatized by the Great Depression and we have good noses for a bargain. Last and certainly not the least, we both have cast-iron—or should we say—stainless steel stomachs." —Milton Glaser and Jerome Snyder, *The Underground Gourmet Cookbook*, 1975. Photo: Milton Glaser

MILTON'S DRAWINGS illustrated almost every "Underground Gourmet" column. Each restaurant was rated based on four categories: Food, Service, Ambience, and Hygiene, on a sliding scale of Excellent to Poor. All of the small establishments listed here have since closed, which sadly is the frequent fate of these wonderful restaurants.

Kitcho 103 West Forty-Fourth Street

Chin-Mi 124 West Forty-Fourth Street

Szechuan Taste 23 Chatham Square

Paradise Inn 347 West Forty-First Street

Dining Commons 33 West Forty-Second Street

Near East Restaurant 136 Court Street, Brooklyn Heights

Texas Taco 694 Third Avenue

The Front Porch 253 West Eleventh Street

Sultan's Table 2337 Broadway

Szechuan Royal 50 West Seventy-Second Street

Cafe Manila 248 East Fifty-Second Street

Chuan Yuan 128 Montague Street, Brooklyn

Chinatown Barbeque House 72 Bayard Street

Wunam Kitchen 806 Second Avenue

Brownies 21 East Sixteenth Street

Alive! Kitchen 11 West Forty-Second Street

Eva's 1556 Second Avenue

Woo Dong 56 West Twenty-Ninth Street

The Brazilian Pavilion 141 East Fifty-Second Street

Foo Joy 13 Division Street

Pot au Feu 123 West Forty-Ninth Street

"The Underground Gourmet" Gets Competitive

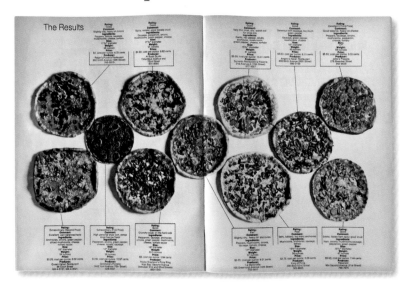

The Results

Igniting debates about the best cheap eats

Every so often we would assemble a panel of tasters to find the best pastrami sandwiches, cheesecakes, beers, and oysters in New York. For the "Pastrami Olympics," we enlisted noted judges: Joe Baum of Windows on the World and George Lang of Café des Artistes, proprietors of two of the most elegant restaurants in the city; publisher and foodie Burt Wolf; Nina Renshaw, a model who jeopardized her career by eating these sandwiches; Ray Hooper, an art director with considerable pastrami-eating savvy; and Murray Miller, a taxi driver who ate a pastrami sandwich every week. At times, members of the magazine staff also got involved (below), such as the time they settled the hotly debated title of best pizza in New York City in "The Underground Gourmet's First Annual Pizzarama" in 1970.

GOLDBERG'S PIZZERIA, the winner of the inaugural Pizzarama (above left), is an example of our city's multiculturalism. Goldberg's created a pizza with sweet sauce and a crust with a distinct rye flavor. Who would think that would be any good? Inevitably, we received several passionate letters refuting our taste. Gemma Fastiggi from Manhattan wrote: "I don't know who your so-called pizza experts are, but I suspect they are mostly non-Italians with appetites jaded by dry martinis, instant breakfasts and Spam."

Photo by Harold Krieger

PASTRAMI OLYMPICS With an advertiser onboard, we sometimes made pull-out posters of various food competitions (opposite). Reprints of this 1973 poster are still sold today.

Photo by Ben Somoroff

Inside the Democratic National Convention (August 26-29, 1968) in Chicago Vice President Hubert Humphrey was nominated on the first ballot, but the chaos outside dominated the TV coverage. Humphrey's campaign for president got off to a rocky start. Antiwar demonstrators and Yippies like Jerry Rubin, Tom Hayden, and Abbie Hoffman objected to his nomination and the Vietnam War. Under orders from Mayor Richard J. Daley to quell the mob, 668 protesters were arrested. Hundreds were hurt. Some blamed the police, calling it a "police riot."

Prague Spring Ends
On August 20, 1968, five Warsaw Pact countries—the Soviet Union, Bulgaria, Poland, East Germany, and Hungary—invaded Czechoslovakia, putting an end to the Prague Spring. Although Alexander Dubček, the Czechoslovakian leader, was allowed to remain in office, his efforts to bring liberal reforms to the communist government were over.

"Hey Jude" Tops Charts
Released on August 26, 1968, "Hey Jude" became the best-selling single ever recorded by the Beatles.

Getting the Picture

Roz Kelly's determination brought back an unexpected scoop.

KELLY'S BUSINESS CARD (left) captured her exuberance. She later went on to appear in *The Owl and the Pussycat*, *The Love Boat*, and *Charlie's Angels*.

Before she became Pinky Tuscadero on *Happy Days*, Roz Kelly was a contributing photographer for *New York*. In 1968, I sent her on a stakeout assignment to photograph Jimi Hendrix, who was playing in town. We knew he was staying at the Drake Hotel, which was very popular at the time with touring bands and Hollywood types such as Judy Garland, Frank Sinatra, and Lillian Gish. We didn't think we could get close to Hendrix, but I figured Roz could just catch him in a paparazzi shot as he emerged from the hotel to go to the concert.

But Roz was determined to get a more interesting picture. Somehow she figured out what suite he was in and knocked on his door. Apparently, a groggy Hendrix opened the door and stumbled back into bed. (Our writer Albert Grossman found out that Hendrix typically woke up at 7 p.m. and "got his head together" around midnight.) Roz recalls that she shook him awake, took a few frames, and rushed back to her studio. The next day she came to the office and presented a contact sheet full of intimate portraits of Hendrix in various stages of playfulness and repose. Roz was truly amazing.—WB

The Blues Today: SuperSpade Raise

By Albert Goldman

"The Hendrix sound identi
artist: rock's resourceful n

Last time I saw Jimi Hendrix onstage, he was playing SuperSpade. His Afro-Annie hair-do looked like it was plugged into his Sunn amp. His country duds—emerald pants, purple shirt, iridescent vest—were drawn from rainbow vats. His music—ominously circling, coiling and striking home—had the motions of a great black snake. Tossing his left-handed guitar over his shoulder, between his thighs or into fast hand spins, Hendrix came on like a flashy western gun slinger. (Sammy Davis would have been proud.) "Flash" was just the word he chose later to nail his own image: "a big flash of weaving and bobbing and groping and maiming and attacking."

Hendrix is camping as a musical mugger, but his sound identifies him as an artist—rock's most resourceful noise sculptor. Mixing fuzz and feedback at *fortissimo* levels, he rears massive acoustic constructions that loom threateningly over his audience. The sound is of a tactile solidity that makes you want to reach out and run your hand around the bend in a blue note. Some of his pieces remind you of totems of scabrous rusty iron; some move like farm machines run amok; some suggest those shiny brass columns and spheres that are breached to reveal a funky interior textured like a toadstool.

Hendrix should have welded some unforgettable assemblages that night at the Fillmore East; but he didn't have his electric mojo working. Every time he'd start to fuse one sound with another, his tandem two hundred watt amplifiers would blow a another sort of fuse . Dancing upstage to make a fast adjustment on the speaker face, then coming down again in a slow split, he got into a *pas de deux* (or was it a *paso doble?*) with his equipment. So graceful were these face-saving vamps, he almost persuaded you that all this fancy footwork was part of the act. "'Jimi Hendrix,' Ladies and Gentlemen, 'in *The Dance of the Dying Amp.*'"

Finally, he
with exasp
much longe
house. Wha
if this colos
standing th
plink of a
nately, he c
and we file
get in for th

After the
and put *Th*
the turntab
iterative, th
shod track
against a
program fo
electrificatio
Futurist sy
I felt I wa
walking alc
its clangorc
open heart
stations an
new factory
of the blue
ments had b
hand worki
would cry c
his pain. W
to the char
the manac
broken by
New Negro
the primitiv
above the
That shout

Hendrix
as he told n
soul there
really the s
and place v
purity of tr
gling and n
new sound
meant man
rience and
Arwhoolie:

him as an
sculptor."

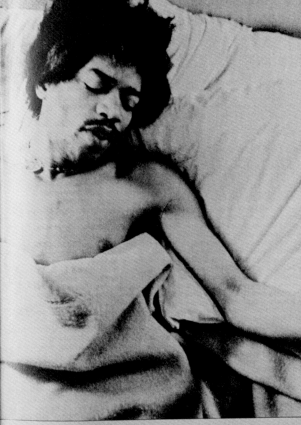

ed in a voice wry
at he couldn't last
y gripped the huge
ppen, we all thought,
symphonist were left
othing but the feeble
fied guitar? Fortu-
he was still audible,
the mobs waiting to
show.
orted, I went home
ndrix Experience on
, abrasive, brutally
suggested the iron-
bulldozer straining
of dirt. Hendrix's
try blues was rural
end products were
of industrial noise.
ome in Pittsburgh,
ld South Side with
etal plants, raucous
es, whirring power
yard engines. This
ought the evolution
e. Those famous la-
abor pains: the field
a Sahara of cotton
his spirits or purge
hollers were joined
orers and prisoners,
ms of work were
s of release. Now a
North had revived
shouting ecstatically
ar of the machine.
dustrial arwhoolie.*
n up in Seattle, and
"there was all kinda
ese, too." That was
grew up in a time
nothing about the
verything was min-
roduce new strains,
ex amalgams that
n the Hendrix Expe-
ar everything from
field holler.

Photograph by Roz Kelly

country frailing** out of Nashville and
dirty hollering from the Delta to the high
tension crackle of the WHO and the sur-
realistic glossolalia of Bob Dylan. Yet
some things were much better realized
than others. Hendrix might make capital
out of his image as SuperSpade, a mythi-
cal Black Man committing acts of violence before fascinated audiences of English and American teenies (his tour
with The Monkees had to be terminated
because the bookers were terrified of his
debauching effect on the little ones). He
could wink at the hipper Soul Brothers
as he stood spotlighted between his hard-
working rhythm section of pale English
boys. (There's an inverted stereotype for
you!) But Hendrix was the greatest living
proof that today Black is Gray.

Apart from his lissome physical grace—
a quality no white rock performer has
ever displayed—Jimi Hendrix is essentially one with the white pop scene wherever it is most advanced, in London or
Nashville or on the West Coast. Like the
last generation of jazzmen, who tran-
scended their Negro origins to become
figures in the international music avant-
garde, playing to almost exclusively white
audiences, working with white sidemen,
studying with white masters and consort-
ing with white women, Hendrix's black-
ness is only skin deep. Nor is he simply
American or English. Every time he starts
to jam, he bends instinctively toward the
East. His guitar becomes a sitar; his
soundscape is enveloped in purple moire.
Listening to track after track in the
cushioned cool of my living room, I began
to sink into a familiar trance. There was,
I realized drowsily, a glittering psychedelic
thread running through even the coarsest
burlap spun by Hendrix's infernal mills.

Having stepped over the threshold of
appreciation, I entered a new zone of
awareness of Jimi Hendrix. I recognized
belatedly that he was the only thing live
and moving on the current rock scene.
Judging from what I had seen and heard
at the Fillmore, he was in that ardent
phase of the creative cycle that trans-

**Frailing: [dialectal for "flailing"] primitive
American guitar technique antedating the
blues.*

JIMI HENDRIX
up close and personal
at the Drake Hotel
(above and left).
Photo by Roz Kelly/Michael
Ochs Archives/Getty Images

ROZ KELLY RECALLS:
"Shooting didn't take
long because he had
other ideas. But
I wanted to get home
and see how my
pictures turned out."

IN THE NEWS

The First Mouse
At the Fall Joint Computer Conference in San Francisco's Civic Auditorium on December 9, 1968, attended by 1,000 computer professionals, Douglas C. Engelbart demonstrated how the mouse he had invented four years earlier could control a computer. Engelbart never received any royalties; his employer, SRI, held the patent, which expired before the mouse became widely used. Both Apple and Microsoft popularized the mouse in the 1980s.

Elvis Makes a Comeback
The Elvis Presley NBC TV special on December 3, 1968, called "Singer Presents—ELVIS" was his comeback. Dressed in black leather, and reunited with the musicians who played with him on his earliest recordings, Elvis re-established himself as a musical force. He had not appeared in public since 1961. It was the most watched show that week.

A Fashionable Question

A comic take on what everybody was thinking

Freelance fashion editor Trudy Owett developed this feature showcasing six emerging actresses, with Brazilian fashion photographer Otto Stupakoff. Trudy produced the entire feature—hired the models, selected the garments, and wrote the text. The article's cheeky title reflects the cultural milieu of the late 1960s, which was in large part defined by the sexual revolution. This was the time of films like *Bob & Carol & Ted & Alice* and plays like *Hair* and *Oh, Calcutta!*

In the early years of the magazine we covered fashion regularly, but eventually we realized that it was not our strength or greatest interest. However, Trudy always found a way to highlight a cultural or political layer that meshed with our editorial character. She once produced a story titled "Black is Beautiful, White is Wonderful," featuring African American models wearing white garments and Caucasian models wearing black clothes. This feature is an example of one of the times when the magazine successfully conveyed fashion information in an amusing manner.

TRUDY OWETT
was a fashion editor at the *Ladies' Home Journal* from 1964 to 1979 and also freelanced for *New York* magazine with stories too racy for the *Journal*. Trudy was an early feminist and a contributing editor to *Ms.* magazine's first edition.
Photo by Susan Wood Richardson

OTTO STUPAKOFF
(1935–2009), a fashion photographer from Brazil, worked for *Harper's Bazaar* in the mid-1960s. In 1972 Otto moved to Paris, working for *Vogue* and leading names in haute couture. More than fifty of his photographs are in the permanent collection of MoMA.

POP CULTURE
Comic books and pop art were important aspects of 1960s American visual culture. Our four-page layout in the form of a comic strip featured up-and-coming actresses. From left, Jenny O'Hara, Shelley Plimpton, Gayle Hunnicutt, Ali McGraw, Jane Merrow, and Lauren Hutton.

Retouching a Masterpiece

A sequel to a provocative study of New York City's East Harlem, also known as "El Barrio"

I n 1966, anthropologist Oscar Lewis published a monumental 700-page study about the life and attitudes of Puerto Rican slum dwellers. Written in the first person, *La Vida: A Puerto Rican Family in the Culture of Poverty—San Juan and New York* traces the travails of the Rios clan, who migrated from the slums of San Juan to East Harlem, known as New York City's "El Barrio." *La Vida* won the National Book Award in 1967 and is hailed as a seminal work on the subject.

Eight months after finishing the field work for *La Vida*, Lewis revisited his protagonists and wrote this epilogue. The story we published focused on the domestic drama of Soledad, the eldest Rios daughter. These drawings are imaginary portraits, rendered in grease pencil on textured paper, evoking a feeling for the emotional turmoil of the characters, matching the strength and liveliness of Lewis's piece.

OSCAR LEWIS (1914–1970) was a professor of anthropology at the University of Illinois at Urbana. His research results led to compelling studies of Mexican and Puerto Rican slum communities.

Photo: The University of Illinois Archives

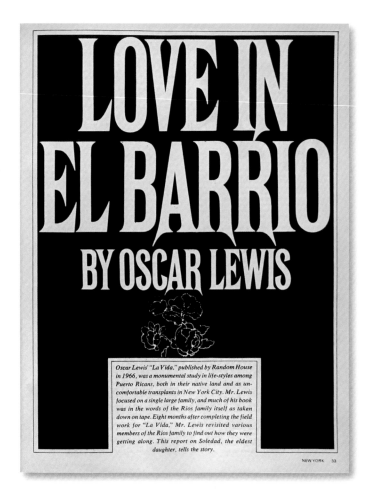

Oscar Lewis' "La Vida," published by Random House in 1966, was a monumental study in life-styles among Puerto Ricans, both in their native land and as uncomfortable transplants in New York City. Mr. Lewis focused on a single large family, and much of his book was in the words of the Rios family itself as taken down on tape. Eight months after completing the field work for "La Vida," Mr. Lewis revisited various members of the Rios family to find out how they were getting along. This report on Soledad, the eldest daughter, tells the story.

NEW YORK 33

IMAGINARY PORTRAITS
The large black-and-white drawings by Milton Glaser (opposite) were supplemented by illustrated initial paragraph breaks (above) throughout the article. The first page of this exceptional story (left) was intentionally designed to be very different from our usual format.

46

"He told me what a fine woman I was and that he loved me. Men! They sure lay it on!"

He begged me so hard that I gave in and stayed. But I couldn't sleep that night. My eyes were wide open. I couldn't get Benedicto out of my mind, thinking that tomorrow he'd be back and when he came in drunk and didn't find me, it was going to be something awful. The thing was that I had started a business, selling perfume, soaps, and all that, and I kept thinking about the piggy bank. I was so afraid!

Well, that night Alberto said again he wanted to marry me. He told me not to worry, that he loved me and was going to be good to me and would make me happy.

I said to him, "I love you. Otherwise I wouldn't have wanted to come here to you."

Then he said, "Go to sleep now. Tomorrow I'll take you to the station."

I was up and dressed at six o'clock the next morning. He took me to the bus station in a taxi and I caught the eight o'clock bus. I rode all night long and was in New York at eight o'clock Tuesday morning.

When I got home the first thing *doña* Nilsa said to me was "Hide yourself, girl, hide yourself! Benedicto is looking for you and you'd better keep out of his way because he'll kill you if he catches you."

"But didn't you tell him that I was out in New Jersey and that I went this morning?"

"That's what I told him, but the girls said you'd been gone since yesterday."

"Oh, my God!"

"He smashed the furniture, but the first thing he did was break the piggy bank and take all the money. I told him he shouldn't do it because the money belonged to your children but he said he didn't care."

The house looked like a hurricane had struck it. I didn't have any feelings left in me and I just lay down. A little while later Benedicto arrived. He knocked on the door and I opened it. Where had I been, he wanted to know. I told him in New Jersey visiting my uncle and aunt.

"You're lying," he said. "You were at the Palladium, dancing. Some people told me."

"It's not true. They're the ones who are lying." Imagine! Somebody had told him I had been up all night drinking and dancing at the Palladium. The thing was taking a different turn from what I had expected.

"Who told you such a thing?" I asked. It was his cousin Joaquín. "It's a lie," I kept insisting.

Well, Benedicto slept on the couch that night. I swear I didn't feel any love for him, not even a little bit. The next morning he got up and left. I felt like I was locked up in a cage. He was supposed to bring me money and I was waiting to see if he would. I was desperate. Then I went out for a few minutes to Rosalia's house and while I was gone he came and took away a saint I had and some bottles of perfume. Toya came running to tell me, "*Mami, mami, mami! Papi* is taking your perfume and the saint."

I rushed down the stairs after him and said, "Benedicto, give me back my perfume and my saint."

You see, he always tries to act like a big shot when he's out with his friends and this time he was with Joaquín and his sister Sasa. So he said, "I'm not giving you back anything. You're nothing but a whore."

I answered, "And you're a dirty sonofabitch. I'm a whore and you're a sonofabitch. Give me those perfumes."

Then the sister came over and said to me, "I don't talk to

"'I don't care if you rot, Beni,' I said. 'You have bad will toward me and get what you deserve.'"

live with me and he kept coming around asking for money. But I swear one thing, I never had relations with him again, not since the day I separated from him.

One day Virginia came to the house to invite me to a party at her place. While she was still here Beni walked in and said to her, "Get out. I'm going to have Soledad."

"Do you still have Beni?" Virginia asked me.

"No, not me," I said. "Don't be such a liar, Beni." I went out of the room with him after me. Wherever I went, he followed. I went in to comb my hair and there he was.

He said that either I should leave Alberto and live with him or I should get money out of Alberto and give it to him. Imagine! What a son of the great whore, that Negro! I said no to him and no and no. Finally, I said, "Leave me alone. Look, I'm going to meet Alberto now and we're going to the party." Well, he followed me all the way into Virginia's house.

At the party we were having a good time, talking, telling jokes, fooling around and dancing. Everybody was drinking except me. Alberto and Beni were sitting down and talking nicely to each other. That made me mad. "You know something," I said to them, "you Alberto and you Beni are a couple of queers."

"What's that?"

"You're queers, black queers, both of you!"

Beni got up to hit me and I stood up ready to fight back.

"Come on," I said to him and he grabbed at me to hit me.

"Come on," I said again.

"You have no business hitting her," said Alberto.

"I feel like letting you have it too," said Beni. Alberto then began shouting, "I want to fight!" He wasn't drunk but he was getting worked up to fight. I said to him, "Start fighting and they'll put you in jail and from there you'll get shipped back to Venezuela. So you'd better calm down."

"No, nobody is going to screw me!"

"Listen, you'd better shut up. You can't even open your mouth here in the United States, understand?"

"I don't give a damn whether I'm in the United States or not."

"Then don't you care whether I'm with you or not? The United States is like any other country, but you have to be legal here, that's for sure. You can't even kick an ash can because if a cop stops you and you get arrested and they ask you for your papers—Where are they? And where will you end up?"

Finally, I seemed to convince him and we took a taxi and went home. But Alberto was furious and went out again to a bar. I warned him not to get drunk and then I went to bed. A short time later I heard a little knock on the door.

"Who is it?" I asked.

"Me, Alberto."

I opened the door and there was Beni. "What do you want?" I said. "Leave me alone. Stop bothering me once and for all."

The next thing I knew he pulled a knife and slashed at my face. I jumped back but he had caught me. When I felt the blood run, the hate rose up in me and set me on fire. I threw myself on him and fought him with my fists while he kept swiping at me with the knife. I got on top of him and hit him and hit him but he cut me again. I don't know how because I was on top of him all the time. My hand and finger were cut and I had another scratch on my head. Not serious. The girls slept through it all. Ana Delia from upstairs called the police and I ran out into the street to look for a patrol car. I said to the policeman in Spanish, "That man there cut my face, that queer!"

Then Beni said to him in English, "Listen, policeman, that

Who Runs Gotham?

Power was Clay Felker's great fascination, and one that many readers shared.

1968 The first power issue

1970 Illustration by Milton Glaser

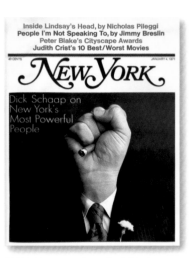

1971 Photograph by Carl Fischer

The power issues were published in an era before the whole idea of lists became a media staple. The cover of the first installment was simply an announcement that we were reporting on the personalities who controlled politics, business, and the arts in the city. Thereafter, our issues became more conceptual and covers conveyed the year's theme. Playing the role of an observer with an ironic tone, these issues became a kind of annual meditation on what power and status really meant.

Our regular contributors, like Tom Wolfe, Gloria Steinem, Nick Pileggi, Richard Reeves, Michael Kramer, Alan Rich, Andy Tobias, Peter Hellman, Edwin Diamond, Edward Costikyan, and Dick Schaap, weighed in on the power game based on their beat. We often assigned David Levine, Robert Grossman, and Ed Sorel to caricature the individual power brokers.

1972 Illustration by Paul Davis

1973 Illustration by Paul Davis

1974 Illustration by Paul Davis

1976 Illustration by Melinda Bordelon

INVISIBLE POWER
Dr. Jack Griffin (played by Claude Rains) removing his bandages in a scene from the 1933 horror film *The Invisible Man* was the inspiration for the 1975 cover (opposite).

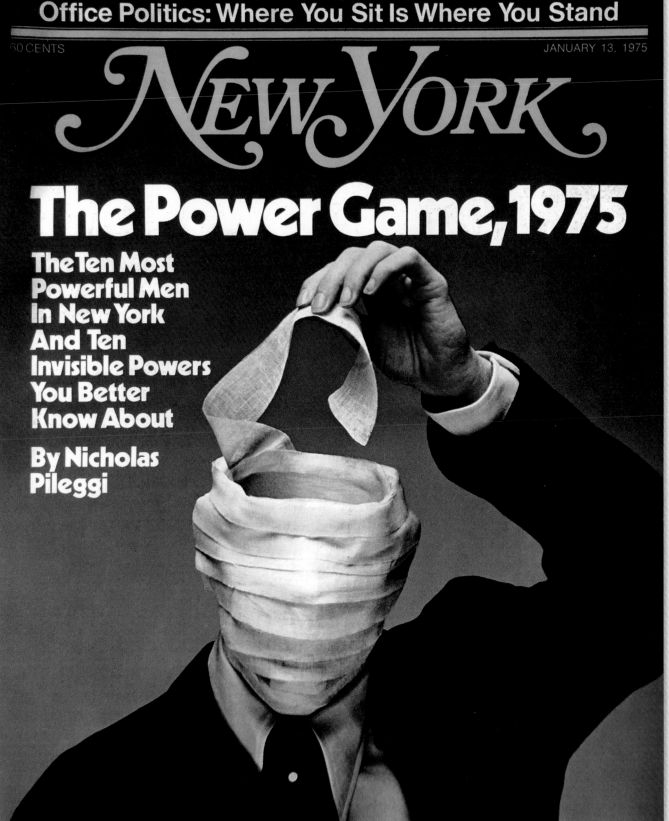

Our Annual Urban Blights and Blessings Awards
Memoir of the Drinking Life, by Pete Hamill
Office Politics: Where You Sit Is Where You Stand

60 CENTS   JANUARY 13, 1975

NEW YORK

The Power Game, 1975

The Ten Most Powerful Men In New York And Ten Invisible Powers You Better Know About

By Nicholas Pileggi

Photograph by Dan Wynn

49

Associate Justice Abe Fortas Resigns from Supreme Court

When Chief Justice Earl Warren told President Lyndon B. Johnson he wanted to retire, LBJ tried to elevate associate Justice Abe Fortas to succeed him. A filibuster was threatened by conservative senators opposed to Fortas. Ultimately, realizing the votes weren't there, Fortas asked LBJ to withdraw his nomination. But as they considered confirmation, senators were troubled by Fortas' finances. He had charged a $15,000 fee for lecturing at American University, which was believed to be funded by his former clients, as well as $20,000 a year for life from Louis Wolfson, a former client under investigation. When they threatened impeachment, Warren urged Fortas to resign, which he did on May 15, 1969. Nixon named Harry Blackmun for Fortas, and Warren Burger for Earl Warren.

Mailer Wins Pulitzer

On May 5, 1969, Norman Mailer was awarded the nonfiction Pulitzer Prize for *Armies of the Night,* which ostensibly deals with the October 1967 anti-Vietnam War rally in Washington, D.C.

BRESLIN'S STATEMENT

"I Run to Win," declaring his commitment: "The last thing, that New York can afford at this time is a politician thinking in normal politicians' terms. . . . The City of New York either gets an imagination, or dies." He and Mailer wanted New York City to secede from New York State and be declared America's fifty-first state.
Cover photo by Dan Wynn

Unleashing Turmoil in Five Pages

Mailer and Breslin launch their quixotic campaign for City Hall.

The mayoral primary is June 17, and already the cliff-hangers have begun. Will the conservative Republicans vote John Lindsay out? Will Badillo persuade enough voters he's really a man of the Left? Whatever became of Robert Wagner? Can Procaccino cry more than Humphrey? And, most of all, are Mailer and Breslin really serious? Turn the page to find out.

Photographed by Dan Wynn

I n the spring of 1968, Norman Mailer and Jimmy Breslin shocked everyone when they announced that they had banded together to run for public office. Mailer, already an accomplished novelist and filmmaker, was vying to be New York City's mayor, and Breslin, a brilliant investigative journalist and one of our most-read writers, sought the office of City Council President.

First of all, you would never put them together in your mind as partners. They may not have even liked each other very much. But Mailer and Breslin got serious enough to the point of recruiting the *Village Voice*'s Joe Flaherty as their campaign manager and opening a campaign office on Columbus Circle.

The black-and-white Dan Wynn portrait of the so-called "Odd Couple," showing Mailer leaning into Breslin, captured their energy so well that it reappeared on their campaign banners.

The beginning was promising. At one event we attended, Mailer gave such a fabulous speech that people in the room thought, "Boy, this guy could actually be the mayor." His eloquence was really compelling and won the crowd with quips like, "If I'm elected, at least the bad news will be couched in elegant language." But just as they began to get traction, they destroyed their own campaign. In one memorable night, Mailer showed up very drunk to speak during a rally at The Village Gate and yelled insults from the stage. Everybody in attendance realized then that their campaign had become ridiculous.

Their high-profile candidacy was a ruckus challenge to the status quo. Mailer and Breslin didn't expect to win but they did want to create some noise. Their campaign slogan: "No more bullshit."—WB

DAN WYNN (1920–1995) was one of the prominent portrait and fashion photographers of the late twentieth century. He covered a wide range of subjects during our nine years at *New York*. During his career he photographed many luminaries from Arthur Ashe to Al Pacino and was also the semiofficial photographer of cooking pioneer James Beard.

Photo: © Dan Wynn Archive and Farmani Group, Co LTD

Covers We Like, 1969

How Shoplifters Are Cleaning Out the City
A Natatorial Guide to Public Pools

40 CENTS   JULY 28, 1969

NEW YORK

Is Lindsay Too Tall To Be Mayor? by Jimmy Breslin

BRESLIN'S OBSERVATION
that John Lindsay was too
tall to be mayor of New York
was an amusing and possibly
true premise. We hired a
model of similar stature,
knowing we could not get
the mayor himself. Cropping
off the stand-in's head
(left) not only was funny but
also convinced some readers
that it was indeed Lindsay
himself. Photographed by
Dan Wynn. Below, a chart
of former mayors ranked by
height and accomplishment,
to support Breslin's theory.

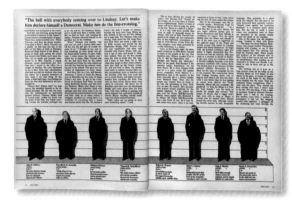

SPECIAL YEAR-END ISSUE

BY JOHN V. LINDSAY
WHY I DIDN'T GET OUT WHEN I COULD

40 CENTS   DECEMBER 22, 1969

NEW YORK

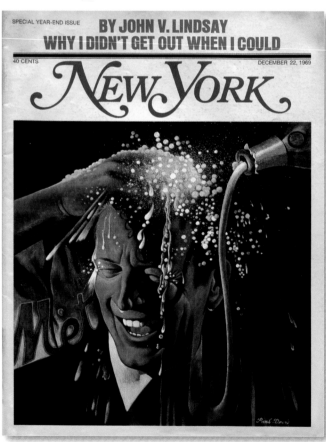

VICTORY When the Mets
won the World Series in
1969, newly reelected
Mayor John Lindsay was
doused with champagne
during the locker room
celebration. Clay Felker
remembered the wire photo
(above) and suggested we
immortalize the moment.
Illustration by Paul Davis

Photo: New York Daily News Archive/
New York Daily News/Getty Images

THE EMERGING FORCE
of women is pictured as a
beautiful female with the
formidable biceps of a
bodybuilder (opposite). The
image is an illusion that
Carl Fischer achieved
without photo manipulation.
He posed actress Ann
Turkel leaning over a
muscular male model to
conceal his head and
her shoulder with her long
flowing hair (below).

40 CENTS

JUNE 9, 1969

New York

The (Liberated) Woman of the Year

You've Come a Long Way, Baby

When Speed First Killed

An illustrated sequence traces the progression of the addictive drug's deadly side effects.

FILM SEQUENCE Five
consecutive illustrations
(above) created a movie
effect. The serpent
springing out of an
amphetamine capsule
(opposite) is an allusion
to the temptation of Eve.

Gail Sheehy wrote a searing two-part series about
a potent stimulant that became America's "drug
of the moment" in the late 1960s. Drawing from
her sister's addiction, Gail outlines how mass dependency
on amphetamines, (a.k.a. speed, uppers, or "pammie"
on the streets) was fueled by the pharmaceutical industry
and doctors who liberally prescribed them as diet pills.
She pitched the story to Clay, noting her access to
doctors, dealers, and druggies who coalesced in the
East Village where she lived.

"My sister was lured by a very handsome, charismatic
medical student into his magic vitamin experiment,"
Gail explains. "She was wigging out across from the
Hell's Angel's headquarters, and I would visit her and
try to bring her out of her stupor. It was really painful."

For the seventeen-page article, I attempted a miniature
film sequence to dramatize the deadly effect of the addic-
tive drug. Gail repurposed one of the interior illustrations
as the cover of her first book, *Speed is of the Essence.*—MG

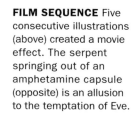

GAIL SHEEHY, a founding
contributing editor to *New
York* magazine, is an
award-winning journalist
and author. Among her
seventeen books is
*Passages: Predictable
Crises of Adult Life*, a
best-selling volume that
has been reprinted
in twenty-eight languages.
Photo: Gail Sheehy

40 CENTS

JULY 21, 1969

New York

The Amphetamine Explosion by Gail Sheehy
An Intimate Story of the
"Magic Vitamin" and Its Consequences

Illustration by Milton Glaser

MILTON RETOUCHING
the pen-and-ink drawings
for "The Amphetamine
Explosion." The vivid hues
of the illustration were
achieved using a color
acetate called "Cello-Tak,"
expertly applied by Milton's
longtime associate
George Leavitt, also
known as the "Man with
the Golden Hands."

Photo by Cosmos Sarchiapone

IN THE NEWS

Libyan Coup d'État
On September 1, 1969, Libyan Colonel Muammar Gaddafi, along with seventy young army officers, overthrew King Idris. The coup, called the Al-Fateh Revolution, abolished the monarchy and established the Libyan Arab Republic.

A Place Called Elaine's

The Literary Saloon As Literary Salon

By Tommy Thompson

What this town needed was the kind of place where a writer could go to nurse a block, or watch the competition goof off—a Toots Shor's for the quality lit set. Then along came Elaine's.

I used to go to Elaine's three or four years ago when everything and everybody was different. George Plimpton came in one night and stood on his hands, and a lot of other people did, too. A fellow brought a lion cub in and leashed it to his table leg—and believe me, Elio, the waiter, set the veal parmigiana down pretty carefully. Some Spanish students in black Toledo capes flew in regularly with guitars and mandolins, making sure they arrived late, when the customers were well lubricated and more generous toward outstretched tambourines. We once watched in discreet fascination as one of the most famous playwrights in the world edged in on his dinner partner, one of the most celebrated male ballet dancers in the world, who was not interested but who was a sport about the advance, and the two moved their chairs gently around the table in a sort of *pas de pasta*. A regular customer who because of a bad accident was condemned to spend his life in a wheelchair drank pretty good anyway, and often danced to the Rolling Stones by scooting his wheelchair around the floor. Bill Anderson, a television producer, came in with a toy pistol and ordered "Everybody drop . . ." and everybody, including Elaine, fell to the floor and then got up laughing. Elaine cashed checks she knew would bounce, or if she wanted to save herself trouble, she just held them until the guy who wrote them could wangle another 200 bucks' advance out of his editor at Random House for the book that was two years overdue.

Elaine discouraged the gay set by the simple expedient of refusing to seat two tables of men side by side. "If you walk into a place cold and you see six tables of fellows lined up, you know it ain't a sales meeting," she said, and she made her point by making groups of lads wait for an hour or two at the bar until a heterosexual juxtaposition could be accomplished. Usually they got annoyed and left, loudly, which was what Elaine wished anyway. She didn't let any working girls in, either, unless they arrived with writers—which can certainly happen now and then—but the models were there every night in pajamas and pants and things with marvelous slashes up and down, all clanking in gold and brass and aluminum, and all generally about six months ahead of Diana Vreeland. I saw my first see-through come sailing through Elaine's front door about 1965, and four of us spent 30 minutes arguing whether the wearer had forgotten her bra, deliberately left it off or was just Peggy Moffitt running one of Rudi Gernreich's outrages up the flagpole.

There were Gauloises Bleues in the cigarette machine, and the toilet was a clean tiny place next to the kitchen so while you stood in line you could talk to the chef and feel the waves of heat—a worthy way to stay off 11th-hour rockiness. Bobby Short was on the juke box—Mabel Mercer, too—and it was the Harvard Club and "21" and Toots' and all the secret private places rolled into one. Elaine served a respectable drink and the bartender remembered your name and preference, and you could get a veal chop past midnight, and nobody even minded the vice squad bounding in now and then, convinced that something *had* to be going on in a place that existed way up Second Avenue at 88th in the heart of the Sauerkraut Belt and which had a yellow canopy and purple walls, besides.

Actually, not much worthy of their attention was going on. Any hustling at the bar was doomed to a sharp cry from Elaine herself ("Hey, cut that out!") and a glower and possible banishment forever if it continued. There was a marathon poker game (chairmanned by playwright Jack Richardson) which Elaine finally closed down because she thought writers should be writing, or drinking, or thinking, or talking, but not gambling, at least not at her establishment. There was an occasional bad drunk, but not many of those, because the one thing Elaine admired—almost required—was "stand-up gents." Such people, she explained, "can sit and drink all night and still pick themselves up and walk out. Most good writers are stand-up gents. Hemingway was." Jason Robards stood up on his chair one night and announced that I was an unethical liar because I had written an article about him and mentioned, in about the 48th paragraph, that he took a drink now and then. But he swayed in mid-accusation and fell toward his tumbler, saved from possible hurt by the quick reflexes of Christopher Plummer; his point was not well taken.

But nothing—not the food, not the drink, not the decor, not the antics of the clientele—nothing was as important as Elaine herself. Elaine Kaufman was her name, and she was the sole reason for her success. There may be tactful words to describe her size, but I can't find them, and besides, the truth is rarely tactful: Elaine was a big woman (she gained over 100 pounds with her success) with a warm and generous face. She wrapped us all in the protection of her bosom, next to the 10s and 20s she continually stuffed there. "You come in here like I used to go to my

22 NEW YORK

Illustrated by David Levine

NEW YORK 23

We asked master caricaturist David Levine to illustrate New York City's most popular literary hangout.

Elaine's, a favorite hangout for the city's writers, actors and power brokers, once stood at Second Avenue near Eighty-Eighth Street. What made the restaurant so great wasn't so much the food (the veal milanese was nothing special) but the people-watching. On any given night, you might catch a glimpse of Jacqueline Kennedy Onassis, Andy Warhol, Woody Allen, Gay Talese, Bruce Jay Friedman, George Plimpton, and Michael Caine, all regulars.

At the center of it all was its owner, Elaine Kaufman, a generous and formidable woman who took kindly to struggling writers. David Levine expertly captured her larger-than-life personality. The lively pencil sketch of the restaurant's interior also showcased his acuity in sketching from life. The article's writer, *Life* magazine entertainment editor Tommy Thompson, was perhaps too hasty in describing Elaine's "decline" in 1969. In fact, the restaurant continued to be a cherished hangout for many writers, artists, filmmakers, and actors for the next four decades.

To commemorate its fortieth anniversary in 2004, Elaine asked me to design a book by A. E. Hotchner about the restaurant and its famous patrons. The restaurant closed just a few months after Elaine passed away in 2010. "The truth is, there is no Elaine's without Elaine," her longtime manager Diane Becker explained. I don't think there's been a place like it since.—WB

DAVID LEVINE (1926–2009) was known for his incisive caricatures in *New York* magazine and every issue of *The New York Review of Books,* always in pen and ink. In this assignment he chose to use pencil alone as he recorded the scene at Elaine's (above). He drew the crowd on a typical night at the restaurant, with Elaine in the flowered dress with a large bow in her hair.
Photo by Walter Bernard

THE RESTAURANT'S ENTRANCE with the bright yellow canopy beckoned "like a lighthouse welcoming a lost traveler," with Elaine standing in the doorway.

ELAINE (right). Tommy Thompson wrote that Elaine had become "the leading literary *patronne* of the world. . . . But nothing—not the food, not the drink, not the decor, not the antics of the clientele—nothing was as important as Elaine herself. . . . She knew that people came to her place to demonstrate they knew and needed Elaine."

The Art of Previewing the Arts

THE FALL PREVIEW
was always a collective effort by the entire staff at the magazine, with a great deal of help from our contributors. Each issue covered theater, television, movies, sports, fashion, music, art, and books.
An example of the illustrated pages (left) from the 1974 Fall Catalogue reflects the format of the London *Sunday Times.*

London's *Sunday Times* magazine inspired our annual cultural guide.

We based the first edition of the catalogue on the design of the London *Sunday Times*, which had a particularly engaging cultural calendar. Each edition was packed with a lot of good writing and original art.

We had a month to work on the catalogue—a luxurious timeline compared to the four-day grind for the regular weekly editions. Every editor got involved in shaping these issues. The fall catalogues really demonstrated how much we depended on illustrations. We had a circle of artists who believed in the magazine and charged us less because they knew we didn't have a big budget. We would often pay around $100 per illustration, which is absurd. We commissioned illustrators like Daniel Maffia, Paul Davis, and Robert Weaver (above), among many others, to create drawings to accompany listings. Decades later, the original illustrations still look exceptional—teeming with graphic wit and great draftsmanship. It's unfortunate that we couldn't print all of them in color at that time.

UNIQUE STYLE
Seymour Chwast, Milton's partner at Push Pin Studios, illustrated six of the eight catalogue covers. The four examples (opposite) show his unique decorative style that set the catalogue apart from other issues. Seymour really understood our vernacular and made a big contribution to the magazine over the years.

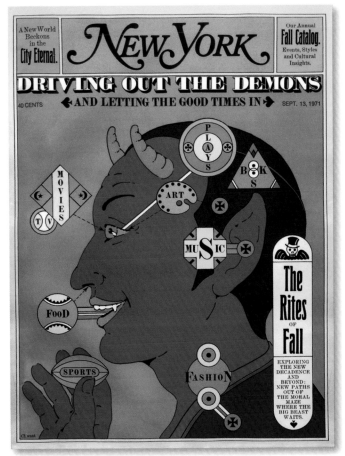

A Failure of the City

HERB GORO (1937–2019) was a photojournalist whose work first appeared in *New York* magazine at the *World Journal Tribune*. Goro (left) subsequently contributed several photo essays to *New York*, including "The Old Man and the Bronx" (January 10, 1972). In 1969, Herb met with Jason Epstein at Random House and showed him samples of the photographs and text of this project. Without hesitation, Random House decided to publish *The Block* in 1970. Goro wanted to "suggest that facile, abstract responses to poverty ignore real problems faced by real people in a real context."
Photo by Herb Goro

A sober portrait of the city's most neglected neighborhood, where residents struggled to survive.

A former social worker, photojournalist Herb Goro, lived in the decaying neighborhood of the East Bronx for over a year and fostered trusting relationships with its residents. Operating like an anthropologist, he recorded their stories of desperation and longing. In words and pictures, Goro delivered an indelible portrait of the East Bronx, then one of the most impoverished and crime-infested areas of the city. "The people of the 'block' live in two rotting tenements separated by a garbage-filled lot," he wrote.

His black-and-white photographs were particularly poignant and powerful. We felt they needed to be seen in a large format. We devoted the entire feature section of the issue—twenty-six pages in all—to Goro's compelling story.

Theodore W. Kheel, a labor mediator who supported Goro's study, keenly noted that the photographs provided "more factual information and understanding about life in the slums than 10,000 volumes of statistics."

Goro, however, stressed that he had certainly not resolved the dilemmas of poverty with this work. "Before anybody can try to solve a problem, they have to know what it's all about," he said. "I'm a photographer. I tried to show."

SIMPLE COVER IMAGE
Herb Goro's photograph showing a figure precariously leaping from rooftop to rooftop on East 174th Street (opposite) was printed as a high-contrast image for dramatic effect.

THE BLOCK was in one of the most densely populated neighborhoods in the country. Herb Goro wrote, "In New York there are countless people, many of them hardly more than children, who live and die like those on The Block. Their struggle is to survive in a city that has no need for them and which barely manages even to keep them alive."

New York

The Block: Portrait of an Urban Disaster

Photographs and Text By Herb Goro

The Block is on 174th Street near Washington Avenue in the East Bronx, part of a 55-block area that is one of the most densely populated neighborhoods in the country. Of the approximately 50,000 people who live there, 48 per cent are Negro, 48 per cent Puerto Rican and 4 per cent elderly white. They are among the one-fifth of all Bronx families with incomes below the poverty level.

This is one of the country's worst health areas, with a significantly high rate of venereal disease and infant mortality (29 deaths per 1,000) and a tuberculosis rate three times higher than the city average. It is also one of the worst crime areas in New York.

The people of The Block live in two rotting tenements separated by a garbage-filled lot. The following text consists of tape-recorded interviews with some of these people (shown in the accompanying pictures), focusing primarily on three adolescents as they come of age and fight to survive. In New York there are countless people, many of them hardly more than children, who live and die like those on The Block. Their struggle is to survive in a city that has no need for them and which barely manages even to keep them alive.

GENEVA, 19, said, "I want to get out of this block because it's filthy. It's too filthy. Just too filthy to raise children. . . . People just throw garbage out the window and the garbage men don't bother about coming collecting it."

Geneva Smith and her one-year-old daughter, Theresa.

Geneva

I was born in Savannah, Georgia, in 1951. My mother and my aunts were living together in something like an apartment building. A two-family house, they called it. My mother says she had a hard time there. You know, there wasn't hardly enough food for us, and she'd take food off her plate to give us. It's just that we had financial problems. That's all. Like money problems. We ran short of money sometimes, ran short of food sometimes, and stuff like that. We came to the city here in 1955 and I was only four.

But we came up to improve our life, you know. Up here we lived in different places before we came to the Bronx, three or four different places—117th Street and Jefferson Place; 155th Street, Washington Heights; Third Avenue and 177th Street. I don't know why we moved so much. I guess we was trying to get a better place, you know. On 177th Street the man didn't want to fit the door, so we moved. It was nice up there, though. Nice neighborhood, clean and everything. The man just didn't want to fit the door, so we left.

I was attending the Dodge High School on Southern Boulevard in the Bronx. Taking the bus, the number 19. Took me straight to Dodge. Then I switched to Roosevelt High, but I didn't finish. I was in the eleventh grade there when I dropped out. Time for my baby. You know, James. My mother didn't say too much about it. She just, you know, she wanted me to go and finish school and make something out of myself. But it was done, and what could she do. She cried a lot. She wanted me to take up nursing training and make something out of my life. She just said she was going to go all the way with me, that's all.

I didn't tell none of my friends 'cause I don't have friends. I have acquaintances. I didn't tell none of them. I told the school in my fifth month I was going down South to a funeral. In September, 1967. And I never came back. I guess they think I'm still down South at the funeral.

I felt guilty in a way, you know, 'cause I knew what I was doing then, and I was making a second mistake all over again. With Theresa, I didn't know what I was doing then. I was young, even younger. You know, my mother had explained everything to me, but I didn't take heed to it until I got Theresa, I guess. I was going to Dodge then. And I went to school through the whole nine months. I didn't start showing until my last month. We got out June the 27th in 1966 and on the 28th Theresa was born. The school

wrote and said I could come back 'cause my mother went and explained to them. So they still promoted me and gave me my award for attendance and my certificate and everything. Nobody knew anything 'cause I went to a doctor at seven o'clock at night. Until I had my certificate and everything.

In September, 1967, after I got pregnant again, I dropped out. My mother took that harder—than the first time, I mean. But now I'm going to school at night—Roosevelt. 'Cause I want to work during the day. But I liked school. I liked it a lot. And I was very smart in school. If I'm interested, I'll do my work. If I don't want to be bothered, I don't want to do nothing. When a subject gets boring, I don't want to do my work.

Me and my brother John's two different people, you know. I do what I want to do, he do what he wants to do. Now I just want to finish high school. That's just my ambition. I want to finish school and make something out of my life, 'cause I got to get a job that's making money. Nursing, that's what my ambition is.

Now then, when I heard Eddie—James' father—was robbing some grocery store, and killed this man—Hector Torres—I just couldn't believe it. I was shocked, you know. I say, "Murder? No, not Eddie." Then I picked up the paper and I saw it. And my mother couldn't believe it either. She don't like Eddie, but she couldn't believe it. And John—he hung around with Eddie—he couldn't believe it. I can't see Eddie doing something like that.

Eddie had come around to see the baby. He said, "I won't be able to see the baby any more." He said, "Here. Take this money and buy the baby a carriage and some clothes, and some food." He didn't say why. He said, "Tell the baby I'm his father. Even though you hate me." I said, "You working or something, you got all this money?" He said, "You'd be surprised what I do." I said, "Yeah, I bet I'd be surprised." And when I saw that paper about the murder, I was surprised!

So now Eddie is in prison and I've got my two children and I'm going to get out and work hard enough to take care of them. I don't think I need no man to help me.

That's why I was so excited when I passed the test for the job at the telephone company. I wanted the job then. So then this woman told me that my baby wasn't old enough, and that I'd have to come back when my baby gets old enough. So it hurt me 'cause I wanted to work then and there. I didn't want to wait for November. She says to come back and I'd get the job right

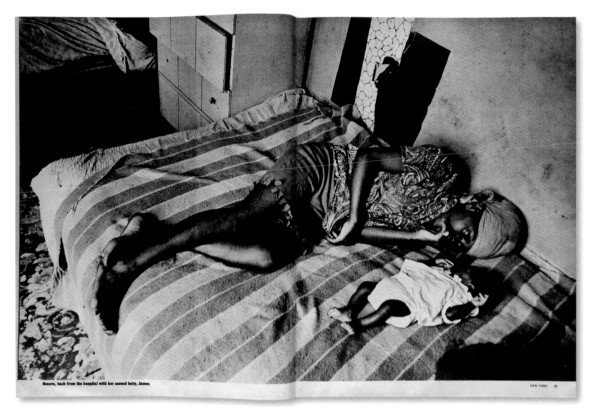

Geneva, back from the hospital with her second baby, James.

GENEVA added, "Now I just want to finish night school. That's just my ambition. I want to finish school and make something out of my life, 'cause I got to get a job that's making money. Nursing, that's what my ambition is."

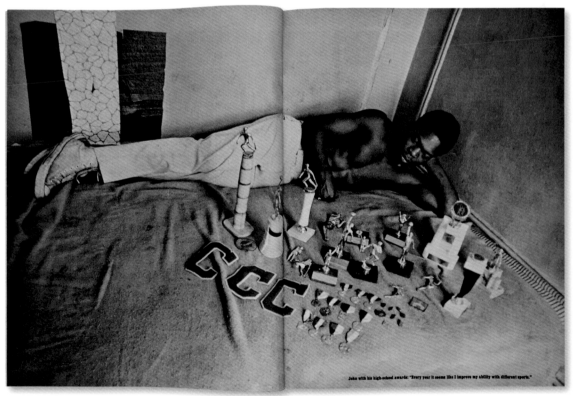

John with his high-school awards: "Every year it seems like I improve my ability with different sports."

JOHN, 21, said, "The main reason I want to go to college is to be an 'All-American.' Unless I get into college, I can't do it. I can't do it in high-school. I don't want to feel that I went to school for 12 years and I have to work for a dollar. . . . I feel like I can help myself. I can help my younger brothers come up better than I was. . . . I want them to have clothes, I mean decent clothes where you don't have to wear the same pants for three days. Or even getting up in the morning and they want to brush their teeth and they ain't got a toothbrush or toothpaste or they even got nothing to eat."

65

Tom Wolfe Goes to (Crashes?) a Party

New York dedicated its entire issue to a 25,000-word satirical essay about the Bernsteins' fundraising party.

SYMBOLIC HOMAGE
We designed the cover and had photographer Carl Fischer arrange three socialites up in arms wearing black gloves, a symbol used by the protesting athletes Tommie Smith and John Carlos at the 1968 Mexico Olympics.

In *Radical Chic: That Party at Lenny's*, Tom Wolfe recounted a political gathering at conductor Leonard Bernstein's Upper East Side residence. Organized by Felicia Bernstein as a fundraiser for "The Black Panther 21" awaiting trial, the occasion allowed New York's wealthiest movers and shakers to mingle with Black Panther Party members, and in effect, help pay their growing legal bills.

Tom slyly managed to crash the reception by replying to an invitation addressed to someone else. In his inimitable style, aided by an ability to take notes in shorthand, he masterfully painted an amusing tableau of Manhattan's elite white guilt or *nostalgie de la boue*, as he puts it. Our issue was published on June 8, 1970, six months after a succession of *New York Times* articles had mocked the Bernsteins. Nevertheless, it caused wide-ranging reactions from our readers as well as from the journalistic community.

We received so many impassioned letters about this article, to the point where we had to run them over several issues. Not only did Tom's reporting divide our readers, but for a time, it apparently dissuaded influential people from hosting cause-oriented gatherings for fear of ridicule. "Unfortunately, many potential contributors run scared," writes lyricist Sheldon Harnick, who was a guest at the party. "Publicity, particularly adverse publicity, frightens them away. . . . And when the publicity (and the mockery!) come from what one considers a sympathetic source, e.g., your magazine or *The New York Times*, the results are devastating."

The photographs by Steve Salmieri, which were not assigned by us, were a most surprising gift. His intimate photographs brought the whole event alive.

TOM WOLFE: "One day I was hanging around a hallway at *Harper's* magazine. . . . I wandered next door into the office of David Halberstam, who wasn't there. Nosily I noticed a rather fancy card on his desk. . . . It was an invitation from Leonard Bernstein and his wife, Felicia, for a reception at their apartment at 895 Park Avenue, corner of Park and 79th Street, in support of the Black Panthers. . . . You were supposed to RSVP to a certain telephone number. So I called it, using David Halberstam's phone, and said, 'This is Tom Wolfe, and I accept.'"
—Tom Wolfe "A City Built of Clay," *New York* magazine, July 6, 2008. Photo by Cosmos Sarchiapone

STEVE SALMIERI: "Late that evening, I got a call from Tom who was already at the party. We met briefly at the *New York* magazine offices, and he got my number from 411—something you could do at that time. I recruited the model who I was photographing to be my assistant because I needed help carry the big umbrella and the lights. Tom had already left when I got there but Felicia Bernstein answered the door, and without question, she welcomed us in."
Photo by Sydnie Salmieri

Radical Chic:
That Party at Lenny's

By Tom Wolfe

"... It's a tricky business, integrating new politics with tried and true social motifs ..."

Do Panthers like Roquefort morsels?

At 2 or 3 or 4 a.m., somewhere along in there, on August 25, 1966, his 48th birthday, in fact, Leonard Bernstein woke up in the dark in a state of wild alarm. That had happened before. It was one of the forms his insomnia took. So he did the usual. He got up and walked around a bit. He felt groggy. Suddenly he had a vision, an inspiration. He could see himself, Leonard Bernstein, the *egregio maestro*, walking out on stage in white tie and tails in front of a full orchestra. On one side of the conductor's podium is a piano. On the other is a chair with a guitar leaning against it. He sits in the chair and picks up the guitar. A guitar! One of those half-witted instruments, like the accordion, that are made for the Learn-To-Play-in-Eight-Days E-Z-Diagram 110-IQ 14-year-olds of Levittown! But there's a reason. He has an anti-war message to deliver to this great starched white-throated audience in the symphony hall. He announces to them: "I love." Just that. The effect is mortifying. All at once a Negro rises up from out of the curve of the grand piano and starts saying things like, "The audience is curiously embarrassed." Lenny tries to start again, plays some quick numbers on the piano, says, "I love. *Amo, ergo sum.*" The Negro rises again and says, "The audience thinks he ought to get up and walk out. The audience thinks, 'I am ashamed even to nudge my neighbor.'" Finally, Lenny gets off a heartfelt anti-war speech and exits.

For a moment, sitting there alone in his home in the small hours of the morning, Lenny thought it might just work and he jotted the idea down. Think of the headlines: BERNSTEIN ELECTRIFIES CONCERT AUDIENCE WITH ANTI-

WAR APPEAL. But then his enthusiasm collapsed. He lost heart. Who the hell was this Negro rising up from the piano and informing the world what an ass Leonard Bernstein was making of himself? It didn't make sense, this superego Negro by the concert grand.

Mmmmmmmmmmmmmmm. These are nice. Little Roquefort cheese morsels rolled in crushed nuts. Very tasty. Very subtle. It's the way the dry sackiness of the nuts tiptoes up against the dour savor of the cheese that is so nice, so subtle. Wonder what the Black Panthers eat here on the hors d'oeuvre trail? Do the Panthers like little Roquefort cheese morsels wrapped in crushed nuts this way, and asparagus tips in mayonnaise dabs, and *meatballs petites au Coq Hardi*, all of which are at this very moment being offered to them on gadrooned silver platters by maids in black uniforms with hand-ironed white aprons ... The butler will bring them their drinks ... Deny it if you wish to,

Felicia and Leonard Bernstein and guest Don Cox

"Everyone in the room is drinking in Cox's performance like tiger's milk, for the Soul"

Nations to be held in black communities, so that we can control our own destiny" ...

Everyone in the room, of course, is drinking in his performance like tiger's milk, for the ... Soul, as it were. All love the tone of his voice, which is Confidential Hip. And yet his delivery falls into strangely formal patterns. What are these black phrases, such as "our Minister of Defense, Huey P. Newton"—

"Some people think that we are racist, because the news media find it useful to create that impression in order to support the power structure, which we have nothing to do with ... see ... They like for the Black Panther Party to be made to look like a racist organization, because that camouflages the true class nature of the struggle. But they find it harder and harder to keep up that camouflage and are driven to campaign of harassment and violence to try to eliminate the Black Panther Party. Here in New York 21 members of the Black Panther Party were indicted last April on ridiculous charges of conspiring to blow up department stores and flower gardens. They've had 27 bail hearings since last April ... see ... "

—But everyone in here loves the *sees* and the *you knows*. They are so, somehow ... *black* ... so *funky* ... so metrical ... Without ever bringing it fully into consciousness everyone over—the fact that he uses them not for emphasis, but for punctuation, metrically, much like the *uhs* favored by High Church Episcopal ministers, as in, "And bless, uh, these gifts, uh, to Thy use and us to, uh, Thy service"—

" ... they've had 27 bail hearings since last April ... see ... and every time the judge has refused to lower the bail from $100,000 ... Yet a group of whites accused of actually bombing buildings—they were able to get bail. So that clearly demonstrates the racist nature of the campaign against the Black Panther Party. We don't say bail anymore, we say 'ransom,' for such repressive bail can only be called ransom.

"The situation here in New York is very explosive, as you can see, with people stacked up on top of each other. They can hardly deal with them when they're amorganized, so that when a group comes along like the Black Panthers, they want to eliminate that group by any means ... see ... and so that stand has been embraced by J. Edgar Hoover, who feels that we are the great-

est threat to the power structure. They try to create the impression that we are engaged in criminal activities. What are these 'criminal activities'? We have instituted a breakfast program, to address ourselves to the needs of the community. We feed hungry children every morning before they go to school. So far this program *is* on a small scale. We're only feeding 50,000 children nationwide, but the only money we have for this program is donations from the merchants in the neighborhoods. We have a program to establish clinics in the black communities and in other ways also we are addressing ourselves to the needs of the community ... see ... So the people know the power structure is lying when they say we are engaged in criminal activities. So the pigs are driven to desperate acts, like the murder of our deputy chairman, Fred Hampton, in his bed ... see ... in his sleep ... But when they got desperate and took off their camouflage and murdered Fred Hampton, in his bed, in his sleep, see, that kind of shook people up, because they saw the tactics of the power structure for what they were.

"We relate to a phrase coined by Malcolm X: 'By any means necessary' ... you see ... 'By any means necessary' ... and by that we mean that we recognize that if you're attacked, you have the right to defend yourself. The pigs, they say the Black Panthers are armed, the Black Panthers have weapons ... see ... and therefore they have the right to break in and murder us in our beds. I don't think there's anybody in here who wouldn't defend themselves if somebody came in and attacked them or their families ... see ... I don't think there's anybody in here who wouldn't defend themselves ...

—and every woman in the room thinks of her husband ... with his cocoa-butter jowls and Dior Men's Boutique pajamas ... ducking into the bathroom and locking the door and turning the shower on, so he can say later that he didn't hear a thing—

"We call them pigs, and rightly so," says Don Cox, "because they have the way of making the victim look like the criminal, and the criminal look like the victim. So every Panther must be ready to defend himself. That was handed down by our Minister of Defense, Huey P. Newton: Everybody who does not have the means to defend himself in his home, or if he does have the means and he does not defend himself—we expel *that man* ... see ... As our Min-

ister of Defense, Huey P. Newton, says, 'Any unarmed people are slaves, or are slaves in the real meaning of the word' ... We recognize that this country is the most oppressive country in the world, maybe in the history of the world. The pigs have the weapons and they are ready to use them on the people, and we recognize this as being very bad. They are ready to commit genocide against those who stand up against

Hard by the million-dollar chatchkas, Don Cox speaks and Leon Quat, a lawyer for the "Panther 21," listens

them, and we recognize this as being very bad.

"All we want is the good life, the same as you. To live in peace and lead the good life, that's all we want ... see ... But right now there's no way we can do that. I want to read something to you:

"'When in the course of human events, it becomes necessary for one people to dissolve the political bands

which have connected them with another, and ...' He reads straight through it, every word. " ... and, accordingly, all experience hath shown, that mankind are more disposed to suffer, while evils are sufferable, than to right themselves by abolishing the forms to which they are accustomed. But when a long train of abuses and usurpations, pursuing invariably the same object, evinces a design to reduce them under absolute

despotism, it is their right, it is their duty, to throw off such government, and to provide new guards for their future security.'

"You know what that's from?"—and he looks out at everyone and hesitates before laying this gasper on them—"That's from the Declaration of Independence, the American Declaration of Independence. And we will defend ourselves and do like it says ... you know?

67

Nixon, Nixon, and More Nixon

The many phases of a polarizing figure

New York was a real anti-Nixon town, and the magazine reflected its mood. Luckily for us, he was a great subject to have fun with. His face had striking, peculiar features, making it ripe for caricature. He had large jowls and a distinctive hairline, and always looked like he needed a shave.

Nixon served as the magazine's antihero throughout his inglorious tenure. From Nixon as a "fiddler of Wall Street" by Paul Davis to Nixon as a lonely piano player by Julian Allen, his gaffes often ended up on the cover of the magazine.

Illustration by Paul Davis

Illustration by David Levine

Illustration by Robert Grossman

Illustration by Alan Magee

Illustration by Haruo Miyauchi

Illustration by Julian Allen

NORA EPHRON
(1941–2012), a prolific
writer, author (*Crazy
Salad, Heartburn, I Feel
Bad About My Neck*) and
film director (*Sleepless
in Seattle, You've Got
Mail, Julie and Julia*), was
a contributing editor to
the magazine. Her *Israeli
Notebook: Thoughts
with the Ceasefire* was
reported from Israel
(December 3, 1973).
In this cover story
(opposite) Nora writes:
"The loyal secretary
who did it for The Boss?
Or the loyal secretary
who was set up? The
tiger or the lady?"
Photo: Nicholas Pileggi

RICHARD HESS, (1934–
1991), an illustrator,
art director, and designer,
painted this American
primitive version of Rose
Mary Woods, Nixon's
secretary (opposite).
Working on an extremely
tight deadline, he
delivered it shortly after
midnight, just hours
before press time. Hess
always maintained that
it was still unfinished.
Photo: Mark Hess

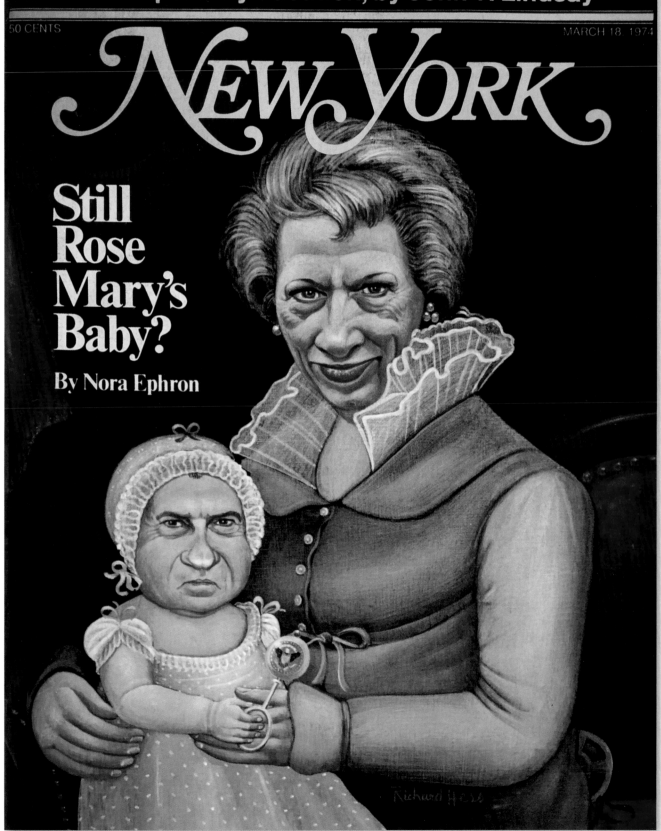

An Incredible Evening With Joey Gallo
Cassoulet in New York? James Beard Spills the Beans
How I Spent My Vacation, by John V. Lindsay

50 CENTS

MARCH 18, 1974

New York

Still Rose Mary's Baby?

By Nora Ephron

THE FUNNIEST Nixon portrait was a gift from the heavens. In 1973, RitaSue Siegel, a subscriber, came to our office bearing a curious shoebox. She claimed to be in possession of a "Nixon eggplant," as she called it. When she unwrapped it, I thought it looked like any ordinary eggplant. She turned it around and Nixon's face appeared! Without any question, that's who God was imitating.

Peggy Barnett photographed it for us. We asked Jerome Snyder, who was a notary public, to certify that we didn't tamper with the Nixon eggplant or perform any photo manipulation. We printed his authenticity stamp (below) along with the photograph. After the photo shoot, managing editor Byron Dobell brought the miraculous eggplant home. His wife, Elizabeth, cooked it for dinner.

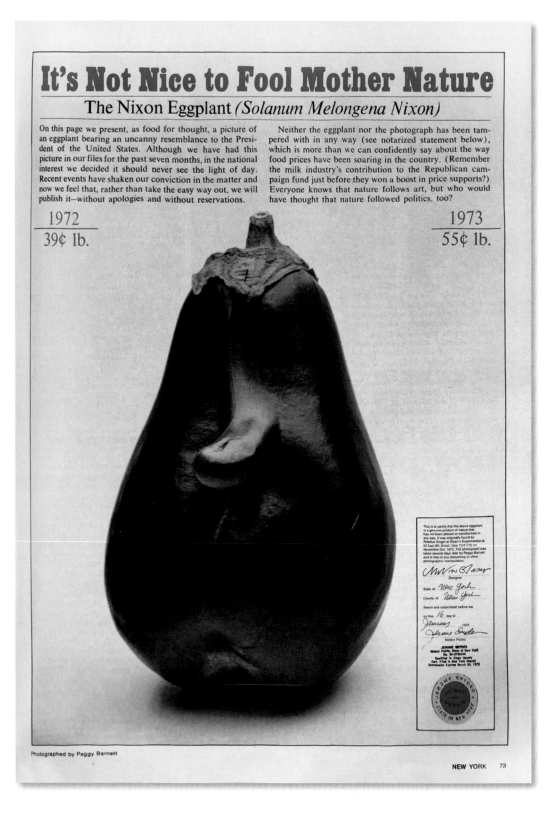

It's Not Nice to Fool Mother Nature
The Nixon Eggplant *(Solanum Melongena Nixon)*

On this page we present, as food for thought, a picture of an eggplant bearing an uncanny resemblance to the President of the United States. Although we have had this picture in our files for the past seven months, in the national interest we decided it should never see the light of day. Recent events have shaken our conviction in the matter and now we feel that, rather than take the easy way out, we will publish it—without apologies and without reservations.

Neither the eggplant nor the photograph has been tampered with in any way (see notarized statement below), which is more than we can confidently say about the way food prices have been soaring in the country. (Remember the milk industry's contribution to the Republican campaign fund just before they won a boost in price supports?) Everyone knows that nature follows art, but who would have thought that nature followed politics, too?

1972
39¢ lb.

1973
55¢ lb.

Photographed by Peggy Barnett

NEW YORK 73

70

DAVID WILCOX painted a recognizable cover portrait (opposite) by just depicting Nixon's hairline. It's an astonishing thing that you can tell who it is even without seeing his face.

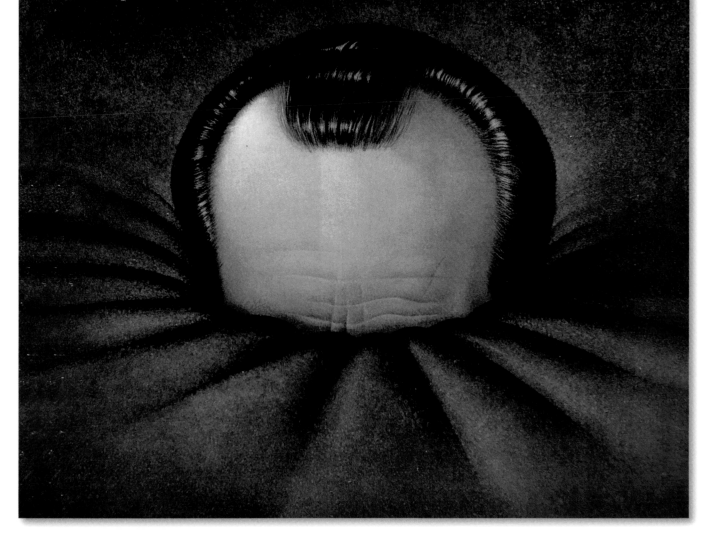

FEBRUARY POSTER-SIZE ENTERTAINMENT CALENDAR

What's Free in February
Does Wall Street Know a Bargain?
by Andrew Tobias

50 CENTS

FEBRUARY 4, 1974

NEW YORK

Is Nixon Finally Going Under?

Why Things Are
Going to Get Worse
Before They Get Worse,
By Joseph Kraft

The Remarkable
Jaworski
Prosecution Team,
By Robert Daley

The Sinister Force
Entangling Al Haig,
By Evans
And Novak

71

A Teenager's Dilemma

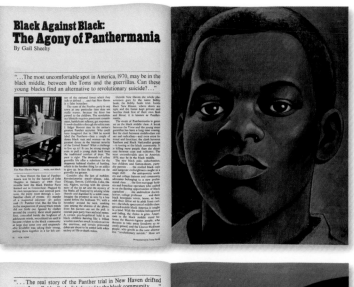

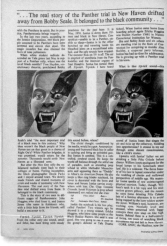

THE BOY AND THE BEAST,
in the striking portraits
by Paul Davis, are symbols
of innocence and violence
(left). These two images
are combined to illustrate
the seduction of the
Black Panther cause on
the cover (opposite).

PAUL DAVIS is an
internationally celebrated
artist and graphic
designer, perhaps best
known for his posters for
the Public Theater. He
grew up in Oklahoma,
attended the School of
Visual Arts, and joined
Push Pin Studios before
starting an independent
career. His distinctive
paintings for magazines
and books have led to
gallery exhibitions and
museum retrospectives
in Europe, Japan, and
the United States. He is
a Fellow of the American
Academy in Rome.

Photo by Cosmos Sarchiapone

Combining two images to dramatize the conflict facing young African Americans

As the Black Panther movement raged across America in
the late 1960s, Gail Sheehy spent six months tracking
a story about a growing chasm within the African American community. It wasn't just whites versus blacks anymore. The
notion that black children should be ready to serve as zealous
revolutionaries for the cause divided middle-class black families.
The paintings by Paul Davis perfectly capture the juxtaposition
between innocence and violence that's at the crux of the narrative.

In Connecticut, where Gail conducted her study, the funeral
of John Huggins, the son of a black judge, brought tensions to a
boiling point. The story is an example of her numerous forays in
"saturation reporting," a mode of journalism that involves deep
immersion in the subject's milieu. "I spent the summer half-living
in New Haven," Gail explains. "Gradually you earn trust because
you're sympathetic to their agony. You really had to prove
yourself for people to open up."

**SHEEHY ON CULTURAL
REPORTING:**
"The great anthropologist
Margaret Mead, who was
my teacher at Columbia
University, gave me my
marching orders as a
cultural interpreter. She
said, 'You don't have to
go to the Fiji Islands, you
can be an interpreter in
your own city. Whenever
there is a revolution or
an assassination or an
epidemic, get there and
you will see your culture
inside out as you rarely
do.' That was incredible
advice. That's what I did."

Jimmy Breslin on the Silent Plurality
Who's Afraid of Jim Buckley? by Dick Schaap
Best of the Jug Wines: A Taste Test

40 CENTS

NOVEMBER 16, 1970

NEW YORK

BLACK AGAINST BLACK: THE AGONY OF PANTHERMANIA
BY GAIL SHEEHY

Covers We Like, 1970

SURVIVAL KIT This issue with the simple universal symbol was the precursor of the handbook series.

ALARM DECAL This fake home alarm sign was cut out and placed by some readers on their front door.

FENCING The Master Fence with a "hot" magazine photographed by Harold Krieger.

SATIRICAL HOMAGE to the breakfast scene from the 1931 film *The Public Enemy* with James Cagney and Mae Clarke, hand-tinted by Saul Weil.

AN OLD JEWISH JOKE A woman is walking, pushing her son in a wheelchair, and someone comes over and says, "I'm so sorry." The woman replies, "For what?" "For your son, he can't walk!" The woman says, "Of course he can walk. Thank God he doesn't have to." We took the writer Jane O'Reilly to lunch to talk about the story, and Milton remembered this old joke. We used that exact punch line on the cover, assuming that a large part of the audience would get it (opposite).

ADAM MOSS, editor-in-chief of *New York* magazine (2004–2019) remembers this cover: "The issue came out in 1970, when I was 13, and I remember yanking it from our mail pile. At the time, I thought it—picture and headline in unison—was hilarious. I still do. The cover taught me that great magazines are steeped in point of view, voice, tone. They live. And seeing that cover for the first time is probably what made me want to make magazines for a living, though I didn't know it at the time."

—*Highbrow, Lowbrow, Brilliant, Despicable: Fifty Years of New York Magazine*

Buckley, the Castle Irishman, by Pete Hamill
The Arrogance of Culture Power
Remaking the Champ, by Gordon Parks

40 CENTS

OCTOBER 26, 1970

New York

Notes on the Paralyzed Generation

"Of course he can walk. Thank God he doesn't have to."

Photograph by Carl Fischer

Third Manned Moon Landing
On February 5, 1971, *Apollo 14* landed on the moon with Commander Alan Shepard; Stuart Roosa, commander module pilot; and Edgar Mitchell, lunar module pilot. Shepard became the fifth person to walk on the moon. The crew returned to earth on February 9 with ninety pounds of lunar rocks and samples.

A Historic Election
Satchel Paige was the first Negro League player voted into the Baseball Hall of Fame, on February 9, 1971.

A Trippy Tale of Medical Malfeasance

We took readers along for an appointment with "Dr. Feelgood."

OUR COVER
(left) featured Alfred Gescheidt's photograph of a masked figure dressed as a doctor with Susan's face reflected in his head mirror. Duane Michals's interpretation of Doctor Feelgood's treatment (opposite) is based on Susan's recollections.

SUSAN WOOD RICHARDSON
is a journalist and photographer. Her work appeared frequently on the pages of *Vogue*, *Look*, *Life*, *People*, and *New York* throughout the 1970s and 1980s. Among the most loved work in her portfolio is a series of unguarded images of then newlyweds John Lennon and Yoko Ono.
Photo: Susan Wood Richardson

The term "Dr. Feelgood" belongs to several notorious physicians in history. Dr. Theodor Morell, who treated Adolf Hitler, and Dr. Max Jacobson, John F. Kennedy's personal physician, are among them. This type of doctor treated any type of ailment—from pimples to impotence—with the liberal use of mood-lifting chemicals, for which their suffering patients gladly paid a typically high price. Susan Wood, an accomplished photographer, wrote an illuminating exposé of three Dr. Feelgoods practicing in Manhattan.

To illustrate the article, Susan's treatment sessions were dramatized in a series of photographs by Duane Michals. We thought his interest in subjectivity and surrealism fit Susan's first-person narrative. Duane often injected some deviation from the assignment we gave him. In this case, his imaginary sequence portrayed Susan's treatment sessions.

DUANE MICHALS
made a mark with artfully manipulated images presented in a sequence of frames. He championed subjectivity and imagination in an era obsessed with photojournalism. Duane's work reminds us that "photography deals exquisitely with appearances, but nothing is what it appears to be," as he puts it.
Photo: Duane Michals

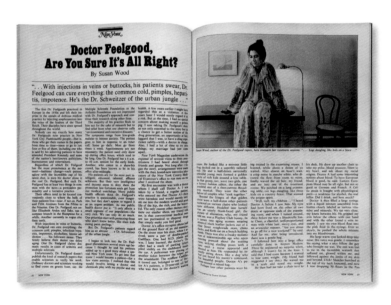

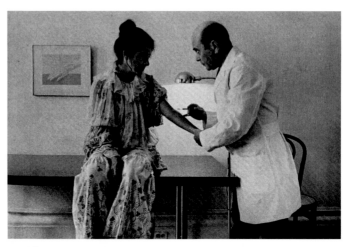

Susan Wood, author of the Dr. Feelgood report, here re-enacts her treatment sessions: ". . . Legs dangling, like kids on a fence . . ."

". . . His warm eyes looked deep into mine. I saw my own blood float into the pink fluid in the syringe . . ."

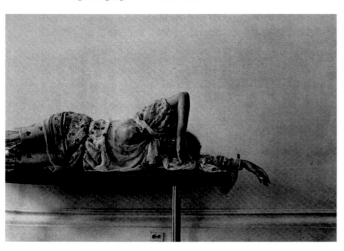

". . . An incredible warmth suffused me, glowed within me, and billowed against the limits of my skin and beyond . . ."

". . . Now I was dropping 30 floors in the Pan Am elevator and spinning on in an undulating thrill . . ."

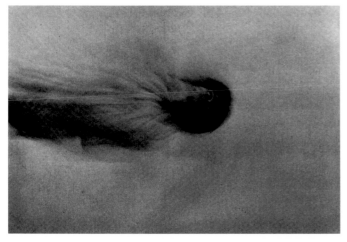

". . . Bad trip. My jaw muscles ached. I felt as if my teeth were loose. I couldn't chew for a week . . ."

". . . I felt drugged and tense at the same time. Whatever appeal the shots once held was gone. Totally gone . . ."

A Clever Idea That Fell Flat

For "New Think: A Way to Solve the City's Problems by Turning Them Upside Down"—we did just that to our logo.

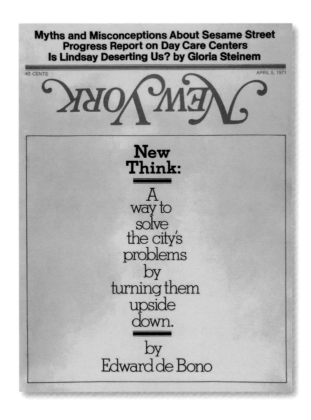

This may have been our worst-selling issue ever. We turned *New York*'s logo upside down to illustrate the concept of Edward de Bono's problem-solving theory called "lateral thinking." De Bono suggests that embracing indirect and creative routes often leads to the best solutions. We thought that turning the logo on its head was a clever way to illustrate his point. Unfortunately, our readers didn't recognize the magazine on newsstands!

In retrospect, if we had taken the Empire State Building and turned it upside down, it would have been a more clearly understood image. There's nothing to hold on to on this cover. You have to be careful when you experiment with novel ideas.

Designing a cover is like telling a joke. First a moment of confusion, where you engage the audience without their complete understanding of what's going on. Then their minds work to put things together until they arrive at the punch line. This happens very quickly on a magazine cover, but the interval is crucial in all of communication. Sometimes it works; sometimes it results in bad sales.

In contrast to the misguided cover, the article presented a real service by highlighting eight of the city's most pressing problems, skillfully illustrated by our community of contributing illustrators.

EDWARD DE BONO
is a Maltese physician, psychologist, philosopher, and author who has done a great deal of research on the thinking process. His book *New Think* was published in 1971.

CRIME IN THE STREETS

Conventional Solution:
More cops; more honest cops.

Lateral Solution:
Instead of more cops, multiply the same number of cops.

Equip police street patrols with special motorcycles that make a distinctive noise. After the noise becomes associated with the police, give away numbers of these motorcycles to teenagers in trouble districts.

Pedestrians carry small alarm buttons. When squeezed, these buttons would emit a sound pitched so high that only dogs could hear it. Train patrolling dogs (or their own or with police) to respond to the sound by running toward it and then attacking whoever moves. The attacker would never know if or when such a button was being used.

Alarm buttons as above, but relaying to police receivers in patrol car or at street corner.

Passersby are unwilling to get physically involved in street crime for fear of getting hurt. But they could still act on passive eyes and ears and they need not even be tough. Give special radio sending sets, for instance, to old people who habitually sit by windows, also to teenagers. The sets would then connect to police patrol points. Direct rewards for reporting incidents.

Pay indigenous street gangs on a bonus-rate basis for decline in street crime in their neighborhoods.

PUBLIC TRANS-PORTATION

Conventional Solution:
More subways and buses—well-maintained and under better control.

Lateral Solution:
Not more buses but more bus space, and split the buses in half.

Fifty per cent of city street area to be given over to the use of buses (and taxis, police cars, fire trucks, ambulances, etc.). Fine anyone else using these streets. Buses to be open platforms with no route and no ride. Completely free. Can be boarded and left at any point (including bus stops and traffic lights). In addition, luxury buses at standard $1 fare. Thus those who want privacy and comfort subsidize the free transport system.

Multi-cabs. Taxis seating twelve people. Standard fare of $1 payable on entry regardless of destination; no change given. Multi-cabs operate in limited areas which is divided up into fixed fare points, each of which is designated by a letter (e.g., Times Square, the Metropolitan Museum). Resident New Yorkers will quickly learn the relevant letters or use special maps displayed in streets (or just a pocket list). The multi-cab has an illuminated board showing four destinations (e.g., K, M, A, B). If you wish to go to any of these you hail the cab and get in. When there are less than four destinations showing on the board, you can hail the cab and add your own destination. Destinations are taken in strict rotation as shown on the board even if this means doubling back on the route. When the cab is full the illuminated board is switched off, as it is presently. No "off-duty" signs. Relief driver is picked up en route.

Maximum use would be made of a subway track if there was a continuous ribbon of a train flowing like a river along the track. Similar effect can be achieved with multiple small trains linked together, not physically but by interlinked controls so that each can follow very closely behind the other and yet start and stop independently. Perhaps eventually a no-stop continuous train with acceleration of passengers at stations to join it in motion.

POLLUTION

Conventional Solution:
Ban automobiles and factories from city.

Lateral Solution:
Don't ban automobiles or even the right to pollute, but simply abolish the free right to pollute.

Automobiles wishing to operate within the city must display the special city license in numbered disk). Cost of this city license varies each year according to the following factors:

1. Average pollution level over the past year.
2. Number of automobiles bearing the license in the past year; cost of licenses increases with number.
3. Whether or not car owner is resident in city.

Normal cost might be in the region of $500 a year for non-residents and $250 for residents. For various fines would be a $10-a-day license. If pollution levels remain static, the tax would automatically escalate by 20 per cent per year.

Parallel scheme for factories.

Every car to have one free parking day a week in the city. Automobile might bear a Monday disk or a Tuesday disk, etc. This would spread load and might encourage commuters to share cars.

RATS

Conventional Solution:
HEW has cut funds from the Rat Control Program run by the Health Services Administration—reinstate funds for existing program and add more.

Lateral Solution:
Try to introduce some self-control into rat population or situation.

Use of sex hormones in bait to sterilize male or female rats (birth control). Or use of concrete tunnel blocks with radioactive ingredients buried in them.

Use of synthetic peptide encephalon (as discovered by Dr. Ungar) which makes rats afraid of the dark. Easier to catch by day—for instance, by trained but free-running terriers.

Research involving transfer of learning in rats. If this is effective, train rats to respond to a tone by seeking it out; then run them toward destination (a Pied Piper fashion, getting rid of them forever).

Breed special edible rats and use to drive out indigenous rats.

Rat-hunting clubs and licenses with rewards for best monthly catches.

Equip and reward teenage rat-catch teams; reward not on limits of rats caught but on rat-free areas.

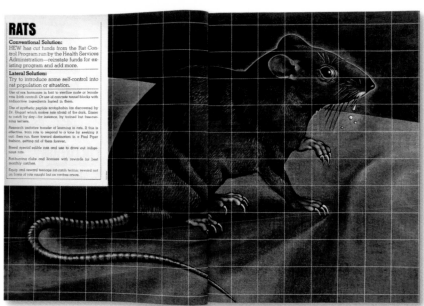

PRISON AND COURT REFORM

Conventional Solution:
Question whole point of prison detention; analyze process by which individual ends up in prison (e.g., drugs, poverty, alienation); work for justice in courts by speeding up bail hearings, sentencing, etc.

Lateral Solution:
Treat crime not as a sin but as social inconvenience.

To avoid court delays, allow criminals to try themselves. Criminal offers his version to a computer programmed to learn. The prosecution does the same. The computer will develop experience in cross-questioning and other courtroom skills. Computer to provide sentence as well. Appeals procedure with provision for increasing sentence if conviction is upheld. First sentence could be relatively small, but for future convictions escalation of sentence is rapid since repetition of computer error becomes less and less likely.

Prisoners to earn a full wage in special prison "cities." Wages to be accumulated to be given to convict in installments after release.

HOUSING SHORTAGE

Conventional Solution:
Build more public housing; offer loans and tax incentives for construction of private housing.

Lateral Solution:
Instead of providing incentives, build in improvement factors.

Paired-building policy. Every building project which is not low-rent housing (e.g., office) to be paired with low-rent project. You cannot build one without the other. Not a matter of paying tax but of actual construction effort so that both projects proceed simultaneously. Original project cannot be used until paired project is also ready for use.

Raise nominal rents. The worse the condition of the property, the higher the rent. But the rent becomes payable in a number of non-cash ways:

1. Incremental improvement to property by resident with supplied materials (e.g., paint).
2. Time spent with "house improvement squads" which move from house to house.
3. Construction work on building project.

Tax people on place of work rather than place of residence. This would prevent city getting poorer as people move out to suburbs.

Fixed proportion laws for lending institutions whereby a certain proportion of their total investments must be in local housing.

DIRTY STREETS

Conventional Solution:
Employ more sanitationmen; more and better equipment.

Lateral Solution:
In order to clean streets it may be useful to dirty them first.

A major difficulty is to determine the effectiveness of street cleaning, for a dirty street may still have been cleaned often. Paper leaves with a specific color for a specific date would be scattered in the streets. It would then be easy to check on the effectiveness of the cleaning by counting the persistence of these leaves (e.g., how many per square yard). For instance, if red leaves were used on June 1 and were still present in high numbers on July 1, then the agency responsible for street cleaning would clearly be at fault. On this basis one could reward or penalize workers, or subcontract street cleaning to private agencies.

Manufacturers could pay a garbage tax at source. This would be based on the garbage potential of the item. The money could then be used to buy garbage (a city resource) from free-lance collectors.

Give street-corner garbage concessions to individuals who would be paid for every street-corner tank that was then hoisted onto a truck.

DRUGS

Conventional Solution:
Legalize drugs (from marijuana to heroin) under strict controls.

Lateral Solution:
Instead of legalizing drugs, legalize and tightly control the [illegal] sale of drugs.

Special "treatment" centers for on-the-spot heroin injection (dispensed in syringes only). Run by state or even by private enterprise. Heroin not free but sold at 50 per cent of prevailing free market price. Proceeds to be used for running the centers and also for rehabilitation centers. At the same center, free dispensing of methadone to another drug capable of coping solely with physical dependence on heroin to remove characteristic dependence desperation.

Infiltrate free market with heroin-B, a mixture of heroin with an additive which cannot be detected on immediate use but which has a cumulative effect. For instance, one might add synthetic estrogen. This is a deterrent to first-time experimenters, who would cast lamination (enlarged breasts, loss of libido, etc.). Perhaps even a rumor of such addition would be effective.

Research into "depot" heroin or methadone on a basis for single-shot drying out technique (one single shot would provide diminishing supply, in place of repeated injections with a smaller amount each time).

Pot smoking licenses with central register open to inspection. Licenses to be paid for yearly with proceeds to help finance drug rehabilitation services. Licenses withdrawn if abused. Illegal to smoke pot without a license or to sell to non-licensees. State sales monopoly.

An Honest but Complicated Cop

Plainclothesman Frank Serpico was the poster child of the New York Police Department's campaign to clear its ranks of corruption in the 1970s.

A whistleblower who wore inventive disguises—from Antoine, the Belgian diamond dealer, to a street sweeper, a British lawyer, and an Amish tourist—Frank Serpico gained notoriety by exposing fellow cops who were receiving payoffs, committing acts of violence, and participating in a range of other crimes.

Detective Sergeant David Durk introduced Robert Daley, a freelance journalist, to Serpico, his former partner. Daley pitched Clay Felker a profile about "an honest cop who was funny and bizarre." As he was just beginning to work on the story, he learned that Serpico was shot in the face during a drug bust in Williamsburg, Brooklyn. There were wild speculations about who could have targeted him. "A high-ranking police official said later, that 'When word came in that Serpico had been shot, this building shook,'" Robert writes. "'We were terrified that a cop had done it.'"

Rather than a photo of Serpico on the cover, we felt that the hospital X-ray showing where the bullet was lodged in his skull made the most impact. We also published one of several death threats disguised as get-well cards that he received and assigned Herb Goro, the astute photojournalist who wrote "The Block" (p. 62), to photograph Serpico. He lived in a tiny, cluttered apartment in Greenwich Village, and did not like to invite friends there. It is a testament to Goro's tenacity and affability that he was able to get a reluctant Serpico's cooperation.

Although it was actually Durk's efforts that led Mayor Lindsey to establish the Commission to Investigate Alleged Police Corruption (the Knapp Commission), it was Serpico's personal story that captivated everyone. Shortly after the article appeared, Police Commissioner Patrick Murphy offered Daley the job of Deputy Police Commissioner, which, to his own surprise, he accepted.

ROBERT DALEY is a novelist and journalist who served as Deputy Commissioner of the New York Police Department in 1971 and 1972, one of the most tumultuous periods in NYPD history. He is the author of thirty-one books, several of which have been adapted for films, including Sidney Lumet's *Prince of the City*.

Photo by Michael Evans/The New York Times/Redux

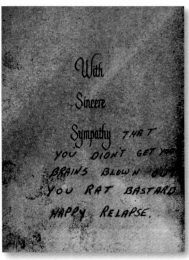

THE COVER (far left) contained more words than usual in order to explain the premise of the story. One of the "get-well" cards (near left) that Serpico received in the hospital.

By Robert Daley

Portrait of an Honest Cop: Target for Attack

"...'When word came in that Serpico had been shot,' said a police official, 'we were terrified that a cop had done it.'..."

The bullet entered the cop's head beside the left nostril and tried to come out his left ear but failed just barely. That was at about 10 p.m. By midnight the cop, Frank Serpico, aged 34, lay behind curtains in a ward in Greenpoint Hospital, and his eyes, opening weakly, focused on Sgt. David Durk beside the bed. Durk and Serpico had once been friends, but had not spoken in a long time.

Serpico took Durk's hand and held on to it. He would not let go.

"Hey," said Durk, trying gently to free his hand. "Take it easy. What's Susan going to say?" Susan was Serpico's girl friend.

Following a commotion in the hall, the curtains parted to reveal Police Commissioner Patrick Murphy, together with most of the top brass of the department. For a while they gazed down at Serpico.

Then, as this crowd departed, an intern wearing a red sweater under his white coat remarked: "What's all the fuss about, just because another cop got plugged?"

A nurse bustled through the curtains saying: "We've got to clean you up, the mayor's coming."

"What does he want?" mumbled Serpico.

"You want to look your best for the mayor."

Serpico said something. She leaned forward to hear it. What he said was, "You've got to be kidding."

By now it was morning. The mayor and entourage entered, looked down at the bed, and departed. "He's too weak to talk," the mayor told reporters. "He's a very brave man."

Two policemen pushed past the protesting nurse: "We're his partners."

They pushed the curtains back along the rods.

"It's all I can do to keep from calling the nurse to have you two thrown out of here," said Serpico. The bullet had plowed through his jawbone, and so the words were slow and slurred.

"Screw you. If that's the way you feel, we won't even give you this."

One of them held up a bag containing Serpico's watch.

The other said: "How do you know what happened? You were unconscious."

"I happen to recall it very vividly."

"No, you don't remember. You were unconscious."

Removed later that day to Brooklyn Jewish Hospital, Serpico was placed in a private room, with a uniformed cop on guard at his door 24 hours a day.

In the hallway, one guard relieved another.

"Don't talk to that guy," the relief said.

"Why not?" asked the other cop.

"Just don't talk to him."

"But I already did."

"I'm just telling you what they told me at the precinct. Don't talk to that guy."

From then on, no guard entered the wounded man's room, or addressed him in any way.

The bullet had entered the sinus cavity, severed a facial nerve and possibly an auricular nerve as well, for one ear was deaf. The bullet had broken into fragments on the jawbone. One fragment had ruptured the cerebral membrane, and then stopped. Another was lodged in the ear canal. The wound had been judged inoperable. A police department investigation was under way to determine if Serpico had

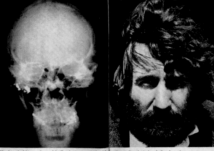

The hospital X-ray showed bullet fragments lodged in Frank Serpico's head. But last rites were premature.

been gunned down in an ordinary way, or set up to be killed.

What the police call Manhattan North is, principally, Harlem. Inspector Paul Delise looked over the 50 men he had just been assigned to command. He knew none of them personally and his first glimpse of Frank Serpico shocked him.

"He was standing in the corner, all by himself. None of the other plainclothesmen would go near him or speak to him. He was being ostracized, but I didn't know that at the time. I looked down at him and I thought: that can't be a policeman. That must be one of their informants here. Serpico had this long unkempt hair, a scroungy beard, and he had an earring in one ear. He wore some kind of Army bush jacket, and sandals with no socks, and he carried this kind of khaki field pack over his shoulder. In the field pack were his guns. He never had less than two guns. The reason he was being ostracized was, he had just locked up some policemen in the Bronx.

"Two days later he came over and introduced himself to me. Meeting him, it was like a breath of fresh air. I knew him by reputation, of course. Here was a man I could rely on. Not that I couldn't rely on the other men, too, but when you're new in a new office you don't know who you can rely on. But I knew Serpico was somebody with a moral code who would stick up for what he believed in. He wouldn't bend to the traditions of the department and the traditions of the men. The other men wouldn't talk in the office when he was there. They were more sympathetic to their friends up in the Bronx."

Delise and Serpico spent most of that winter crouched on rooftops or standing at windows in condemned buildings observing and photographing gambling operations across courtyards. Serpico had the habit at this time of munching on grapefruit halves in the street all day, an additional disguise, and sometimes Delise would follow a trail of grapefruit rinds across rooftops to find Serpico. Because no one else wanted to partner Serpico, Delise often did. Most men of Delise's rank—and age—will not go on rooftops any more, but Paul Delise enjoys it. For this reason, and because he will not take bribes, Delise is known in the Department as St. Paul.

Once he and Serpico trailed a Harlem gambling syndicate to an abandoned store where payoffs were being made. Because a lookout was posted out front, they came at the store through back alleys, over the rooftops and then down the stairs from the roof. The store had a side door onto a hallway. Delise waited there; presumably Serpico would flush them into his arms. Serpico came out the front door of the building and tried to enter the store. But the lookout had given a signal, and the door was slammed in his face and barred.

So Serpico heaved a garbage can through the plate glass window and went in after it. Holding four men at bay, Serpico let Delise in the side door. But a crowd now gathered in the street and began calling threats in the gaping window. They had guns out there, the voices claimed, and when the two cops came out they would be shot. The prisoners began to make threats, too, and this was an especially tough street.

Delise had a walkie-talkie, but it wasn't getting through. They waited an hour and a half with their prisoners inside that abandoned store. When the menacing crowd out front diminished somewhat, Serpico sneaked out the side door and up over the roof again, found a pay phone, and called in a radio car. "He was a unique type individual," says Delise. "He was very serious. He always did the dangerous thing."

When I first met Frank Serpico the beard was temporarily gone, but the hippie haircut and the earring remained. This was at a dinner party at Durk's house. Serpico came in packing two guns, one of them a fourteen-shot automatic which, stuffed in his belt, must have weighed ten pounds, not to mention the pain it gave him in the side. As he entered this room (and all other "friendly" rooms) I was to see him enter) his first act was to lay the automatic on a bookshelf and hitch his belt two notches tighter. Only then would he smile and shake hands.

He had recently come off what cops call the "pussy posse." The job of this detail is to lock up prostitutes. The law says the girl must explicitly solicit a man, and must either touch him lewdly or explicitly promise sexual acts, if the arrest is to be legal. But the girls are extremely wary, they smell cops from a great distance, and so most cops assigned to the posse simply leap out of cars, grab the girls off street corners and then testify in court to a criminal solicitation which never took place.

Not Serpico. He had to get the girl legitimately, or not at all.

The quota was one girl a night. Easy duty, unless you work at it. Serpico went out each night furnished with foreign airline tickets, a foreign accent, and foreign labels sewn in his clothes. One night he was Pierre, the diamond merchant from Antwerp. The next night he would be José, the Madrid dealer in heavy machinery. Each night he would circle in on a girl and admit he had just made a business killing, it was his first time in New York, and he wanted a little fun.

Still the girls were wary.

At Durk's party, he told us how he had picked up a girl outside the Barbizon. In a heavy French accent, he invited her into the bar for a drink.

She squeezed up close to me, bumping me with her hip, trying to feel my piece. I wasn't wearing it on my hip; I had a little revolver in my pocket.

Still, she made no sexual advance. Despite Serpico's beard, the earring

Photographed by Herb Goro

Serpico shares his cluttered Village apartment with a sheepdog and sometimes a girl.

"...The prostitute fixed Serpico with a cold, cold eye. 'You're dirty,' she said, 'but you're good.'..."

and the accent, the girl was obviously suspicious.

"You are Belgian?" said the girl.

"Zat iz right."

"They speak French in Belgium."

"Yes, they do."

"Vous parlez français, alors," said the girl.

After a moment's silence, Serpico said: "Oui, je parle français. Vous parlez français?"

"Oui."

"How iz it zat a pretty girl like you spik French?"

"I'm from Quebec."

"You spik French wiz a very beautiful accent," said Serpico.

"Where are you staying?"

Serpico waved his bogus hotel key. "At ze Americana. Perhaps you like to come wiz me to my hotel."

"Oh, what lovely small feet you have," said the girl. "What size shoes?"

"Forty-four," said Serpico without hesitating. This was the European equivalent of a size 11.

"Could I see your passport?"

Pointing out that he wore the Order of Lenin in his buttonhole, and zat ze party was not popular in zis country, Serpico said: "Tzerefore I do not like zat people examine my papers too closely."

Apparently convinced at last, the girl suggested they repair to Serpico's hotel. Fine, but she still hadn't mentioned price or an explicit sexual act.

"It will cost you something."

"Not too much I hope."

"One hundred dollars."

"I do not wish to purchase you, only to rent you for a little while."

"Quality is expensive."

"What you do, how we say, special?"

"Would you like a little soixante neuf?"

Ah, an explicit sexual offer that Serpico already planned to write up just that way. He couldn't wait to get to court to hear the judge holler: What the hell is soixante neuf?

By now they were in a taxi aimed toward the Americana. At this point Serpico withdrew his badge and in the same thick French accent said: "Zis has gone far enough. I am, how you

Photographs by Herb Goro

81

Survival Guides to the City

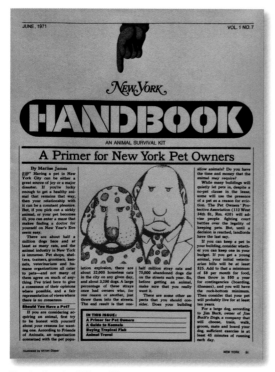

Illustration by Milton Glaser

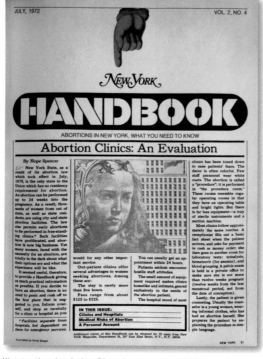

Illustration by Anita Siegel

Illustration by Oliver Williams

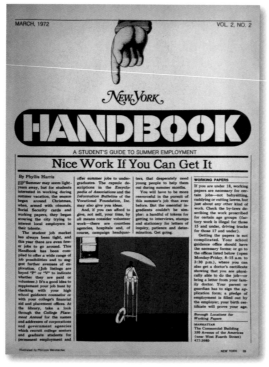

Illustration by Philippe Weisbecker

THE HANDBOOKS took the magazine's service mission to another level. Edited by Nancy Newhouse, the *Handbook* was a monthly deep dive about one topic that concerned New Yorkers at the time—from pet care and hospitals to summer jobs. They were really like consumer reports. We printed them as inserts with the idea that they could serve as stand-alone reference guides. Nancy recalls one edition that riled some readers. "The one that was quite daring at the time—and one can hardly imagine such a thing today at all—was the evaluation of abortion clinics. The author, Hope Spencer (a Rockefeller, if you please), researched them all herself."

NANCY NEWHOUSE was a senior editor and the "Consumer Handbook" editor at *New York*, overseeing a wide range of topics. She joined *The New York Times* in 1977 as the first editor of the new "Home" section. In 1989 Nancy became editor of the "Travel" section and the *Sophisticated Traveler* magazine. She was made a Chevalier of the Ordre national du Mérite by France in 1998.

Photo by Cosmos Sarchiapone

Our House Poet

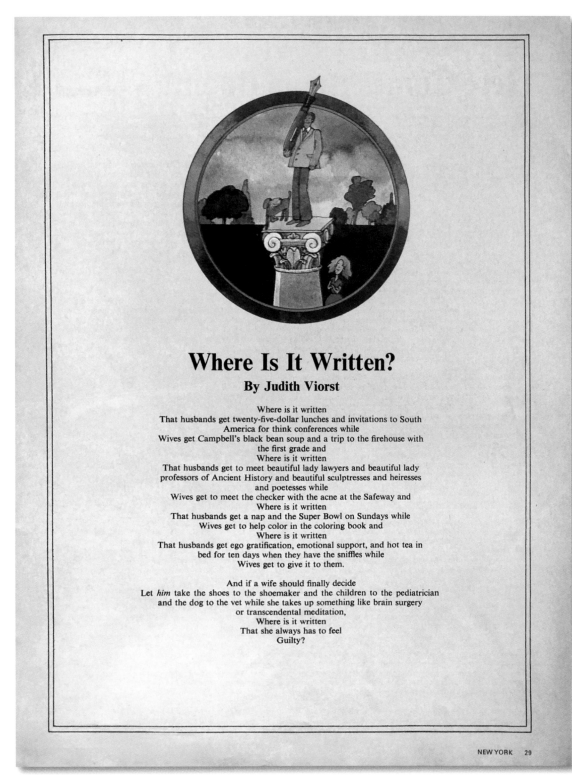

Where Is It Written?

By Judith Viorst

Where is it written
That husbands get twenty-five-dollar lunches and invitations to South
America for think conferences while
Wives get Campbell's black bean soup and a trip to the firehouse with
the first grade and
Where is it written
That husbands get to meet beautiful lady lawyers and beautiful lady
professors of Ancient History and beautiful sculptresses and heiresses
and poetesses while
Wives get to meet the checker with the acne at the Safeway and
Where is it written
That husbands get a nap and the Super Bowl on Sundays while
Wives get to help color in the coloring book and
Where is it written
That husbands get ego gratification, emotional support, and hot tea in
bed for ten days when they have the sniffles while
Wives get to give it to them.

And if a wife should finally decide
Let *him* take the shoes to the shoemaker and the children to the pediatrician
and the dog to the vet while she takes up something like brain surgery
or transcendental meditation,
Where is it written
That she always has to feel
Guilty?

Illustration by Tim Lewis

JUDITH VIORST was in her thirties when her first poem appeared in *New York* magazine. That event changed her life, she says. Judith has since written a total of forty-three poetry and prose books for children and adults and raised three sons, "thanks in large measure to a husband who never made me feel guilty when he went to the supermarket and the shoemaker."
Photo by Mark Baldwin

Louis Armstrong Dies
The funeral service for Armstrong, sixty-nine, on July 10, 1971, was held in the small brick Congregational Church in Corona, Queens, four blocks from where he lived with his wife, Lucille. Five hundred people packed into the crowded pews, including New York City Mayor John Lindsay and his wife, Mary; Moon Landrieu, the mayor of New Orleans; and Governor and Mrs. Nelson Rockefeller. Singer Ella Fitzgerald attended but did not sing. Peggy Lee sang the Lord's Prayer. Al Hibbler sang "Nobody Knows The Trouble I've Seen." Fittingly, the service concluded with, "When the Saints Go Marching In!"

Hustlers with Chutzpah

Gail Sheehy's reporting called for photo documentation of the alarming spread of prostitution—and violence—in the city.

A new breed of prostitutes emerged in New York City in the summer of 1971. Street walkers, who tended to congregate near the Waldorf Astoria hotel, took to "swindling, mugging, robbing, knifing, and occasionally even murdering their patrons," Gail Sheehy reports.

Wearing a hooker's costume and working from 10 p.m. to 4 a.m. over the course of three weeks, Gail interviewed colorful characters such as a prostitute she calls "Redpants," "Sugarman" the pimp, a "pros-hotel" operator named Jimmy Della Bella, and Bobby, the night guard on the Lexington Avenue door at the Waldorf. The series of photographs that accompanied Gail's exposé was taken by Burt Glinn, who at that time didn't want to be credited in the magazine. Shooting with a long lens from a high perch, Burt captured (and time-stamped) a real-life transaction on Lexington Avenue.

Soon after the story was published, *The Washington Post* accused Gail of fabricating the story's protagonist. Unbeknownst to her editor Jack Nessel, Clay Felker had decided to delete the first paragraph of the story where Gail disclosed that the Redpants character was a composite of several prostitutes she interviewed. "It was a big mistake on my part," admitted Clay months later. "She was explaining her method, and it got in the way of the flow of the narrative."

Braving the backlash, Gail wrote five more vividly-reported articles about the effect of prostitution on the city. The series won her the New York Newswomen's Front Page award and a contract from Delacorte for her 1973 book *Hustling: Prostitution in Our Wide Open Society.*

HUSTLING The violent nature of the new breed of prostitutes and pimps is symbolized on the cover in words and Carl Fischer's photographs (far left). Pimp style was captured by Burt Glinn (near left).

NEW AMMUNITION (opposite top) Carl Fischer illustrates a new police tactic of taking Polaroids of suspected prostitutes to use in court.

EAST SIDE BUSINESS (opposite bottom) Burt Glinn's time-lapsed sequence captured classic transactions, which lasted about fifteen minutes.

WIDE OPEN CITY/PART I
THE NEW BREED

By Gail Sheehy

"...They don't just dispense pleasure. These girls swindle, mug, sometimes murder their patrons. And police drives against them are about as effective as pacification programs in Vietnam . . ."

By ten at night they have ringed the streets around the Waldorf like an anklet of Zircons. Horseface, Little Tiffany, Dutchman: the street names they assume are impersonal and sexually neutral. Like their work. Three play decoy for the hotel's private guard while two slip upstairs in the service elevator. They cruise the corridors, knocking on random doors. *Hiya, sugar, want company? Don't say no or I might have to scream 'rape.'* The guest flashes on how his prominent name will look in the morning papers. "PUBLISHER TANGLES WITH V-GIRLS." It's a twenty-dollar touch, work-free!

Zoom back down to the East Lobby. Powder up in the mirror wall, keeping an eye on the ballroom elevators. *Okay, I'll be up after your banquet, Congressman—just give me your room number.*

Then out the 49th Street door, working in pairs now to lure some dumb Iowa daddy up to a trick pad in the Belmont Plaza. *You take a shower first, sweetie, then we gonna do you like you never been done before.* And while he is panting his fantasies under the hot spigot, it's El Splito! Airmail his clothes down the air shaft and run like hell with the wallet because, as anyone knows, Daddy Iowa is too moral a man to make a scene in the altogether. What a score! Five hundred and a wad of credit cards; tomorrow the cards will be sold to a fence down the street from the Waldorf.

Tell all the weary girls plugging their lives away at 99 a week for Ma Bell, tell them their future lies in the street.

These are working girls of a violent new breed. They work on their backs as little as possible. More often they work in cars, with partners, and in hallways and in the open on sidewalks running through our carnal theater district and surrounding our grand hotels. The bulk of their business is not the dispensation of pleasure; it is to mug, rob, swindle, knife, and possibly even to murder their patrons.

Petty crimes have always been associated with prostitution, but only in the last year have New York's working girls, as they call themselves, made a habit of violence. Early this spring police began a crackdown because of a rash of news reports of attacks sprung by this new breed of hookers on their unassuming tricks.

All within a month . . . Pasquale Bottero, 50, a visiting glass manufacturer from Cúneo, Italy, was stabbed to death outside the Hilton Hotel; hundreds of prostitutes were questioned. Franz Josef Strauss, former defense minister of West Germany, was mugged and robbed and his career tarnished back home by a nasty scuffle with three oddly masculine prostitutes in a car outside the Plaza. Charles Addams, the cartoonist, was the victim of a particularly malicious act, also executed by a group of car-borne hookers. They stalked him past Bloomingdale's. He refused to turn around. Prostitutes, living in a permanent condition of humiliation, are hypersensitive to insult, and the cruelest insult, of course, is to be ignored. So when Charles Addams refused to turn around, the girls splashed

a little acid on the back of his head. Symbolic rape, it could be called. For in a crazy, incoherent form the message of women's lib has seeped through to prostitutes. Why give one's body into the bargain when men go about crime so much more directly? Why not attack the john, take his money and be done with it?

The public has become aroused. This is not the sort of behavior one expects from ladies of the evening.

Policemen are currently flashing their newly issued Polaroids in the startled faces of streetwalkers. The photographs will supposedly supply evidence in court. A *New York Times* editorial charges that not since the Jimmy Walker era 40 years ago has midtown appeared so "wide open" to prostitutes, pimps, pornographers and human degradation of intolerable variety. Mayor Lindsay plans a drive against all such "abuses."

Ordinarily, police drives against prostitution are about as effective as pacification programs in Vietnam. Police respond to the immediate public outcry. Their "street sweeps" last only until the courts are choked with insubstantial cases and a louder cry comes back from the district attorney's office to the police commissioner's office: lay off. Meanwhile, the girls evicted from one territory simply move to another, wait for calm, and return. The local populace supports them. One expects they always will.

But a few weeks ago the whistle was blown by a disgusted judge. Two women, flaunting between them 32 previous

New ammunition in court: police have started to take Polaroid pictures of suspected prostitutes.

. . . our photographer found it was business as usual on the East Side. The transaction was classic: girl solicits, steers john to hotel, follows to consummate deal. Time elapsed: about fifteen minutes.

Only one complaint from Kimp— her teenaged sons are beginning to ask what kind of work she does up in New York. "I tell them I work for the city."

Sugarman beckons Redpants across the hall of this modern high-rise in the Murray Hill section where he keeps his gals. He pays the $350 rent; two girls share an apartment and at least one generally has a child with her. He lives in a better pad on a higher floor but in the same building, for purposes of surveillance.

"Now you're gonna meet the hustlingest dame in Sugarman's agency. College girl, real class. She was a track star at this dum-dum nun's school of hers. She can outrun anybody—cars, cops, anybody 'cept Sugarman of course."

He rings. "Road Runner?"

A pair of dark eyes, painted beneath with zebra stripes, peer around the door. "Hello, you bastard. I'm busy."

A child is crying in the dimness behind Road Runner. The young woman is nude except for a Catholic medal on a chain.

"Redpants here needs employment." Sugarman spins the new girl around by the hair. "She's a model."

The eyes narrow in appraisal. How old? Is she clean? Any habit? Any experience on the street? Sugarman answers for his probationer, whose attention is wholly distracted by the apartment. Though sparsely furnished and humorless, it is, in the eyes of a girl from a rooming house in Detroit, the quintessence of glamor.

Road Runner reaches for the girl's cardboard suitcase. "I'll try her out in the Lindy tonight and see what she's got." The door shuts.

Grinning, strutting, enormously pleased with himself, Sugarman sweeps Redpants off to dinner and double Scotches at a First Avenue bar in the Seventies. She notices that everyone knows him here. And that all the men wear the same hat. Whether it's Panama straw or felt, trimmed with peacock or parrot feathers, its big plate brim is tipped at a preposterous diagonal. This is the street pimp's cockscomb, the big bad dude Capone hat.

Redpants is not quite sure what she is into, but Sugarman is so kind . . .

"We got a little family here, see?" he purrs. "You don't have to be lonely no more."

Wonderland! In the Belmont Plaza drugstore Road Runner is now outfitting her with eye expanders, false lashes from Andrea's European Hair collection. She chooses Exotics Black, which are clumped like shrubs. Then a gloss of Pearl Drops toothpaste, her pick of six varieties of hair dryer, and birth control pills. Road Runner explains the pills must be taken every day of the month to obliterate any flow and its interference with business.

What's this? One whole window is devoted to the display of foot remedies, Dr. Scholl in his vast orange inventory, and on the counter, tonight's feature: For Feet's Sake refresher spray. Redpants laughs.

"Must be a lot of old folks aroun' here."

Road Runner looks at her recruit in astonishment. "You're a working girl now. We walk!"

This is the first time Redpants confronts her position directly. She panics. Shrinking back, retreating from Road Runner, she flies into the street. Running does not help. She is still a captive of her motives. Every girl on the verge of turning out must pass through this quick hell, wrestling with the urges and illusions which have brought her this far. A pimp often drugs a girl at this point. Or he has sex with her and makes her feel needed, then suggests she have a few "dates" for pay, hoping that the customers will reinforce her sense of being wanted. Or the girl herself continues to observe the lifestyle of the prostitutes around her until she learns the value of criminal behavior and takes

Shall We Start a Magazine? Part II

Ms., the first national magazine for and by women, was launched in our pages.

Bound within our December 1971 issue is the historic premiere of *Ms.* magazine. Cofounded by Gloria Steinem and a group of female journalists, the iconic publication fueled the feminist movement and forever changed the conversation around gender politics in the United States and beyond.

Gloria says her weekly "The City Politic" column in *New York* served as a dry run for the kind of perspective-shifting journalism championed by *Ms.* "I could write about politics for the first time, and in the way we experience them in daily life," she says. "Indeed, that column was the beginning of my understanding that there also needed to be the first national magazine that was actually owned and controlled by women."

Clay told Gloria that he would pay for the printing and distribution of the inaugural edition if he could publish thirty pages in *New York*'s year-end double issue. "I doubt we would have been able to afford national distribution of a preview issue without Clay's generous offer," Gloria says. The *Ms.* staff did everything to pull the insert together. Our only contribution was freeing our assistant art director, Rochelle Udell, to work on it; assigning Carl Fischer to photograph the cover; and cheering them on.

Finding their audience quickly was a great concern for the *Ms.* founders. "We were so worried about disgracing the [women's] movement that we cover-dated it 'Spring,' even though our first issue came out in January, in case it languished on the newsstands," Gloria recalls. "As I was interviewed on a call-in show in L.A., a viewer called to say she couldn't find the preview issue on the newsstands. I called Clay in a panic, thinking it hadn't been shipped. Clay called me back to say it had sold out." It became instantly clear that *Ms.* struck a chord. The 300,000 test copies sold out in a matter of days. Within weeks, they received over 25,000 subscription orders and 20,000 reader letters.

GLORIA STEINEM
Iconoclastic feminist, activist, and writer Steinem was a founding staff member of *New York*. In 2013, President Barack Obama awarded her with the Presidential Medal of Freedom, the highest civilian honor in the United States.
Photo: Gloria Steinem

ROCHELLE UDELL
served as art director for the *Ms.* preview issue while she was assistant art director at *New York* magazine. She then went on to *Harper's Bazaar*. For twenty-two years she worked at Condé Nast, art directing *Vogue*, editing *SELF*, and starting Condé-Net, its digital publishing group with Epicurious.
Photo: Rochelle Udell

An early staff meeting at the offices of *Ms.* magazine.
Photo by Michael Alexander, courtesy of Gloria Steinem

MIRIAM WOSK
(1947–2010) was a skilled commercial illustrator, working for *Esquire*, *New York*, *The New York Times*, *Mademoiselle*, and *Vogue*. In the 1970s she moved to California and concentrated on her personal artwork.
Photo: Adam Gunther

Ms. magazine cover illustration by Miriam Wosk, photographed by Carl Fischer

THE LONG SURFACE atop the flat files was the location of most meetings at *New York*. The art department was "The Kitchen" of the magazine where all the ingredients came together and made "the weekly meal." Here, editors and production personnel are discussing ad placement. Included are editorial director Jack Nessel, Walter Bernard, production assistant Frank Sullivan, art assistant Lynne Milnes (at desk), production director Bill Gallagher, editor Clay Felker, and editorial directors Sheldon Zalaznick and Byron Dobell.

Photo by Charles Denson

Shirley the First
Shirley Chisholm, the first African American major-party candidate for president of the United States, came in fourth, with 152 delegates supporting her candidacy at the July 1972 Democratic National Convention in Miami Beach. The first African American woman elected to the U.S. Congress in 1968, who served seven terms, said she faced "more discrimination as a woman than for being black" in her campaign for president.

Cold War Chess Match
On July 11, 1972, the long-anticipated chess match between Boris Spassky of the Soviet Union and American champion Bobby Fischer finally took place in Reykjavík, Iceland. Final score: Fischer, 12½; Spassky, 8½.

Jane Fonda in Hanoi
Actress Jane Fonda posed for a photo in Hanoi next to a North Vietnamese anti-aircraft gun on July 15, 1972. The antiwar advocate was called a traitor by some.

A Bloody History

This three-part series on the Mafia wars defined how we would subsequently present complex historical events.

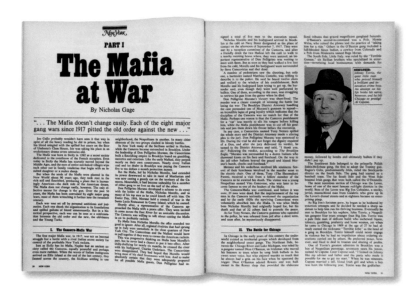

NICHOLAS GAGE was an investigative reporter for *The New York Times*, specializing in organized crime and official corruption. He is the author of *The Mafia Is Not an Equal Opportunity Employer* (1971) and the autobiographical best-seller *Eleni* (1983). He was the executive producer of *The Godfather Part III*.
Photo: Nicholas Gage

In lieu of using news photographs, which were hard to come by at the time, we asked our contributing illustrators to re-create scenes detailing Nicholas Gage's study of the "bloody and convulsive struggles" in the coming of age of the Mafia in America. Our illustration team consisted of Harvey Dinnerstein, Alex Gnidziejko, Burt Silverman, Paul Davis, James McMullan, Richard Hess, and Mark English.

This was the first time we used illustrations to re-create scenes of important events that were known to have taken place but were not recorded by photography. To some degree, we were reviving an old magazine form. Publications like *The Saturday Evening Post*, for instance, used illustrations to portray events in both fiction and fact. The critical requirement of this form lies

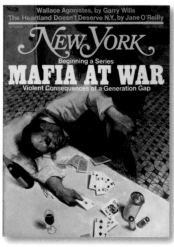

in the illustrators' ability to paint scenes that are both dramatic and believable.

Their artistic interpretation didn't diminish the article's credibility. Of course, there's an assumption that photographs would be more authentic, but we never got a sense that any of these dramatizations were implausible. Readers accepted the way we presented them. Here we show six paintings from the series.

THE KILLING OF JOE THE BOSS (opposite). After many attempts on his life, Joe the Boss Masseria dies with six bullets in his back on April 15, 1931, following lunch and a card game in a restaurant with his trusted right-hand man, Lucky Luciano. Luciano was conveniently out of sight in the men's room at the time. Illustration by Harvey Dinnerstein

HARVEY DINNERSTEIN is a classical realist painter and teacher. Painted from life, many of his images show intimate, poignant views of the people and buildings of his native New York. His work is in many private and museum collections, including the Lehman Collection of the Metropolitan Museum of Art.
Portrait by Harvey Dinnerstein

made up of the leading Mafia bosses in the country. In the wake of all the bloodshed there were many hard feelings within families, and Luciano established the position of consigliere (counselor) to protect the soldiers from the vengeance of their superiors. There were six consiglieri in New York, one each from the Five Families and one from Newark. Before the murder of a soldier was authorized, the charges against him had to be brought before the consiglieri for their approval.

Luciano scorned regional rivalries and made his own no. 2 man a Neapolitan—Vito Genovese. He also forged bonds of cooperation with such non-Italian criminals as Dutch Schultz and Meyer Lansky.

V. The Genovese Campaign

The Mafia entered a period of relative calm and prosperity under the rule of Luciano, who ensconced himself in elegant style at the Waldorf-Astoria under the name of Mr. Charles Ross. Even when Prohibition was repealed in 1933 and unemployment became a problem throughout the underworld, Luciano, with customary foresight, moved the Mafia to new and profitable rackets such as numbers and prostitution.

But this blissful state of affairs could not go on indefinitely. In 1934 Luciano's underboss, Vito Genovese, got involved in a murder and was careless about covering his tracks. Then a crusading special prosecutor named Thomas Dewey brought Luciano to trial on charges of compulsory prostitution. The underworld was stunned when, in 1936, their leader was sentenced to 30 to 50 years. (In 1945 he was paroled and deported to Italy, where he died of a heart attack in 1962.)

After the conviction of Luciano, Dewey turned his attention to Genovese and Genovese decided it was the perfect moment for a long visit to Italy. Along with his toothbrush he packed $750,000 in cash. The onset of World War II made it impossible for Genovese to return, and he spent the war in Italy as one of the greatest admirers of Mussolini, donating $250,000 to the Fascist party.

With both Luciano and Genovese temporarily indisposed, the mantle fell on the shoulders of Frank Costello, Luciano's no. 3 man. Costello preferred to use political power rather than guns and muscle and he began collecting politicians the way Luciano collected silk underwear. Soon he had all of Tammany Hall in his pocket.

Things were going along swimmingly for the Luciano family when, in 1945, word went around that Vito Genovese was coming back. Don Vitone, as he was sometimes called, had been arrested in Italy and finally brought back to the States to face trial for that old clumsy murder. Soon after his arrival, however, the key witness, who was in protective custody, discovered too late that someone had substituted poison for his stomach-ache tablets. The indictment was dismissed.

Now that he was back on American soil and no longer facing a murder rap, Genovese set his mind to seizing power back from Costello. He moved very slowly, however, biding his time. Meanwhile, he was living in Lucullan splendor with his wife Anna in a $175,000 mansion in New Jersey filled with $250,000 worth of bibelots, including a bed with a swan back made of Lucite and dishes of 24-carat gold and platinum. Don Vito's domestic life was not serene, however, and Anna divorced him in 1952, charging, among other things, that he had once knocked out two of her front teeth at a party.

Despite his domestic problems, Genovese concentrated on winning as many of the Luciano family as he could away from Costello. He appealed to the more conservative in the family and, knowing that Costello was popular with the capos, tried to fan discontent among the soldiers.

THE KILLING OF
ALBERT ANASTASIA:
A close Costello ally,
Anastasia tried to win
back his associate's
position for him. The
ruthless Anastasia was
rewarded for his
effort by gunmen who
murdered him in the
barber shop of the
Park-Sheraton Hotel.
Painting by Burt Silverman

THE KILLING OF
BIG JIM:
The vice lord
of Chicago is shot
to death in
the vestibule of his
café on May 11, 1920,
as he waits for
a shipment of illegal
whiskey.
Big Jim Colosimo,
old-fashioned and
newly in love,
failed to see the profit
potential inherent
in Prohibition. His
timely murder made it
possible for his
nephew, Johnny Torrio,
to modernize
Chicago rackets.
Painting by Alex Gnidziejko

THE KILLING OF ALBERT ANASTASIA

A close Costello ally, Anastasia tried to win back his associate's position for him. The ruthless Anastasia was rewarded for his effort by gunmen who murdered him in the barber shop of the Park Sheraton Hotel. Illustration by Burt Silverman

THE KILLING OF BIG JIM

The vice lord of Chicago is shot to death in the vestibule of his cafe on May 11, 1920, as he waits for a shipment of whiskey. Illustration by Alex Gnidziejko

ALEX GNIDZIEJKO illustrated for most major magazines until he moved to Maine in 1985. Inspired by the Dutch and Flemish masters, he uses egg tempera oil emulsion to bring stunning depth and a three-dimensional quality to his realist paintings. His work is in many public and private collections, including the Smithsonian Institution.

Photo by Paulette Gnidziejko

THE KILLING OF JOEY GALLO:
Blamed for planning the shooting of Joe Colombo, Gallo is shot to death and his bodyguard wounded at 5:30 a.m. on April 7, 1972, in Umberto's Clam House in Little Italy. Gallo was celebrating his 43rd birthday with people close to him, including his bride and her young daughter. A Colombo associate named Joseph Luparelli later turned himself in to the F.B.I. saying that he waited outside in a getaway car while four Colombo men took part in the Gallo killing.
Painting by Burt Silverman.

THE KILLING OF JOEY GALLO

Blamed for planning the shooting of Joe Columbo, Joey Gallo is shot to death and his bodyguard wounded at 5:30 a.m. on April 7, 1972, at Umberto's Clam House in Little Italy. Illustration by Burt Silverman

THE SHOOTING OF FRANK COSTELLO: *The successor to Lucky Luciano was walking through the lobby of his apartment building on May 2, 1957, when he heard someone say, "This is for you, Frank." The speaker was a henchman of Vito Genovese, who wanted Costello's job as Mafia boss. Costello was only wounded, but he got the message and took an early retirement.*
Painting by Paul Davis.

THE SHOOTING OF FRANK COSTELLO

The successor to Lucky Luciano was walking through the lobby of his apartment building on May 2, 1957, when he heard someone say, "This is for you, Frank." Costello was only wounded, but he got the message and took an early retirement. Illustration by Paul Davis

93

THE NIGHT OF THE SICILIAN VESPERS: *The purge of September 10, 1931, was brilliantly planned by Lucky Luciano, who modernized the Mafia overnight by wiping out the old-timers or "Mustache Petes" as they were contemptuously called by the young Americanized Mafiosi. During the bloodbath nearly 40 of the Old Guard were executed in ingenious various ways.*

Painting by James McMullan

THE NIGHT OF THE SICILIAN VESPERS
The purge of September 10, 1931, was brilliantly planned by Lucky Luciano, who modernized the Mafia overnight by wiping out the old-timers, or "Mustache Petes," as they were contemptuously called by the young Americanized Mafiosi. Illustration by James McMullan

Covers We Like, 1972

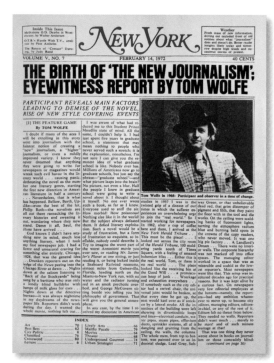

OUR NEWSPAPER format didn't sell well. The logo was too small and the magazine was unrecognizable.

CUT OUTS of five staff members were placed in a bowl of pasta, no retouching. Photograph by Ben Somoroff

GAEL GREENE'S sensual theme (opposite) was underlined by our homage to a popular Tabu perfume ad, which was based on a painting by René Francois Xavier Prinet (detail below). George Lang, a restaurant consultant, and his wife, Karen, a publishing executive, posed for the cover photograph by Carl Fischer.

THE MONEY CHAIR
Milton loved this chair, painted on by David Wilcox, so much that he took it home. Photograph by Armen Kachaturian

CELEBRATING THE GRAPE
A wine catalogue by New York's oenophiles. Photograph by Henry Wolf

Buying Without Fear at New York's Auction Houses
Tubal Ligation: Why and Why Not

50 CENTS

SEPTEMBER 25, 1972

NEW YORK

The
Kitchen
As
Erogenous
Zone
By
Gael
Greene

**Apartment Living
Is Easy If You Know How**

Custom-Designed,
Hold-Everything Closets

The Best Handymen
in Town

Un-Cute Children's
Furniture

What Department Store
Decorators Can Do For You

25 Objects You Shouldn't
Do Without

Anatomy of a Supermarket

Translating the customs and curiosities of a Chinese food emporium

Socio-Gastronomic Notes on a

Chinese Grocery

If you want a cold can of Rheingold, you can go to the neighborhood deli; if you want bok choy, you'd do well to try Chinatown. If you want both, United Supermarket, a well-stocked and authentically Chinese emporium with the inevitable city touches, is the place to go. But unless you speak fluent Cantonese, or are already a master of Chinese cooking, you may need some help. Milton Glaser, *New York*'s design director, and writer Frank Ching have come up with a guide to Chinese food shopping that is also a small-scale study of the effects of New York City on an ancient foreign culture. Since all you may be looking for at United (84 Mulberry Street) is some dried seaweed, you might not notice the employees (who work a twelve-hour day) having a coffee break in the back. If you're in line at the checkout counter behind a Cantonese couple, take note—in China, shopping is the exclusive province of women; in New York, however, men and women shop at United seven days a week. And, along with their imported won ton wrappers or six-month-old thousand-year eggs, they may be buying the mainstay of their diet: 25-pound bags of Texas-grown rice.

Photographed by Steve Meyers

NEW YORK 55

THE OPENING PAGE (left) of our dissection of United Supermarket featuring a twenty-five-pound bag of Texas-grown rice. The four-page presentation (opposite) of the market's complexity with as much information as we could possibly cram in. Looking back, the design of the layout seems to be inspired by the periodic table of elements.

I've always loved Chinese food. I think that it's an incredibly sophisticated cuisine. Writer Frank Ching and I roamed Chinatown and picked up anything that looked unusual or significant. We called the report "socio-gastronomic notes" because it was as much about the culinary curiosities as it was a study of a vital immigrant enclave that was mysterious to the rest of the city because of the language barrier.

With the help of the gracious owners of United Supermarket at 84 Mulberry Street, we charted exotic-sounding ingredients such as Tientsin cabbage, dried lotus root, and thousand-year-old eggs. We also included a wonton recipe, a few Cantonese words that might come in handy when shopping, and a profile about its industrious employees. The layout is as fully packed as the grocery aisles.

As our editors describe it, cooking Chinese food was a "household sport" during this time. In 1972, President Richard Nixon embarked on a historic diplomatic visit to China and opened people's minds about the cuisine. During a televised banquet hosted by Prime Minister Zhou Enlai, Americans saw Nixon sampling dishes like shark fin soup, roast duck, and lotus-seed sweet porridge. This resulted in an instant boom in Chinese restaurants in New York. Michael Tong, the enterprising owner of Shun Lee Palace on East Fifty-Fifth Street, even re-created the menu within twenty-four hours and sold an eight-course prix fixe meal for $25 a head—that's equivalent to $150 today. *The New York Times* called Nixon "the greatest salesman for Peking duck."—MG

FRANK CHING is a journalist and an expert in U.S.-China diplomatic relations. While working as a correspondent for *The New York Times*, he wrote "China: It's the Latest American Thing," about a wave of Sinomania that swept the United States on the eve of Richard Nixon's diplomatic visit to Beijing in 1972. He opened *The Wall Street Journal*'s first Beijing bureau in 1979 and is the author of four books.
Photo by Mike Sakas

STEVE MEYERS, a young photojournalist, was assigned to this feature. We gave him an especially large photo credit because of his extremely patient and diligent work recording the hidden treasures in the United Supermarket.

98

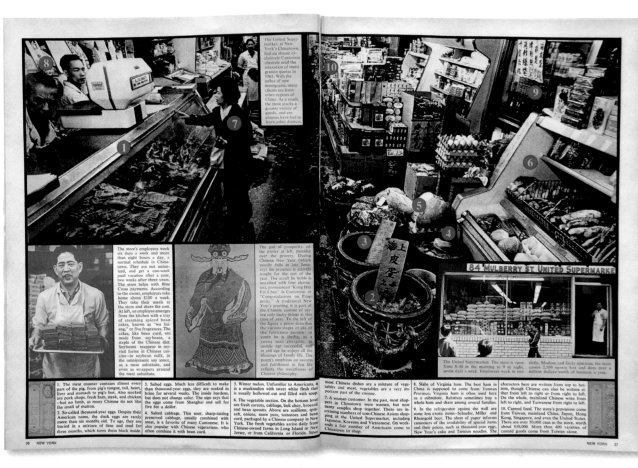

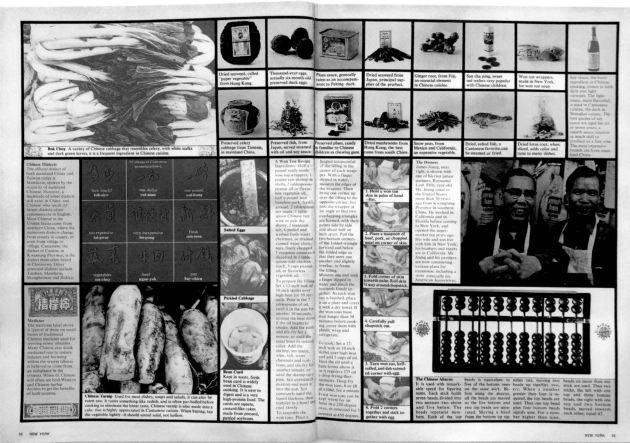

A Disturbing Premonition

Jack Javits, a Burnt-out Case? by Richard Reeves
An Eater's Guide to Italian Street Festivals
The Most Powerful Black in Town, by Nicholas Pileggi

50 CENTS   MAY 27, 1974

NEW YORK

What Are Your Chances of Surviving A High-Rise Fire?

FIRE HAZARD
The cover (left) depicting
a possible rescue by
helicopter, which sadly
wasn't possible in 2001.
Magee's painting (oppo-
site) illustrates the futility
of the firefighters below.

We unwittingly pictured the horror of a future tragedy.

In 1974, the film *The Towering Inferno* ignited a widespread
paranoia about being trapped in flaming high-rise buildings.
This fear was especially acute in New York, the city of sky-
scrapers. Residential high-rise buildings were just beginning to
pop up all over during this period, and as Byrna Taubman points
out in the article, the city was woefully unprepared to cope
with such a catastrophe. She wrote, "It can take over an hour to
evacuate a 50-story building; the World Trade Center would probably take three hours, providing, of course, that no one panicked."

Illustrator Allen MaGee painted an image that's quite eerie
to look at now because it so closely resembles the scene at the
World Trade Center on 9/11, 2001. If you look at photographs of
the tragedy, you can see that the hijacked planes crashed into
the twin towers just about where he painted the billowing smoke.

On the cover we were trying to link what was fresh in people's
minds and encourage New Yorkers to think about emergency
readiness. In hindsight, the city could never have been prepared
for what was to come.

ALAN MAGEE began
working as an editorial
and book illustrator in
New York in 1969.
Later, Magee started
to concentrate on his
personal paintings and
since 1980 has had
annual one-person shows
throughout the United
States and Europe.
Magee's works can be
seen in many public
collections including the
Fine Arts Museums
of San Francisco, the
Museum of Fine Arts,
Boston, the Art Institute
of Chicago, and the
National Portrait Gallery.
Photo by Monika Magee

IN THE NEWS

Rabin Becomes Prime Minister of Israel
When Yitzhak Rabin formed the seventeenth Government of Israel on June 3, 1974, it was the first time that it was led by a native-born Israeli. Rabin was born in Jerusalem, prior to Israeli independence, when it was the British Mandate of Palestine.

Criminals, Fools, and Heroes

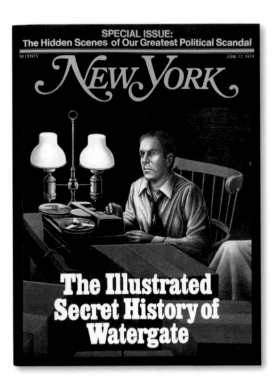

H. R. HALDEMAN, the White House Chief of Staff, listens to the presidential tapes in awe (left). Illustration by Roger Hane

Over three issues, we dramatized the conspiracy that gripped the nation two months before Nixon resigned.

With multiple writers, researchers, and no fewer than nine illustrators involved, it was our most ambitious illustration reportage project since "Mafia at War." We spent a lot of time meticulously reassembling the faces and places associated with the historic Watergate break-in of the Democratic National Committee's headquarters two years prior. The list of critical minutiae, as our editors said, was endless.

The editors described the project's purpose: "Tapes on Watergate we have aplenty and books, and enough printers' ink to float the *Queen Elizabeth*, but in an era when we're surrounded by images, when Sam Erwin's eyebrows are as familiar to us as the Manhattan skyline, we realized that we are still missing an accurate picture of the right- and wrong-doers plotting and carrying out criminal or foolish acts."

We obsessed over details such as where Nixon wore his flag lapel pin, the color of White House counsel John Dean's suit, down to the view outside the Oval Office windows. We chose the illustrators with the inventiveness and patience to make something out of these historical notes. Together with our in-house illustrator Julian Allen, who did most of the paintings, we asked Jim McMullan, Alex Gnidziejko, Burt Silverman, David Wilcox, Roger Hane, Richard Hess, and Harvey Dinnerstein to work on various aspects of the story. Melinda Bordelon was a new addition to this roster and she fit right in beautifully.

AARON LATHAM, a writer and journalist, was a senior editor at *New York* magazine. He was also a regular writer for *Rolling Stone, Esquire,* and *The New York Times*. His work includes the screenplays *Urban Cowboy* and *Perfect* and the novels *Code of the West, Orchids for Mother,* and *The Cowboy with the Tiffany Gun*. Photo by Cosmos Sarchiapone

J. EDGAR HOOVER (opposite top) confronts Attorney General John N. Mitchell. Illustration by Burt Silverman

E. HOWARD HUNT (opposite bottom) photographs Lewis Fielding's office building. Illustration by Julian Allen

July, 1970

J. Edgar Hoover Opposes Nixon's Intelligence Plan

F.B.I. Director J. Edgar Hoover confronts Attorney General John N. Mitchell in Mitchell's office to protest the President's plan to use the F.B.I. to gather domestic intelligence by unprecedented extralegal methods.

During the period of national unrest following the invasion of Cambodia in 1970, perfervid conservative 29-year-old White House staffer Tom Charles Huston nurtured and then proposed an astonishing plan which was approved by Richard Nixon. Huston and the White House wanted to establish an intelligence agency for permanent, extensive surveillance of antiwar activists, minority leaders, foreign diplomats, and other persons considered threats to "national security." The plan authorized garnering of information by such illegal means as bugging, burglary, and opening mail. On June 5, the President held an Oval Office meeting of the heads of the F.B.I., the C.I.A., the National Security Agency, and the intelligence component of the Defense Department, to discuss the Huston plan. Hoover, ostensible head of the project, heavily annotated his copy of the plan with objections. Nevertheless, the White House sent the participating intelligence agencies a "Decision Memorandum" on July 23. Hoover promptly arranged a meeting with Mitchell. Hoover refused to participate in the plan unless he was given written permission to violate the law, which Mitchell and/or Nixon refused to give. Hoover's motives for refusing to cooperate are still unclear, but few Hoover-watchers imagined his motives were other than self-protective. Mitchell, now cautious, urged the administration to bow to Hoover's demands. Huston, who still supported the plan, was transferred to another part of the White House staff. On July 28, five days after issuance, Haldeman asked that the intelligence agencies return their copies of the plan. However, neither Huston nor Mitchell nor White House counsel John Dean (who replaced Huston) can remember seeing orders that actually canceled the plan. If the Huston plan was scuttled, the unprecedented commitment to such measures remained—a commitment which eventually led to the burglarizing of a Beverly Hills psychiatrist's office and the Democratic Committee headquarters in Washington.

Painting by Burt Silverman   NEW YORK   49

August 25, 1971

The Plumbers Prepare to Rob Dr. Fielding

E. Howard Hunt removes his miniature camera from a tobacco pouch to make a "vulnerability and feasibility" study of psychiatrist Lewis Fielding's office building, in preparation for stealing the doctor's files on Daniel Ellsberg. G. Gordon Liddy poses in front.

Right after the publication of the Pentagon Papers, the secret history of U.S. involvement in Vietnam, Richard Nixon delegated White House counselor John Ehrlichman, who delegated aides Egil Krogh and David Young, to investigate alleged security leaks independently of the F.B.I.

G. Gordon Liddy, counsel to the Committee for the Reelection of the President, and E. Howard Hunt, White House consultant and an ex-C.I.A. man, were recruited as part of the group that became known as the Plumbers. Among their early targets was Daniel Ellsberg, who had acknowledged leaking the Pentagon Papers to the press. Hunt and Liddy set about compiling a "psychiatric profile" of Ellsberg that would "destroy his public image and credibility."

A week after their preliminary photographic reconnaissance of Fielding's Beverly Hills office, Hunt and Liddy returned with three accomplices from Miami. On the evening of September 3, two of them, posing as deliverymen, were able to leave a suitcase in Fielding's office. The suitcase contained a camera, light, and film for photographing Ellsberg's records. After midnight, the three Miami men broke through a window and forced the door to Fielding's office. (Hunt had stationed himself outside Fielding's home; Liddy was driving around looking for police.)

The operation was futile in its immediate objective, for there is still dispute as to whether or not Ellsberg's file was ever found. And the break-in continued to backfire on the administration. When the Watergate-Fielding connection was finally made during the 1973 Pentagon Papers trial, Judge Matthew Byrne dismissed the case against Ellsberg. And on May 24, 1974, Federal Judge Gerhard Gesell ruled, in the trial of those accused of violating the civil rights of Dr. Fielding, that even if the break-in *had* been a matter of national security, the President's power to conduct foreign affairs does not include the right to enter homes and offices without a warrant.

Painting by Julian Allen

Painting by Julian Allen   NEW YORK   53

January 27, 1972

Gordon Liddy Makes a Modest Proposal

George Gordon Liddy, general counsel to the Committee for the Re-election of the President, shows charts of an elaborate intelligence-gathering scheme to (left to right) White House aide Jeb Stuart Magruder, Nixon's lawyer John Dean (the man who had brought Liddy into CREEP), and John Mitchell in the attorney general's Justice Department office.

Liddy's half-hour show and tell—the genesis of the Watergate break-in—was presented with his typical flamboyance. (He had, a former associate recalled, "a brilliant capacity to turn the most routine and monotonous case into what would appear to be an earth-shattering event.") This time his plan was, in fact, earth-shattering. His colorful, professionally drawn charts, headed with such code names as "Gemstone" and "Target," outlined plans for extensive political espionage: wiretapping, electronic surveillance, mugging and kidnapping radicals who might cause trouble at the Republican National Convention. Liddy suggested renting a yacht in Miami, then hiring call girls to compromise members of the Democratic National Committee. Liddy's last chart was a summary of his proposed expenses and activities. He wanted $1 million for the job.

Liddy, who claimed to have spent $7,000 on his handsome charts, was disappointed that his proposals were not accepted immediately, but on February 4, he returned to Mitchell's office and offered a scaled-down plan (the Democratic headquarters at the Watergate and D.N.C. Chairman Larry O'Brien were mentioned as possible targets) with a budget of $500,000.

In his Watergate testimony, John Dean said, "I probably should have been much more forceful in trying to stop the plan." Mitchell swore that the plan "was rejected again." But when Samuel Dash, the Ervin committee's chief counsel, asked Magruder, "Would it be true to say that at least Mr. Liddy was encouraged to continue in his planning?" Magruder replied, "Yes, I think that is correct."

On March 30, Liddy submitted a third proposal, with a price tag of $250,000. Magruder claims that Mitchell approved the plan. Mitchell denies this. Nevertheless, on June 17, 1972, one part of Liddy's plan did take place: the burglary attempt on the D.N.C.'s Watergate headquarters.

March, 1972

Dita Beard's Change of Mind

E. Howard Hunt, his red wig askew, interviews I.T.T. lobbyist Dita Beard in her Denver hospital room.

On February 29, 1972, columnist Jack Anderson reported that the Justice Department had dropped an antitrust case against I.T.T. in return for a $400,000 pledge to help underwrite the 1972 Republican National Convention. Anderson's source was a memo, written and authenticated by Dita Beard, which stated: "Other than permitting John Mitchell, Ed Reinecke, Bob Haldeman, and Nixon . . . no one has known from whom that 400 thousand commitment has come. . . . Mitchell is definitely helping us, but cannot let it be known."

The Senate Judiciary Committee, concerned about Richard Kleindienst's handling of the I.T.T. case, reopened hearings on his confirmation as attorney general. Dita Beard was to testify, but she was suddenly whisked off to a Denver hospital by G. Gordon Liddy, too "ill" to talk.

White House Special Counsel Charles Colson sent a disguised E. Howard Hunt to Denver. Claiming to represent "high levels of the administration," Hunt bearded Beard from 11 P.M. to 3 A.M. on her memo.

A few days later, on March 17, Dita Beard issued a sworn statement which said: "Mr. Anderson's memo is a forgery, and not mine." But, in 1973, the Senate Watergate hearings finally linked the President and Mitchell to the I.T.T. settlement.

April 19, 1971

Nixon Gives an Order on I.T.T.

President Nixon orders Deputy Attorney General Richard Kleindienst to drop the appeal on the I.T.T. case.

In July, 1971, instead of going ahead with its landmark antitrust test case against the International Telephone and Telegraph Corp., the Justice Department announced an out-of-court settlement. No one announced that I.T.T. had just pledged $400,000 to the 1972 Republican Convention.

On February 29, 1972, columnist Jack Anderson linked the contribution and the case. In March, Kleindienst insisted "I was not interfered with by anybody at the White House." In October, 1972, however, he told Special Prosecutor Archibald Cox a very different story:

On April 19, 1971, Kleindienst recalled, White House domestic counselor John Ehrlichman had called and told him that the President did not want him to file the government appeal on the I.T.T. case. Kleindienst refused to comply. Nixon himself called next. "Listen, you son of a bitch," he said. "Don't you understand the English language? Don't appeal that goddamn case, and that's all there is to it."

Kleindienst went to John Mitchell, and told him that he would resign rather than drop the case. Later, Mitchell told Kleindienst, "I've talked to your friend [Nixon]. He said do anything you want on antitrust cases." Kleindienst filed the appeal, but before it could be argued, the Justice Department settled with I.T.T.

54 NEW YORK   Paintings by Julian Allen   NEW YORK 55

June 17, 1972

The Arrest— 'Are You Police?' Asked McCord

Around 2 a.m., on the sixth floor of the Watergate Office Building, Sergeant Paul Leeper (holding gun at left, over glass partition) and Officers John Barrett (peering around partition at right) and Carl Shoffler of the Washington, D.C., Second District Casual Clothes Squad, catch and arrest (left to right): Bernard Barker, James McCord, Eugenio Martinez, Frank Sturgis, and Virgilio Gonzalez.

Why, given their ultimately successful efforts to bug two phones there, did they break into Democratic National Committee headquarters a second time? According to James McCord, in testimony before the Senate Watergate committee a year later, the team had three objectives: to photograph additional documents and, as long as they were there, to see why one of the bugs was not working and to supplement the phone bugs with a device that would transmit conversations held anywhere in a senior committee executive's office.

It was his understanding, McCord testified, that these objectives were determined by former Attorney General John Mitchell himself. McCord said he got that impression from Gordon Liddy. John Mitchell subsequently denied all responsibility. Liddy has offered no testimony at all.

Whoever the final authority, the whole operation came to light only when Frank Wills, a 24-year-old security guard, decided to call the police after discovering tape on a door lock in the Watergate garage. Because of his call, the entire conspiracy began to come apart early in the morning of June 17, 1972, when James McCord, his hands in the air, asked, "Are you gentlemen Metropolitan Police?"

It seems clear, though, that the administration did its best to prevent disclosure. On June 14, 1973, almost exactly one year to the day after the arrest of the "Watergate Five," Jeb Magruder, posted from the White House to work on the Nixon re-election committee, told the Ervin committee: "The cover-up began . . . when we realized there was a break-in. I do not think there was ever any discussion that there would not be a cover-up."

Part II of "The Illustrated Secret History of Watergate" will appear next week.

Painting by Richard Hess

GORDON LIDDY (opposite top) shows charts of an intelligence gathering scheme to White House aide Jeb Stuart Magruder, lawyer John Dean, and Attorney General Mitchell. Illustration by Julian Allen

DITA BEARD (opposite, bottom left) interviewed by E. Howard Hunt, changes her mind. Illustration by Julian Allen

NIXON (opposite, bottom right) gives an order to Deputy Attorney General Richard Kleindienst. Illustration by Julian Allen

THE ARREST (top) of five burglars at 2 a.m. in the Watergate Building. Illustration by Richard Hess

GORDON LIDDY (left) approaches Attorney General Richard Kleindienst to ask him to get Watergate burglar James McCord out of jail. Illustration by David Wilcox

June 22, 1972

Martha Mitchell Is Manhandled But Unsilenced

In a Newport Beach motel room, Martha Mitchell's bodyguard rips out the telephone cord just after Martha tells U.P.I. reporter Helen Thomas "They don't want me to talk."

Martha Mitchell, wife of John Mitchell, the head of CREEP, was fed up with being considered a security risk. "Can you believe," she later told a reporter, "that a man can walk into your bedroom, take over, and pull the phone out of the wall? . . . [They] threw me down on the bed . . . and stuck a needle in my behind." She was being punished because "they're afraid of my honesty."

And the government had good reason to be afraid. During the panic that followed the Plumbers' arrest in the Watergate, incriminating files were destroyed, flat denials of wrongdoing intoned, and John Mitchell, who was in California when the arrests took place, flew back to Washington and announced on June 19 that James McCord had been fired by CREEP and that his "apparent actions . . . [were] wholly inconsistent with the principles upon which we are conducting our campaign."

When Mitchell left California, he'd persuaded Martha to stay behind with her bodyguard, Steve King. Martha Mitchell knew and liked James McCord. She also knew that there was nothing "inconsistent" about his participation in the Watergate break-in. Desperate to reveal what she knew, on June 22 she called Helen Thomas to say that she was "sick and tired of the whole operation." Then Ms. Thomas heard her say "You get away" to someone in the room, and the line went dead.

Three days later, Martha called again. She was still a "political prisoner," she announced, and she had given her husband an ultimatum: give up politics or give up his wife.

Several days went by, then Martha was on the phone again, this time from the Westchester Country Club, in Rye, New York. "I'm black and blue," she said. "I love my husband, but I'm not going to stand for all those dirty things that go on."

By this time, John Mitchell wanted to get out, too. On July 1, 1972, aware he and John Dean were likely to bear most of the responsibility for the break-in, he resigned.

40 NEW YORK   Painting by Julian Allen

Summer, 1972

"Deep Throat" Whispers The Secrets

Bob Woodward, a reporter for The Washington Post, awaits a still unidentified government informer, "Deep Throat," in a deserted underground garage in or near Washington late one summer's night.

Bob Woodward and Carl Bernstein, despite White House attempts to discredit their stories and besmirch their paper ("shabby journalism," announced White House Press Secretary Ron Ziegler), managed to penetrate the miasma of secrecy surrounding Watergate, win The Post a Pulitzer, and shake the foundations of the United States government. The young reporters broke essential parts of the story by carefully cultivating sources of information and then ardently protecting their sources' identities.

Perhaps their most important source was a government official at first known only to Woodward. Woodward and Deep Throat (so dubbed by a Post editor) had devised complicated rituals which enabled them to communicate without being detected. When Woodward wanted a meeting he would position a flowerpot on his apartment balcony. Deep Throat would draw, or have drawn, a clock face on page 20 of Woodward's home-delivered New York Times to indicate a meeting time. Woodward would take at least two taxis and then walk to the concrete catacombs of an underground garage where they met, usually at one or two in the morning. Deep Throat, for security and other reasons, refused to reveal too much—even to Woodward. (Woodward and Bernstein suggest in their book, All the President's Men, that "he felt that the effect of one or two big stories . . . could be blunted by the White House.") Deep Throat did not state, but hinted, directed, or confirmed.

However, one evening Woodward and Deep Throat sat on the garage floor until almost 6 A.M. Deep Throat, in an unusually impartive mood, told the reporter of plans to discover The Post's sources, attempts to wreck political campaigns, and the existence of a web of over 50 people who were involved in gathering intelligence for the White House. Characteristically stopping short, he observed that some of what had occurred was "beyond belief." He had already warned Woodward, "They are all underhanded, and unknowable."

42 NEW YORK   Painting by Julian Allen

MARTHA MITCHELL (top) is manhandled by her bodyguard Steve King. Illustration by Julian Allen

DEEP THROAT (left): Bob Woodward, a reporter for *The Washington Post*, awaits an unidentified government informer. Illustration by Julian Allen

ANTHONY ULASEWICZ (top left) receives instructions from Herbert Kalmbach to make secret cash payments to a Watergate conspirator. Illustration by Melinda Bordelon

A SECRET DISCOVERED in a plane crash (left). Firemen find an attaché case that belonged to passenger Dorothy Hunt, who died in the crash, containing $10,000 in $100 bills. She was the wife of E. Howard Hunt. Illustration by James McMullan

ARCHIBALD COX (top right) refuses Nixon's ultimatum on October 18, 1973. Attorney General Elliot Richardson resigned rather than fire Cox on Nixon's order. Illustration by Melinda Bordelon

MELINDA BORDELON (1949–1995): Soon after Melinda arrived in New York from Texas, we selected her to illustrate part of the Watergate series. Though she was unknown to us, her portfolio was so impressive that we trusted her with this big assignment. Melinda went on to illustrate for major magazines including *Harper's*, *Esquire*, and *Playboy*.

Photo: the Bordelon family

Covers We Like, 1974

30-SOMETHINGS leaping into the future was the first story in Gail Sheehy's series, which led to her book *Passages*. Photograph by Carl Fischer

INSIDE SOHO Our guide to the new hot district of New York. Illustration by Haruo Miyauchi, after Toulouse-Lautrec

THE KISSINGER RIDDLE Henry Kissinger as the Sphinx, in the midst of Middle East negotiations. Illustration by Melinda Bordelon

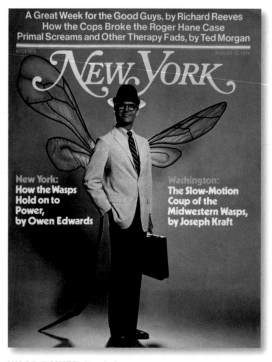

WASP POWER An obvious representation of the privileged white male. Photograph by Carl Fischer

MARTHA MITCHELL (opposite) was a colorful bit player in the Watergate scandal. The gabby wife of U.S. attorney general earned the moniker "The Mouth of the South" for leaking information to the press. Our design editor Joan Kron schemed this head-turning idea with fashion writer Priscilla Tucker. They hired fashion photographer Francesco Scavullo, a small squad of make-up artists and photo retouchers to give Martha a beauty makeover. Joan recalls how the story landed on the cover: "It was my job to plan the annual Christmas Shopping Guide and I proposed making it based on price with gifts from $1 to $1,500. I had read that a Francesco Scavullo beauty photo costs $1,500— a huge sum at the time— and even ordinary people were buying them. It was Priscilla who suggested Martha. When the photo came in, I brought it to Clay and he went crazy. In his inimitable brilliance, he said we are not saving this for the Christmas gift issue. We're making it a cover story and Priscilla and I were to write it together. Scavullo worked his magic. It was Clay's and Milton's genius to make it a story on its own."

JOAN KRON is a writer and documentary film director. A former senior editor of *New York*, she went on to write about design for *The New York Times*, fashion for *The Wall Street Journal*, and plastic surgery for *Allure*. She is the author of three books and co-author of the groundbreaking *High-Tech: the Industrial Style and Source Book for the Home* (designed by Walter Bernard). She premiered her first documentary, *Take My Nose . . . Please!* in 2017.

Photo by Charles Denson

Farewell to Pro Football, by David Halberstam
Abba Eban: Campaigning at Columbia
Why Bill Simon Is in Trouble, by Andrew Tobias

60 CENTS

DECEMBER 16, 1974

New York

Martha Mitchell Transformed!

To Find Out How, See Page 60

Photograph by Francesco Scavullo

The Reporter Nixon Hates Most, by Aaron Latham
I Lost It at a Diet Spa, by Gael Greene
Wall Street's Newest Hustle, by Andrew Tobias

50 CENTS

JANUARY 21, 1974

NEW YORK

THE AGONY OF A LOSING SEASON

A LAMENT for the Jets' coach Weeb
Ewbank's last and losing season. The
injured Joe Namath "Suffered for Us All."
Photograph by Harry Benson

EXODUS We used many staff members as models to help defray the cost of building the elaborate set. Photograph by Carl Fischer

An Outrageous Proposal

Ken Auletta argued that some of the biggest and most respected figures in the city were guilty of financial fraud and deserved to pay a personal price.

In 1975, Ken Auletta exposed collusion among corrupt officials and corporate executives in what was dubbed as the "greatest financial fraud in city history." With the incendiary cover headline "Should They Go to Jail?," his article implicated high-profile personalities such as U.S. Treasury Secretary William Simon, New York City Mayor Abe Beame, his predecessor John Lindsay, and David Rockefeller, among others.

It was an important news premise, so our challenge was to find a compelling way to present it on the cover. Ken recalls how it was solved: "Milton was in the meeting, and on a sketch pad he quickly drew a picture of officials behind prison bars and attached a headline close to the one finally chosen. I was in awe. Milton's idea transformed my piece into a must-read. My only contribution was to insist on making the headline a question, not a declaration that they should go to jail."

Fleshing out Milton's idea, illustrator Julian Allen masterfully captured the fear on each politician's face with his usual precision. For the inside opening pages (above), we asked him to arrange the men in question in a quasi-police station lineup—an obvious and effective solution.

This piece eventually became part of Auletta's first book, *The Streets Were Paved with Gold,* published in 1979.—WB

KEN AULETTA, who worked on Robert Kennedy's presidential campaign, joined *New York* magazine as a contributing editor in 1975. His interests were politics and urban affairs. He was also a weekly political columnist for the *Village Voice* and the author of twelve books, including *Frenemies* (2018). Auletta has been the "Annals of Communication" columnist for *The New Yorker* since 1992.

Photo: NYU/Philip Gallo

Ten Pages of the Best New York Kitchen Equipment
From The Cooks' Catalogue
The Fall and Rise of Hollywood's Hottest Producers

75 CENTS

DECEMBER 1, 1975

NEW YORK

These Men and Others May Have Participated in the Greatest Financial Fraud in City History
Should They Go to Jail?

Illustration by Julian Allen

Covers We Like, 1975

DETERMINED We gathered the Citizens Committee for New York City on four hours' notice to be photographed by Carl Fischer.

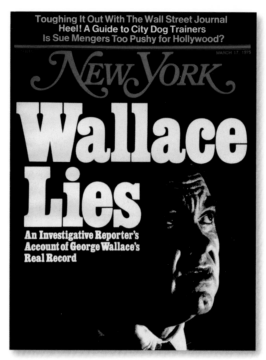

OUR BOLD HEADLINE dramatized Steve Brill's assessment of George Wallace. Photograph by Charles Moore, Black Star

IMMIGRANTS Harvey Dinnerstein's haunting painting captured the great early twentieth-century wave of Jewish immigration.

ARTIFACTS of the New Age of Pot and what legalization would mean in 1975. Photograph by Carl Fischer

ANDY WARHOL'S ATTITUDE is evident in his willingness to pose in a closet to promote his new book (opposite). "As soon as I became a loner in my own mind that's when I got what you might call a following."
—*The Philosophy of Andy Warhol*

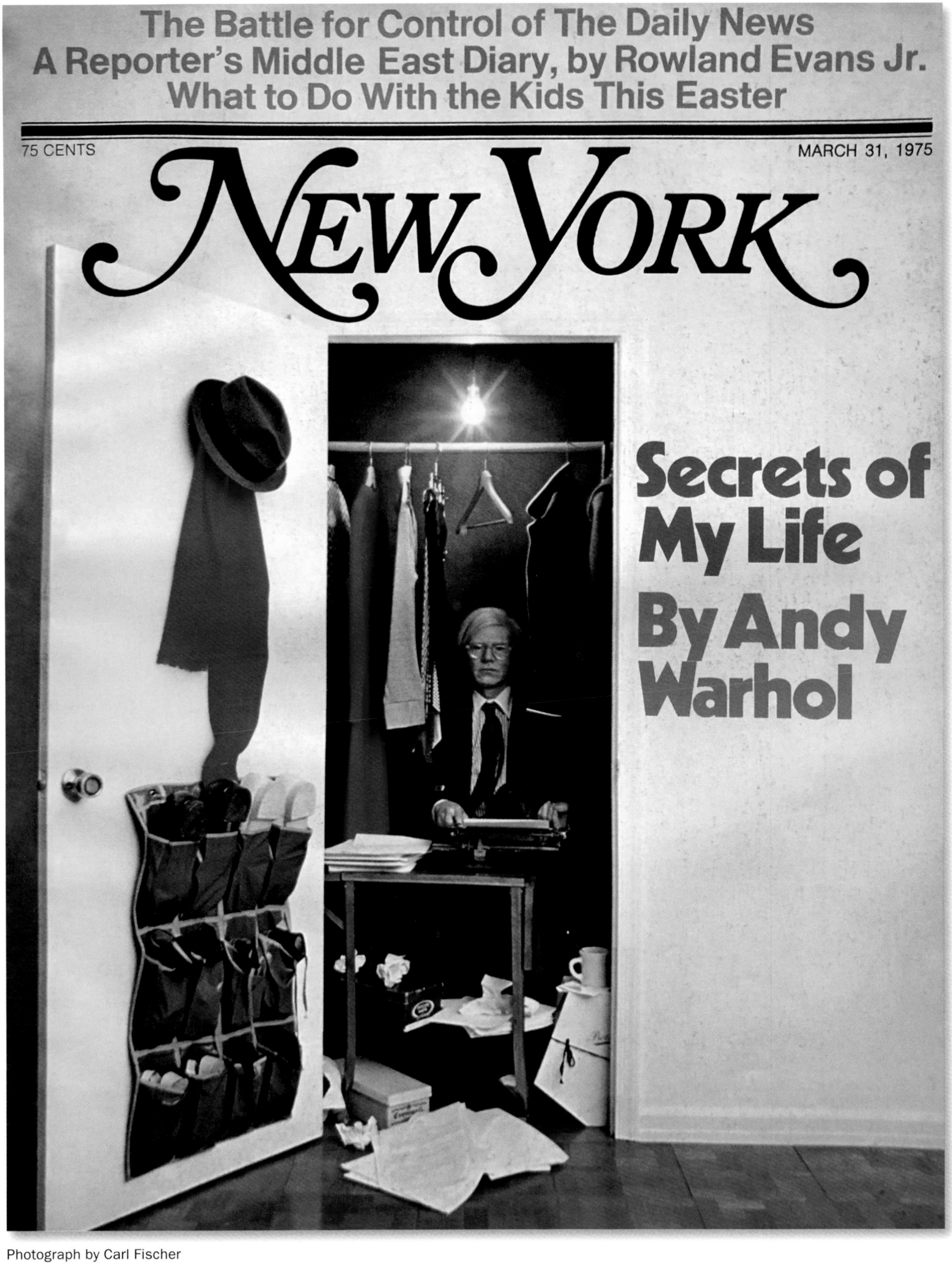

The Battle for Control of The Daily News
A Reporter's Middle East Diary, by Rowland Evans Jr.
What to Do With the Kids This Easter

75 CENTS

MARCH 31, 1975

NEW YORK

Secrets of My Life By Andy Warhol

Photograph by Carl Fischer

"Even New Jersey Looks Good from Here."

Fine dining soared to new heights at Windows on the World.

Reception: Concierge Joseph Scialom (sixth from right) and 297 others make up the staff that runs the Windows on the World.

The Most Spectacular Restaurant in the World
By Gael Greene

"...Windows on the World is a triumph. No other sky-high restaurant quite prepares you for the astonishment of these horizons..."

THE RECEPTION STAFF of Windows on the World (left), photographed by Burt Glinn, welcomes readers to the eleven-page report by Gael Greene.

THE COVER Illustration (opposite) depicts our focus, the dazzling 107th floor of the World Trade Center, offering a beautifully designed bar and restaurant with stunning views.

There was never a more ambitious restaurant than Windows on the World. Occupying the entire 107th floor of the World Trade Center, the place was designed to overwhelm with its grandeur and marvelous details.

Being so high above Manhattan had the effect of making you feel that you were the "ruler of some extraordinary universe," as our food critic Gael Greene puts it. She visited the restaurant before it opened to the public in 1975. Although she was lukewarm about the menu, the view was without question spectacular. She writes: "Even New Jersey looks good from here. Down below are all of Manhattan and helicopters and clouds. Everything to hate and fear is invisible. Pollution is but a cloud. A fire raging below Washington Square is a dream, silent, almost unreal, though you can see the arc of water licking flame. Default is a silly nightmare. There is no doggy doo. Garbage is an illusion." Many say that the restaurant single-handedly redeemed the World Trade Center's reputation; its architectural design was fiercely despised by many New Yorkers at the time.

Burt Glinn's photographs captured the restaurant's elegance. He zoomed into the beautiful place settings, popped into a menu-planning meeting, took portraits of the Windows on the World staff, and, of course, featured that peerless skyline at various times of the day. We crammed as many of Burt's pictures as we could into the layout. It's unfortunate that our color printing wasn't up to today's professional standards.

GAEL GREENE
was *New York*'s restaurant critic from 1968 to 2001. Apart from reviews of the city's prominent dining establishments, she developed lively features such as "Everything You Always Wanted to Know About Ice Cream But Were Too Fat to Ask," "The Mafia Guide to Dining Out," and "Nobody Knows the Truffles I've Seen." Her book *Blue Skies, No Candy,* was published in 1976. Gael cofounded Citymeals on Wheels in 1981; the charity delivers over two million meals to homebound senior citizens each year. She is credited with coining the word "foodie" in 1980.
Photo: Gael Greene

116

Who's Holding Up Solar Energy? by Andrew Tobias
Why Front-Runners Keep Stumbling, by Richard Reeves
Fanny Pants: Summer's Newest Erogenous Zone

75 CENTS

MAY 31, 1976

NEW YORK

The Most Spectacular Restaurant in the World

How a Brilliant Restaurateur
Created a Masterpiece on the 107th Floor
Of the World Trade Center
By Gael Greene

Illustration by Nicholas Gaetano

"Windows" creator Joe Baum: Nobody has ever called him less than a genius.

Changeable Feasts
Dishes on the Grand Buffet table in The Restaurant change every day. Eat all you want for $7.95 on weekdays; weekends, the spread ($9.75) is even more elaborate.

44 NEW YORK/MAY 31, 1976

The complexity of restaurants is very fascinating from a design perspective. Everything is connected—you can't separate the comfort of your seat from the hors d'oeuvres. I was a consultant to Joe Baum, the city's preeminent restaurateur of that time. I designed logos, plates, wall murals, promotional materials—really anything that he felt wasn't quite resolved.

The Windows logo reflects the complexity of this restaurant. I wouldn't necessarily take this approach today. It can't be reduced to a simple shape. But you really remember it. The blue and yellow motif of the tableware was designed to create an interesting pattern when pieces were piled one upon another.

I enjoyed working on Joe's restaurant projects over the years. Aside from Windows on the World, he was the brains behind iconic New York establishments such as the Rainbow Room, the Four Seasons restaurant, and Aurora. Joe tended to intimidate his restaurant staff but was actually very gracious and caring. We became very good friends, and his smiling picture still hangs over my desk.—MG

BURT GLINN (1925–2008) began his career as a photojournalist for *Life* magazine before becoming a freelancer who worked for major magazines, most notably *Holiday*, *Esquire*, *Geo*, *Travel and Leisure*, *Fortune*, and *Paris Match*. Eclectic and technically proficient, Glinn was one of Magnum's prolific photographers. He was president of Magnum Photos from 1972 to 1975 and was re-elected to the post in 1987.
Photo: Elena Glinn

WINDOWS ON THE WORLD

THE WINDOWS LOGO
and an example of the tableware (left)

118

the Four Seasons, is on loan from the Culinary Institute of America (CIA), hiring bakers, setting up the commissary bakeshop, perfecting his achingly piquant lemon tart. A tall blonde with Campbell Kid curls works beside him. The entire staff is an emancipator's dream—male and female, assorted colors, eclectic backgrounds.

"Oh God, I hope it will be good," says Joe.

The Club is the showpiece of a com-

liant but they weren't willing to make the capital investment." So $21 million was budgeted for creating food service. (The Club itself is only $300,000 to $400,000 over its $7.5-million budget, Tozzoli reports.) Now nine companies were interested enough to bid. Joe Baum among them. But Hilton International's bid offered the most profitable balance for the Port Authority. It didn't require exceptional intelligence for H. I. president Curt Strand to form Inhilco to run the system with his old

The Plan
Below, one of the working drawings used in planning the 107th floor. The shaded areas on the perimeter are the public spaces. The core contains the work spaces and building services.

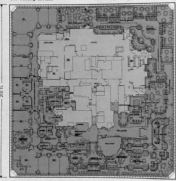

The Grill
At right, the international cooks' table in The Grill (called, after three o'clock, The Hors d'Oeuvreries). Various chefs preside in rotation. Here, Sadaharu Doira does the sushi, Gudny Paulsen the smørbrød.

munity of WTC restaurants and carry-outs designed to feed the complex's 50,000 employees, 80,000 visitors . . . 50,000 lunches a day, mostly $2 or less, in 35 locations. It was early deemed impractical to parcel out parts of Baum's feeding scheme to individual owners. A tribe of operators would quickly tax truck docks, elevators, and garbage disposal. But when WTC director Guy Tozzoli presented Baum's plan and construction estimate to food industry giants, no one was interested. "I hadn't planned to spend a dime building The Club," Tozzoli recalls. "Everyone thought Joe's plan was bril-

Cornell Hotel and Restaurant School classmate Joe Baum as president. Same salary plus a percentage. Net profits go 85 percent to WTC, 15 percent to Inhilco.

"Tozzoli is a feisty guy with a good eye," says Baum. "He gets things done. He protected the integrity of our idea. Ask him how the windows got wider." "The steel was going on, already 40 stories up," Tozzoli recalls. "And I saw how thick the mullions were and I realized we were building a view restaurant with a limited view. I called our architect, Yamasaki, and he refused to change it." Tozzoli built a win-

People and patterns: Pastry chef Albert Kumin, assistant Rena Smith, chef André René, Italian cookware, receptionist Beverly Rouse, chairs by Warren Platner in the West Parlor, $2.50 soap.

The War Room
On the 106th floor, just below the restaurant, Barbara Kafka, Joe Baum, Alan Lewis, and Kevin Eraly spent days on end plotting menus in what they came to call the war room. "Working with Joe," says Barbara Kafka "is fascinating, aggravating...and rewarding. He can drive you out of your skull. That Talmudic mind looks at everything from every side. He always expects more than you can do. And you do it."

The Liquor Library
By day it's called "The Great Bar," by night "The City Lights Bar," and, in addition to mind-bending views of New York Bay, it boasts a "library" of 1,000 different labels of spirits—among them 150 kinds of Scotch, 76 kinds of gin. No matter where in the bar your table is, the mirrored ceiling lets you watch your drink being poured. And if you're in a hurry, the waiter will bring you something to eat at the counter.

Touches: Dessert tables, place setting in Grill, coat checking, brass accent, captain Felicia Lee, liquor sentinels in the bar, and details of The Cellar in the Sky, a small restaurant that's also a working wine cave.

dow mock-up in his office and brooded. "For six months we argued, then finally I said, 'Sorry, Yama.' Yamasaki visited The Club two weeks ago. "'You were right,' he told me. That made me feel good."

Two thousand names were suggested for the restaurant. "A marble contractor named Robert de Lazzero came up with the winner," Tozzoli remembers. "We were down in Puerto Rico. Caterina Valente was singing 'Windows of the World' . . . he turned it around a little."

Joe Baum wanted to call it "For Spacious Skies." For a while he even signed letters "For Gracious Skies, Joe Baum."

The member-recruitment brochure was irresistible—a seductive lyric of homemade potato chips, live trout, lead baffles for conference-room walls with no ears, never a soggy lettuce leaf, the concierge-miracle-maker. Not even the WTC's fiercest critic, Theodore Kheel, could resist. "Since my office is above Canal Street, the dues were only $100. What a buy," Kheel rejoices.

"On April 12th, 1976, the incredible Club at the World Trade Center will open its doors," the brochure declared. "We'd scheduled it three times and postponed it. We just had to pick a date," Baum recalls. "It will be a private luncheon club the likes of which the city has never seen."

The State Liquor Authority ruled it would not. The SLA demanded full public access at all times. A compromise was finally reached—120 non-members would be admitted at lunch for a $10 cover, plus $3 for each of their guests . . . The Restaurant would be open to all, no cover, from three on. and weekends. Baum is bitter. SLA chairman Mike Roth (offices in the WTC) paid a $15 entrance fee and got a window seat at lunch the first Friday in May.

The architect is the one in blue jeans —Warren Platner, calmly supervising a colleague with a staple gun on a ladder in Suite F. "We are putting doodads on

the wall," he says. "As architects we like to do the whole thing." Most of the artwork is still to come. "We held off ordering till we knew there'd be money left in the budget to pay for it." If there hadn't been? "We'd have done without." Platner looks like a country hick. Yet he has created a quietly sophisticated environment, so splendid the eye need not seek a window for joy.

Without a trained eye or Platner as guide, you might not see the elaborate repetition of points in a square, the subtle distinction of velvet and wool and rattan and brass, the pattern of curve, the unlikely grayed-Easter-egg color in The Grill . . . nothing makes noise.

"There are no compromises here," Platner says, watching in fascination as two lingering drunks, holding each other up, navigate the mirrored glass of his Gallery, coming from the bar. "We had to trim our design and keep trimming to keep it within the inflationary spiral. That is the cheapest acoustical tile you can buy. We have acres of plasterboard. That way we can afford silk and gold leaf and brass and pink marble."

Cynics who long ago gave up quality forever will have to think again.

Joe Baum believes in consultants. James Beard has been Joe's giant muse for two decades. Jim fantasizes, spinning sense-numbing fancies by cassette:

"There must be croissants that float in the air . . . fresh sorbets every half hour . . . fish hash I adore . . . blueberry slump and apple grunt and gooseberry fool . . . crab cakes luscious and hot and wonderful . . . last night I had a lamb ragout so wonderful you just wanted to cuddle it in your arms." And Joe wades through "all that excitement" asking, "What can I do? What's possible?"

All week the bodies have assembled in what will soon be Inhilco's 106th-floor offices—naked now except for Joe's desk and cookbooks on the floor, ringing the room. It's time to plan the dinner menu. Barbara Kafka, Baum's resident muse, calls up to The Club

DETAILS Burt Glinn meticulously photographed every detail of this spectacular restaurant.

The Scene Is Real, the Story Not So Much

A fabricated account of Brooklyn's disco scene inspired the Hollywood hit movie *Saturday Night Fever*.

JAMES McMULLAN has created images for magazines, books, record covers, U.S. stamps, murals, and animated films. McMullan is best known for the over eighty posters he has done for the Lincoln Center Theater. He has illustrated a popular series of children's books, including *I Stink!*, a monologue by a garbage truck, written by his wife, Kate McMullan. Along with his illustrated memoir, *Leaving China*, his other books are *Revealing Illustrations*, *High-Focus Drawing*, *The Theater Posters of James McMullan*, and *More McMullans*.

Photo by Cosmos Sarchiapone

There were grumblings among the magazine's young staff that Clay didn't get out of Manhattan enough to get a sense of the other boroughs. Partly in response to this criticism, we published a story about the vibrant nightclub scene in Brooklyn.

Nik Cohn, who was renowned for his insightful coverage of London's rock-and-roll world, pitched this story based on his initial visits to these working-class disco clubs. We thought Jim McMullan was the ideal illustrator for the assignment because he had a mastery of capturing the reality of a moment. In the tradition of the visual reportage style that distinguished the magazine, we asked him to operate like a journalist and paint what he saw.

Jim's illustrations really transported you to the club scene. Consider the illustration (above) showing Vincent, the story's protagonist, and his sidekick behind him. The degree of distraction on the sidekick's face is so palpable. Jim captures his darting glances and a kind of detachment from the figure in the foreground. The ability to record this nuance gives this painting life.

We had Jim's paintings in hand, but Nik had missed his deadline entirely. Clay called him and threatened to run the story as a portfolio of paintings. His first draft arrived two weeks later.

NIK COHN is a British journalist and author who has published many articles, novels, and music books. His report on the disco scene in *New York* was the basis for the film *Saturday Night Fever*. Cohn was a columnist for *The Guardian* in the mid- to late 1990s. His book *Triksta: Life and Death and New Orleans Rap* was published in 2007.

Photo by Allan Tannenbaum

Nigel Dempster, the World's Boldest Gossip
Governor Carey Hits Rock Bottom, by Ken Auletta
The Mid-Life Crises of 'Time' and 'Newsweek'

75 CENTS   JUNE 7, 1976

New York

Tribal Rites of the New Saturday Night
By Nik Cohn

"...The guard dogs went berserk; they hurled themselves full force against the gate..."

THE SCENE OUTSIDE
the disco "Ascension" (above). Jim made up the name at Clay Felker's request. It was in fact the 2001 Odyssey.

S oon after we published "Tribal Rites," Hollywood producer Robert Stigwood called to inquire about buying the rights.

We later found out that Nik fabricated much of the report! Vincent (John Travolta's Tony Manero) was an amalgam of London clubgoers and an anonymous figure he saw outside the 2001 Odyssey Night Club in Bay Ridge. In a mea culpa to *New York* in 1997, Cohn wrote: "When we pulled up outside the club, a drunken brawl was in progress. Just as I opened my side door, one of the brawlers emerged from the pack, reeled over toward the gutter and threw up, with fine precision, all over the side of the cab and my trouser legs. I took it as a sign. Quickly slamming the door I ordered us back to Manhattan. The following weekend, I went back to 2001 Odyssey and this time we got past the door. I didn't learn much, though. The noise level was deafening. . . . None of my attempts at striking up conversations got beyond the first few sentences. . . . Plus, I made a lousy interviewer. I knew nothing about this world, and it showed. Quite literally, I didn't speak the language. So I faked it.

"If not for James McMullan's illustrations, the story may have never seen daylight."

". . . He looked at her legs with a strange smile, a smile that made her want to run . . ."

tongue. Then he smacked right into the fence itself, and this time the dogs flung back with such frenzy, such total demonic fury, that even the steel bonds were shaken and the whole gate seemed to buckle and give.

That was enough. Somewhat chastened, though they continued to giggle and snicker, the Faces moved on. Behind them, the dogs still howled, still hurled themselves at the wires. But the Faces did not look back.

When they reached the car, they found Vincent already waiting, combing his hair. "Where were you?" asked Gus.

"Watching," said Vincent, and he climbed into the back, out of sight. Inside 2001 Odyssey, there was no more music or movement. The dance floor was deserted. Saturday night had ended, and Vincent slouched far back in his corner. His eyes were closed, his hands hung limp. He felt complete.

Another Saturday night. Easing down on Fifth and Ovington, Joey parked the car and went into the pizza parlor, the Elegante. Vincent and Eugene were already waiting. So was Gus. But John James was missing. Two nights before he had been beaten up and knifed, and now he was in the hospital.

It was an old story. When the Double J got home from work on Thursday evening, his mother had sent him out for groceries, down to Marinello's Deli. He had bought pasta and salad, toilet paper, a six-pack of Bud, a package of frozen corn, gum, detergent, tomato sauce, and four TV dinners. Paid up. Combed his hair in the window. Then went out into the street, cradling his purchases in both arms.

As he emerged, three Latins—Puerto Ricans—moved across the sidewalk toward him and one of them walked straight through him. Caught unawares, he lost his balance and his bag was knocked out of his arms, splattering on the curb.

Produce scattered everywhere, rolling in the puddles and filth. The frozen corn spilled into the gutter, straight into some dog mess, and the Latins laughed. "Greaseballs," said John James, not thinking. All that was on his mind was his groceries, the need to rescue what he'd lost. So he bent down and began to pick up the remnants. And the moment he did, of course, the Latins jumped all over him.

The rest was hazy. He could remember being beaten around the head, kicked in the sides and stomach, and he remembered a sudden sharp burn in his arm, almost as though he had been stung by an electric wasp. Then lots of shouting and scuffling, bodies tumbling all anyhow, enormous smothering weights on his face, a knee in the teeth. Then nothing.

In the final count, the damage was three cracked ribs, a splintered cheekbone, black eyes, four teeth lost, and a deep knife cut, right in the meat of his arm, just missing his left bicep.

"Three greaseballs at once," said Gus. "He could have run. But he wouldn't."

"He stuck," said Vincent. "He hung tight."

Judgment passed, the Faces finished their pizzas, wiped their lips, departed. Later on, of course, there would have to be vengeance, the Latins must be punished. For the moment, however, the feeling was of excitement, euphoria. As Eugene hit the street, he let out a whoop, one yelp of absolute glee. Saturday night, and everything was beginning, everything lay ahead of them once more.

But Vincent hung back, looked serious. Once again he had remembered a line, another gem from the screen. "Hung tight," he said, gazing up along the bleak street. "He could have got away clean, no sweat. But he had his pride. And his pride was his law."

Donna loved Vincent, had loved him for almost four months. Week after week she came to Odyssey just for him, to watch him dance, to wait. She sat in a booth by herself and didn't drink, didn't smile, didn't tap her foot or nod her head to the music. Though Vincent never danced with her, she would not dance with anyone else.

Her patience was infinite. Hands folded in her lap, knees pressed together, she watched from outside, and she did not pine. In her own style she was satisfied, for she knew she was in love, really, truly, once and for all, and that was the thing she had always dreamed of.

Donna was nineteen, and she worked as a cashier in a supermarket over toward Flatbush. As a child she had been much too fat. For years she was ashamed. But now she felt much better. If she held her breath, she stood five-foot-six and only weighed 140 pounds.

Secure in her love, she lived in the background. Vincent danced, and she took notes. He laughed, and she was glad. Other girls might chase him, touch him, swarm all over him. Still she endured, and she trusted.

And one Saturday, without any warning, Vincent suddenly turned toward her and beckoned her onto the floor, right in the middle of the Odyssey Walk, where she took her place in the line, three rows behind him, one rank to the left.

She was not a natural dancer, never had been. Big-boned, soft-fleshed, her body just wasn't right. She had good breasts, good hips, the most beautiful gray-green eyes. But her feet, her legs, were hopeless. Movement embarrassed her. There was no flow. Even in the dark, when she made love, or some boy used her for pleasure, she always wanted to hide.

Nonetheless, on this one night she went through the motions and nobody laughed. She kept her eyes on the floor, she hummed along with the songs. Three numbers went by without disaster. Then the dancers changed, moved from the Walk to something else, something she didn't know, and Donna went back to her booth.

Obscurity. Safety. She sipped Fresca through a straw and fiddled with her hair. But just as she was feeling stronger, almost calm again, Vincent appeared above her, his shadow fell across her just like in the movies, and he put his hand on her arm.

His shirt was pink and scarlet and yellow; her dress was pastel green. His boots were purple, and so were her painted lips. "I'm leaving," Vincent said, and she followed him outside.

His coat was creased at the back. He didn't know that, but Donna did; she could see it clearly as they walked out. And the thought of it, this secret weakness, made her dizzy with tenderness, the strangest sense of ownership.

"What's your name?" Vincent asked.

"Maria," said Donna. "Maria Elena."

A YOUNG WOMAN (above) observes the dancing and waits to take to the dancefloor inside the Odyssey.

THE SCENE INSIDE (left) "This trio at the table attracted me for the way the girl in the silver top and with the amazing hair held the attention of the other two."—JM

MCMULLAN ON HIS PROCESS:

After the first night visiting the 2001 Club and photographing the young people dancing and sitting around, my contact sheets came back completely black, no images. I realized I would have to go back and use a flash on my camera to pierce the gloom of the dark rooms. On that repeat visit to the club, I knew that confronting people with aggressive bursts of light from my flash would be more challenging than moving around the room discreetly taking shots with available light, so I introduced myself to the club manager very self-importantly as "on assignment from *New York* magazine," and he gave me permission to photograph the patrons. I managed to assume the role of the unstoppable professional and fired away all over the club. What the prints revealed when I got them back from the processor were nuances of expression, loneliness or insecurity, that people had not bothered to hide in the dim light of the club. These details made the information much more psychologically provocative to me than I had expected. Also, the strange shadows that the flash

had created along the edges of the figures went from being an annoying photographic glitch to an aesthetic opportunity. These echoing black perimeters flattened the images and gave them the patterned effect of a Japanese print.

I began to see the paintings I would do as carefully constructed puzzles, with their realism interrupted and made more psychologically expressive by the unrealistic black edges.

The basic change for me in the way I created the disco images was that I worked from my photographs without changing details. I trusted the instincts that had led me to take each of the photographs at that particular instant and that my reaction to the scenes in the club was a legitimate story in itself.

The careful realism I used in the disco paintings suited the journalistic intent of the assignment and taught me a level of patience in building up an image that I hadn't had before. It gave me a new confidence in my use of photography and in embracing the role of a journalistic illustrator.

McMULLAN'S PHOTOGRAPH of the disco scene (above left) provided information for his illustrations.

THE RESULT (middle). Jim's illustration based on the photograph, taking advantage of the flash bulb effect. A detail of this illustration was used for the cover.

MOVIE STILL from the film *Saturday Night Fever* (opposite). McMullan's illustrations are believed to have been a guide for the staging of scenes in the film.

THE WAR OF WORDS CONTINUED

As could be expected, letters poured in after Nik's shocking admission. McMullan took issue with how his illustrations were characterized in the article. The two hashed it out in the magazine's December 22–29, 1997, "Letters" column.

JIM WROTE: "Nik Cohn's piece on the true story of his trip to the Brooklyn discos in 1975 establishes his credentials as a writer of fiction once and for all ["Saturday Night's Big Bang," December 8]. I was with him that night, and I'm amused to read that my 1972 Audi got turned into a gypsy cab, that Tu Sweet was just a witness to a fight and not the catalyst for it by dancing with the wrong young woman, and that the illustrations I did were simply a nudge to Clay Felker to print the piece and not, in fact, the visual journalism that preceded Cohn's writing. There's some kind of symmetry going on here. Twenty years later, Nik Cohn had another chance to tell the truth."

NIK RESPONDED: "James McMullan is both right and wrong. We did indeed spend an evening together in Brooklyn discos, and it was essentially as he describes. But that was not my first journey to 2001 Odyssey. The night described in my recent piece—the night which McMullan disputes—occurred earlier, as others will confirm. On the question of his illustrations, I don't know on what grounds McMullan feels slighted. As my article clearly stated, the disco story might never have seen daylight without them. They were not, however, an inspiration for my own writing as he seems to imply."

PICKING PICTURES
At *New York* magazine, a meeting discussing a contact sheet of Burt Glinn's photographs. From left to right: Walter Bernard, Tom Bentkowski (assistant art director), Dorothy Seiberling (senior editor), Burt Glinn, Byron Dobell (editorial director), and Milton Glaser.

Photo by Cosmos Sarchiapone

Covers We Like, 1976

THE POISONED TONGUE The devil and the serpent are allusions to the mean-spiritedness of gossip. Like every cover, the challenge here was to create a symbolic equivalent for something that's very difficult to represent.—MG

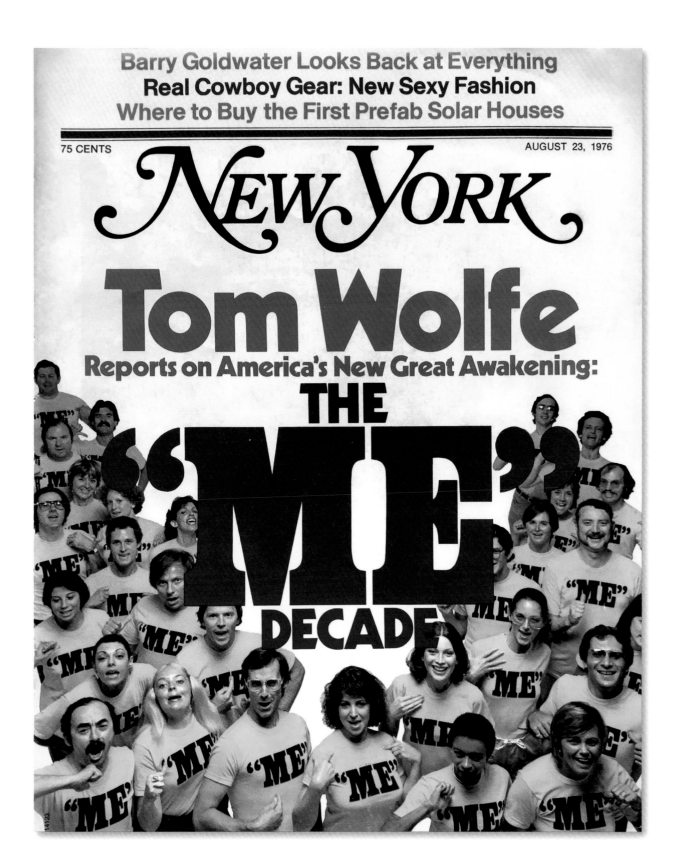

THE "ME" DECADE was defined by Tom Wolfe. We printed
T-shirts and enlisted our staff and friends to pose for the cover.
Photograph by Harold Krieger

Robert Weaver (1913–1991)

To observe a moment and make you believe a pencil sketch as you would a photograph: this was Robert Weaver's gift.

ROBERT WEAVER (left). When he died in 1994, *New York Times* art critic Roberta Smith aptly summarized Robert's genius: "His style combined loose, rough-hewn rendering, deft abbreviations and sometimes elements of collage, with a startling degree of realism that seemed to capture of essence of any face or pose without resorting to photographic detail."
Photo by Todd Gangel

TO CATCH A THIEF
Weaver went down to Police Headquarters on the first day that the force's brand-new computer system was installed to speed up response time. He recorded the scene (above) from the time of a reported robbery to the thief's apprehension.

GRAFFITI AT HARVARD
For "Adam Smith's" article about the Harvard Business School in turbulent times (opposite), Robert's collage technique captured the mood on campus.

U nlike other illustrators who relied on reference pictures, Robert liked to go out and capture a scene on the spot. This was possible because he could draw like a dream. His sketches, sometimes presented in a collage, had a journalistic quality and an immediacy that convinced you that you were actually witnessing something unfolding.

Robert had an expert narrative sense that helped define *New York* magazine's visual reportage style. Through acutely observed visual notations, he showed how artists can embrace a reporter's mindset and be agents of truth, in the same manner writers and photographers can. "The journalistic approach in art is nothing more complicated than a desire to tell a story, describe an event or illustrate a mood," he wrote in *The Art of Humorous Illustration.* "The illustrator has experienced something and he desires to reproduce it. Many painters simply don't have this desire, but an illustrator who doesn't have it cannot very well serve the course of journalism."

A beloved teacher, Robert was a longtime faculty member at the School of Visual Arts. "The Weave," as some students affectionately called him, championed drawing from life. "Any on-the-spot sketch would provide a welcome sparkle to the printed page," he said. "I believe, then, that the artist could restore to the journals a visual excitement, a more personal view of events, and, finally, a more honest one."

That's exactly what he did for us.

131

On the beach at Coney Island, 1974, courtesy of the Forum Gallery

ON THE BEACH
David loved Coney Island and could be found most summer mornings painting the "women in shmatas." He also played tennis regularly at The Heights Casino in Brooklyn, where we would deliver manuscripts for him and pick up his artwork. Caricature of Joe Namath, 1969 (below).

David Levine (1926–2009)

One of the great caricaturists of our time was an early and frequent contributor.

David Levine excelled not only as a caricaturist, where he is unparalleled, but also as a watercolorist. Unlike myself, who's always had to struggle with likeness, he could draw any face accurately. He did the most astonishing tricks in the realm of caricature and is truly up to the level of Honoré Daumier in that genre. I don't think he's acknowledged enough for his brilliance.

If we couldn't figure a visual treatment for an article, we'd say, "Give it to David. He'll do a portrait!" We knew he'd always get something on time and beautiful. His lyrical watercolors were totally separate from his wacky pen-and-ink drawings. He was equally good at both.—MG

If we had to illustrate a personality who was well known but not particularly interesting—say a candidate for comptroller—David would be among the first illustrators to come to mind. He was accommodating, quick, and exceptionally prolific. We used him in the magazine frequently, but I was also impressed to see his work in so many other publications, including *The New York Review of Books*, where he made his mark.

In 1974, I joined the Painting Group organized by David and Aaron Shikler. Every Wednesday night, the group of about twenty-five artists of all skill levels met at a loft in Soho to paint from a live model. Watching David produce a watercolor portrait inspired everybody.

Neil Leifer and I produced a documentary titled *Portraits of a Lady* featuring Justice Sandra Day O'Connor sitting for the group. At the time, David was turning eighty and had developed macular degeneration, a disease that robbed him of the ability to adequately see the model. Nevertheless, David still led the group every week and sat among us talking about Degas, Sargent, and Daumier. After giving a precise critique, he always offered encouragement. "Keep playing," he'd say.—WB

PORTRAITS OF POWER
Ted Kennedy (top) from "Teddy or Not" by Richard Reeves, 1974
Alexander Haig (middle) from "Has a Sinister Force Corrupted Alexander Haig?" by Evans and Novak, 1974
James Angleton (bottom) from "Politics and the CIA—Was Angleton Spooked by State?" by Aaron Latham, 1975

CHAMPS
Levine's group portrait celebrating the New
York Knicks' NBA championship in 1973.

Robert Grossman (1940–2018)

ROBERT GROSSMAN
in his studio in SoHo in
Manhattan (left).

Photo by Jan Welt, courtesy of
Alex Emanuel Grossman

Witty and politically savvy, Grossman
energized *New York*'s political coverage
over the years.

Three covers of *New York*
magazine displaying
Grossman's masterful
airbrush style.

Robert Grossman was a cartoonist at heart. A graduate
of Yale University's Fine Arts Program, he was the editor
of *The Yale Record*, which is today the oldest running
humor magazine in the world. He was a kind of natural comedian,
a joke teller, and also had such a strong visual sense that his
work was always of a sort that made you pay attention. Grossman
said, "Uglification is not my idea of caricature. Monstrous people
who want to terrify us probably like being portrayed as monstrous and terrifying. To me, it's better to show the bully as the
frightened baby he probably is."

Bob's illustrations invigorated the magazine's "City Politic"
section and various middle-of-the-book features over the years.
He had such insightful and well-formed opinions about politics
that we gave him the entire column, opposite, in several issues.

Bob was also a master at airbrush painting and really led
the revival of this nineteenth-century commercial art tool. Until
then, airbrush was mostly considered a photo-retouching technique. We published several covers by Bob that demonstrated
how he elevated it to a lively artistic medium. He used this technique when he created that wonderful twisted plane illustration
for the theatrical poster of the 1980 slapstick comedy *Airplane!*

In the 1970s, Bob began experimenting with sculpture and
made wonderful political busts. He received an Oscar nomination
for the charming 1977 claymation film *Jimmy the C*, featuring
Jimmy Carter singing Ray Charles's "Georgia on My Mind."

BILL CLINTON IN CLAY
Robert used many
materials for his sculptures,
but in the 1990s he primarily
used red clay, used
for designing cars, which
he coated with primer
and acrylic paints. The
sculpture (above) of Bill
Clinton, at 8.5" tall,
was sent to us as a gift
from Bob in 1998.

THE CITY POLITIC
One of several full-page
columns written and
illustrated by Robert
(opposite). He also
illustrated almost every
"City Politic" column by
others from 1968 to 1977.

THE CITY POLITIC

LIBBY AND SAM

Julian Allen (1942–1998)

JULIAN ALLEN in his New York studio. His work for the magazine included many "secret histories" and re-creations. Among them were "The Illustrated Secret History of Watergate," "The Secret Deal of the Oil Cartel," "The Illustrated Story of the Great Israeli Rescue," and a variety of mafia crime-related stories.

Photo: the estate of Julian Allen

BATTLE OF MANHATTAN
Julian did a series of paintings commemorating the Revolutionary War's battles in New York City. He illustrated the historical events by painting over contemporary photographs by Henry Groskinsky.

THE YOM KIPPUR WAR
Shortly after Julian arrived in New York, we sent him with Nora Ephron to the Sinai desert to cover the Yom Kippur War in the tradition of "soldier artists" embedded with U.S. troops during World War II. Unfortunately, Julian was injured during a bomb explosion. While recuperating in the hospital there, Julian sketched evocative portraits of Israeli and Arab soldiers wounded in battle (at right and opposite).

Julian so impressed us with his intelligence and skills that we offered him a contract to move to New York from England.

Clay and I had an idea to bring back illustrative journalism in a sort of nineteenth-century style, probably best exemplified by Winslow Homer's newspaper illustrations for *Harper's Weekly*. Although the circle of new American illustrators was outstanding, most were not really focused on representing a kind of objective reality. I had been taking notice of some unusual illustrations that appeared in two British magazines, *The Observer* and the *Sunday Times Magazine*. They had an objective, almost neutral quality that intensified their sense of being "real." The effect was powerful. Many illustrators conceal the photographic origins of their work. Here, those references were intensified and because of our belief in the reality of photography, the images were convincingly authentic. The creator of those paintings was Julian Allen.

I flew to London with the idea of offering him a six-month contract to become our staff illustrator specializing in reportage. He had a Humphrey Bogart-like persona; his few carefully chosen responses were defined by a sense of coiled energy. Within a very short time he was on his way to New York. That was June 1973.

Julian's ability to create convincing illustrations of unwitnessed events became his trademark. With very few exceptions, no other illustrator was capable of creating the deadpan, seemingly objective paintings as well as he could. A man of few words, he was a born storyteller. He was capable of painting a beautiful picture, but in his work beauty was an occasional by-product. His ability to focus on the narrative heart of a story was unexcelled.

Julian developed a brilliant career working for other publications, including *Rolling Stone*, *Time*, and *Vanity Fair*. His enthusiasm for his work never diminished. In his all too brief life, his contribution to the field of illustrative journalism established a standard that continues to inspire our profession.—MG

Courtesy of *Julian Allen: A Retrospective*, exhibition brochure, MICA, 2006

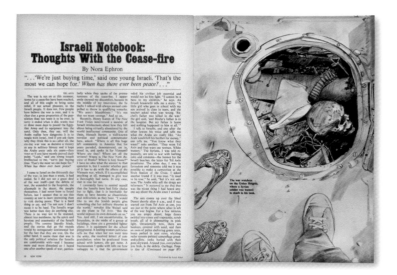

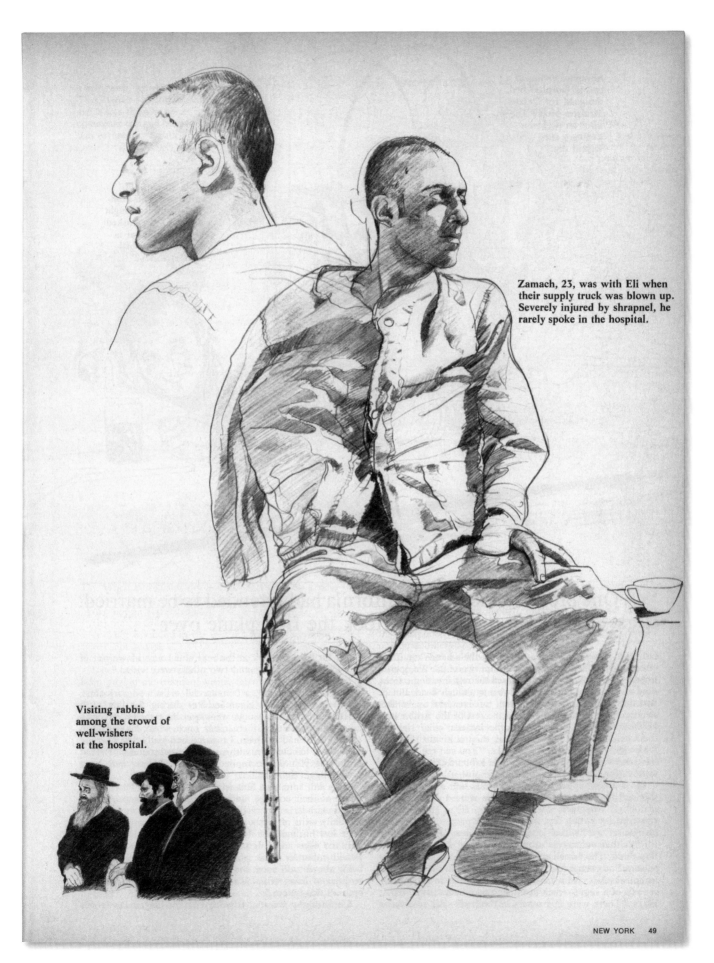

Zamach, 23, was with Eli when their supply truck was blown up. Severely injured by shrapnel, he rarely spoke in the hospital.

Visiting rabbis among the crowd of well-wishers at the hospital.

We worked separately after leaving *New York* magazine in December of 1976. The seven magazines noted in this chapter were designed independently.

Audience

Paris Match

Time

Adweek

The Atlantic Monthly

The Sophisticated Traveler

Fortune

CHAPTER

New Opportunities on Bigger Stages

LATE NIGHTS
Playing darts while waiting for late-breaking stories or incoming photographs after midnight at *Time* (above). From left, Tony Libardi, Walter Bernard, and Rudy Hoglund.

I will never forget the day Clay Felker stood on a desk to tell us that he had failed to stop Rupert Murdoch's hostile takeover of *New York* magazine. The news was devastating. We all gathered at an Irish bar that evening and together with our families, mourned the end of a joyful era. Though Murdoch offered to keep the staff intact, I realized that it was time to leave. Nothing would be the same.

I met with Murdoch shortly after he took over in January 1977. When I informed him about my intention to resign, he agreed to give assistant art director Tom Bentkowski a chance at the job. In turn, I agreed to be a consultant to the new editor, James Brady, for three months.

Leaving something that has been part of your working life for nine years is a bit depressing. Our close team of editors would all go off in different directions. We all had to adjust to life without Clay's large presence and the literary trio of Milton, Byron (Dobell), and Shelly (Zalaznick), our top editors. But before I could decide what to do next, *Time* magazine called with an opportunity to art direct a major national magazine. I would do it without Milton, my teacher and mentor, coming to the rescue whenever I got stuck. It was the right time to work on my own.

I spent three months preparing a redesign for Henry Grunwald, managing editor of *Time*. Happily, it was well received and I was slated to join the staff on the sixth of June. Just before I was to start, I was given a memo from Henry listing "a few changes" he wanted in the design. Since I had agreed to come aboard only if the design had been accepted, his request came as a shock. I knew if I agreed to make these changes I would lose control over the graphics.

I wrote to Henry explaining that he owned my redesign and could do anything he wanted with it, but I only agreed to work at *Time* if I could implement the design I thought we had both agreed on. If he had second thoughts, I understood, but I could not accept the job under those circumstances.

Lucky for me, Henry decided his requests were not all that important, so I came on board. I believe this helped me establish some authority within the editorial team.

My tenure at *Time* gave me the confidence that I could pursue magazine design independently. Over the next three years I designed four magazines: *The Atlantic, Adweek, Fortune,* and *The New York Times' The Sophisticated Traveler.* My experience working in various newsrooms gave me new insights into working with different personalities and talents. I learned to listen, to give my opinion, and to help get things done.—WB

The end of *New York* magazine presented an opportunity to start something else. I maintained my personal relationship with Walter and Clay and continued to see them on social occasions. But I admit that I had lost interest in magazines at the time of the takeover. I feel nervous about doing the same thing day after day.

I don't remember this time as being terribly traumatic, but it probably helped that my attention was focused on another big project. In 1977, I was in the thick of a top-to-bottom redesign of Grand Union, a supermarket chain owned by Sir Jimmy Goldsmith, who incidentally, once entertained the idea of acquiring *New York*.

Those years as a magazine designer informed my approach to supermarkets. The word for "magazine" is derived from the French *magasin*, meaning storehouse—a word that could also describe a supermarket. An idea lifted from editorial design: Why not put a "table of contents" at the entrance of Grand Union? It was a reversal of the old supermarket design principle: Make them walk through the entire store to find things to buy along the way. Mine was: Make it easy to find everything. Customer will like the experience and come back more often. Being on the consumer's side provided the philosophical basis for this job, as it did for *New York* readers.

The key to designing magazines and supermarkets is affection. You have to make the people feel that they like it, almost in a personal way. The emotional dimension of communications is very powerful. You have to offer something beyond the functional purpose. It's a simple idea; you'd think more people would consider it.—MG

A GROCERY'S TOC
The aisle index displayed at the entrance of Grand Union is essentially a "table of contents" page, applied to a supermarket setting. It's a wayfinding device derived from magazine design.

THE GIANT PEAR
I took every opportunity to inject something amusing for the customer, whether in packaging design or in the giant fiberglass pear installed outside Grand Union's flagship on Eighty-Sixth Street. That delightful sculpture by Jordan Steckel became a beloved neighborhood icon and escaped vandalism for many years. For a magazine feature, I was photographed hugging a smaller prototype of the pear (above).
Photo by Benno Friedman

The Short Life of an Elegant Idea

Surviving without advertising is challenging, even for a magazine with best-selling authors.

A IS FOR *AUDIENCE*
The first issue (left), without a name on the cover, was published in January 1971, with a cover illustration by Tim Lewis. The cover of the July-August 1972 issue (opposite) featured a 1939 Ford customized by Guy Spoonley, photographed by Steve Meyers.

This bimonthly magazine was a rarity. *Audience* had no ads and was sold only by subscription. It didn't try to persuade anyone to do anything and existed simply for the pleasure of its readers.

Cofounders Tim Hill and Geoffrey Ward envisioned a bimonthly periodical that would serve as "an open-ended chronicle of America's taste, as reflected in superb fiction, poetry, lavish portfolios, and eloquent articles." Indeed, *Audience*'s list of contributors read like a who's who of literary stars, Margaret Atwood, W. H. Auden, Jorge Luis Borges, William Faulkner, Jack Kerouac, Arthur Miller, Vladimir Nabokov, and Philip Roth among them. Another remarkable element was its distinguished editorial board, which included Charles Eames, Philip Johnson, and Marisol.

For a so-called "little magazine," *Audience* had grand ambitions when it came to graphic design. Seymour Chwast and I aspired to surprise readers with adventurous illustrations and high-quality papers. The printing was beautiful for the early 1970s. The absence of ads allowed us to design each issue without unplanned interruptions. In short, it was a dream assignment. Each issue was hardbound, which, in our minds, inspired readers to save them. *Audience* was really a cross between a magazine and a book.

But survival without advertising proved too difficult, and *Audience* died bravely in 1973. Though it only lasted for a little over two years, the magazine connected with a sizeable readership. It once had 60,000 subscribers who paid $15 ($90 in 2019) for an annual subscription.—MG

TIM HILL, editor-in-chief of *Audience*, has worked at *American Heritage* and *Aperture* magazine. As editor of the New York Graphic Society (Little, Brown & Company), he has published numerous illustrated volumes, including books by Ansel Adams and Andrew Wyeth.
Photo: Tim Hill

GEOFFREY C. WARD was a founding editor of *Audience*. He has won several Emmy Awards, five for his collaboration with Ken Burns and two for his work on PBS's *The American Experience* series. His 1989 book, *A First-Class Temperament: the Emergence of Franklin Roosevelt*, received the National Book Critics Circle Award and was a finalist for the Pulitzer Prize.
Photo by John Isaac

Collage by Tom Tome, courtesy Dorn and Smokler

Illustration by Barbara Nessim

THE HARDCOVER BINDING, without the necessity for advertising on the back, gave us a wonderful opportunity to design unusual covers all of one piece and with no cover lines as well. Aside from the logo, the only text was on the spine.

Photographs by Dennis Chalkin

Photograph by Mike Salisbury

"Interiors/Exteriors," a portfolio
of drawings by Saul Steinberg

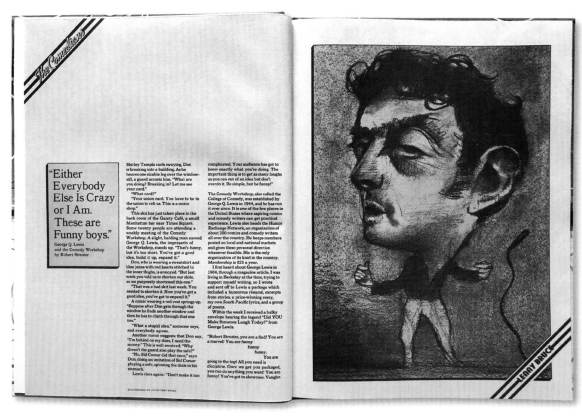

Robert Strozier's report on the Comedy
Workshop. Lenny Bruce illustration by
Julio Fernandez

146

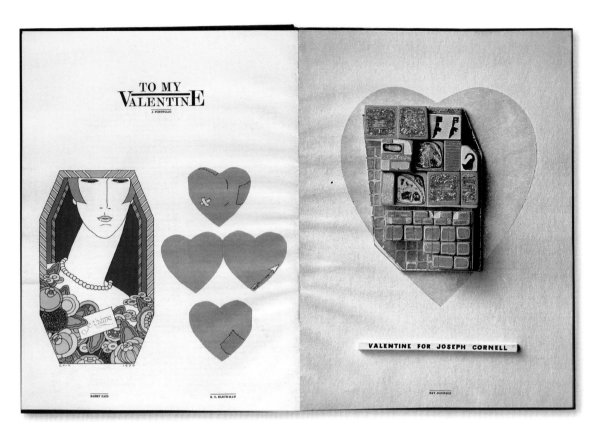

A portfolio of valentines, from left, by
Barry Zaid, R. O. Blechman, and Ray Johnson

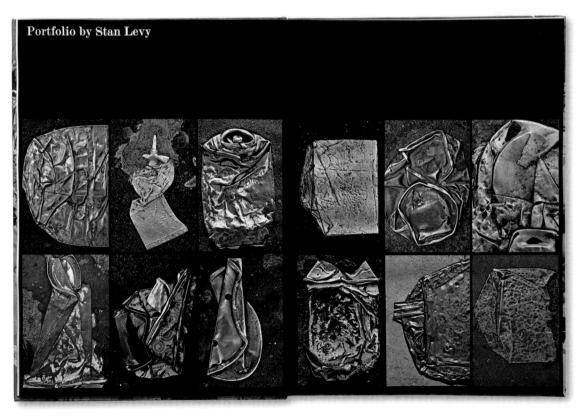

A portfolio of crushed aluminum cans
Photographs by Stan Levy

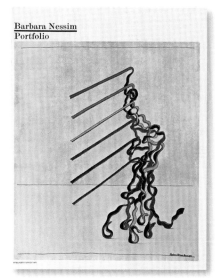
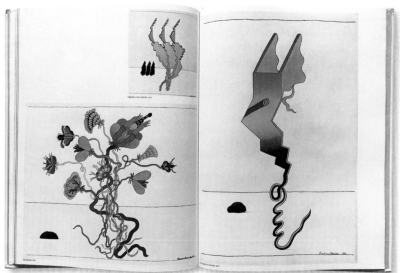

Barbara Nessim
Portfolio

A five-page portfolio of paintings by
Barbara Nessim

City Rat by Edward Hoagland

Photographs by Steve Salmieri

A series of photographs by Steve Salmieri
accompanied "City Rat," an essay by
Edward Hoagland.

"The Renewal" by Andrew Ward.
Illustration by Seymour Chwast

Martin Mayer's report on the
chain motel process, illustrated
by Arno Sternglass

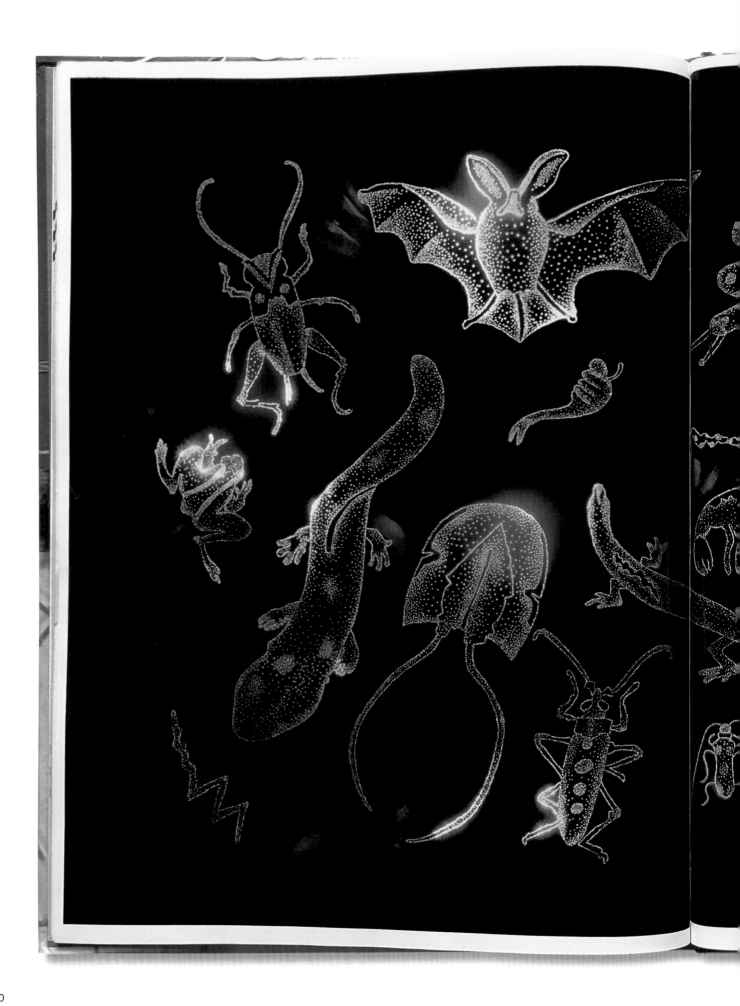

Notes from Inner Space

Three Caves in Southern Missouri by C. W. Gusewelle

They have come on a brittle winter afternoon — Roy and Jeannette with their frozen smiles — to see if this time they might make a union that no man will put asunder. Have come to the very place where Prince Buffalo, a Big Hills Osage, took to wife and may even have bedded sweet Irona who was of the Little Hills faction.

Buffalo and his Irona have gone to dust, but the greatness of their love lives on under the careful stewardship of Eddie Miller, the manager of Bridal Cave. In the twenty-three years since the cave was opened to the public, five hundred sixty-six couples have said their vows there. The pictures of some of them are displayed on the walls of the souvenir shop on the bluff above the cave entrance.

"You'll be the five-hundred-sixty-seventh," Eddie Miller tells Jeannette and Roy. "It's a world record." And though his grin is fixed, the groom's eyes go bugging in absolute wonderment from face to face and finally to the shelves of gewgaws, looking anywhere to discover *Why me?*

"Yeah, but how many of them's still married?" one of the men, husband of Roy's niece, asks Eddie Miller.

"Listen here," Jeannette says, "if he thinks he's gonna divorce me he's outa his head."

The bride's father is wandering among the shelves.

"Hey, c'mere," he calls. "Lookit here." He is holding a box with a cellophane window and three corncobs inside. Two reds and a white.

In an Emergency, it says, *Break Glass. Directions: Use red cob first. Then use white cob to see if you need other red cob.*

"Gimme a dollar and I'll sing for you," Roy's nephew-in-law tells him.

The bugging eyes fix on him. "I'll give y' five dollars *not* to sing."

Eddie Miller is watching through the window.

"I guess the preacher hasn't forgot," he says, and the bride's face gets a sudden no-funny-business look. But Eddie meant it for a joke. "He'll be along pretty soon."

A car pulls into the gravel parking area, bearing customers — a boy in buckskin and a girl in saucer-sized pink sunglasses. They come into the heated building and give Eddie their dollar seventy-five apiece.

"When's the tour start?" the boy asks.

"Right after these folks get married," Eddie tells him. "You might as well see the wedding and start from there."

"Crazy," the boy says. He looks at his girl.

"Crazy," she agrees.

ILLUSTRATED BY MILTON GLASER

IN THE NEWS

Last Manned Moon Mission
From 18,000 miles above the Earth, the Blue Marble image of planet Earth was taken on December 7, 1972, by the crew of *Apollo 17*, Gene Cernan, commander, Ronald Evans, command module pilot, and Harrison Schmitt, lunar pilot. It is one of the most reproduced photos in history. The *Apollo* trajectory made it possible for the first time to photograph from the Mediterranean Sea to the South Polar ice caps, the coastline of Africa, and the Asian mainland. While it was the last lunar mission for *Apollo 17*, it was the first time the spacecraft had a nighttime liftoff.

PONG Released
On November 29, 1972, Nolan Bushnell, cofounder of Atari, released PONG, the first commercially successful video game.

My Weekend in Paris

Twenty-four hours to redesign *Paris Match* was a crazy idea, but why not?

The redesign of *Paris Match* is a designer's fantasy. I was already in Paris for business in November 1972 when I got a call from Jean Prouvost, the magazine's remarkable publisher. Prouvost—"patron" to his employees—asked if I could overhaul the entire publication over the weekend. I would usually ask for two or three months for this kind of assignment, but this was an irresistible challenge.

The first consideration was the masthead. It seemed like a crime to get rid of that logo. The issue was how to tell readers that we were going to give them everything they'd known in the past, except with something extra. My solution was simple: fold down the left corner and say "Nouveau." It's a trick from packaging design. I told editors that in America, sales increased by 20 percent every time the word "new" appears on a package.

I redesigned the interior pages to make it more journalistic looking. I noticed that their old formula varied from page to page with no attempt at unity. My intention was to make it clear and more direct. I eliminated frivolous decorative elements and introduced bold, gothic letters for headlines and a system for headlines and subheads. The main challenge was establishing and maintaining a consistent system, which I thought was more important than inventiveness.

I remember we started at 5:30 p.m. on a Friday and worked with the magazine's very cooperative staff until the wee hours of the morning, breaking only for a few dozen oysters. We reconvened early on Saturday and worked straight through until 8 p.m. I don't speak a word of French, but somehow we worked through the language barrier and actually met Prouvost's deadline. The redesign was launched the following week. In the end, I was thrilled. When I left the offices of *Paris Match* that evening, I walked out into the streets and said to myself, "Paris, now you owe me one!"—MG

THE TRIM size of the new *Paris Match* with the revised logo was reduced to be ¾" shorter than the previous size, saving paper costs.

LA GRANDE BATAILLE DES BUSINESSMEN DU NU

Hefner contre Guccione :
l'empire de « Playboy » est menacé par
un Sicilien aux allures de « parrain »

L'opération la plus sensationnelle de l'histoire de la guerre des
magazines du nu se déclencha à la fin de la nuit historique
du 30 novembre au 1er décembre. Dans les rues de toutes les
villes italiennes, à l'heure où le pavé n'appartient plus qu'aux der-
niers clients des night clubs et aux voitures de laitier, les camion-
nettes qui livrent les journaux aux kiosques distribuè-
rent leur contingent d'explosif : le numéro 12 du nouveau magazine pour homme « Playmen ». Lorsque le jour se leva pour de
bon et que le soleil éclaira les pages luxueusement imprimées en
couleur de ce mensuel qui s'est donné pour tâche de s'emparer
du public de la péninsule avant que l'organisation américaine
« Playboy » ne lance une édition italienne, les premiers acheteurs
qui feuilletaient leur numéro tout neuf se trouvèrent face à face
avec Jackie Onassis, complètement nue, de face et de dos, et
encore de dos, et encore de face, montrant à l'univers entier une
intimité surprise par d'impudents condottieri de la photographie.
Le fait qu'un journal ait osé montrer le nu intégral de Jackie,
dans tous ses détails, démontrait aux yeux du monde que maintenant les limites qu'on croyait les dernières étaient dépassées. Ainsi
se trouvait du même coup révélée en pleine lumière, la guerre que
se livrent depuis des mois, des magazines américains spécialisés
dans le nu et qui oppose deux hommes acharnés à conquérir
l'hégémonie dans un domaine où roulent d'énormes intérêts :
Hugh Hefner de « Playboy », Charles Guccione de « Penthouse ».
Il n'y a pas si longtemps, l'Amérique vivait encore dans une
décence heureuse, respectable et prude, veillée par les pèlerins du
May Flower et corsetée par les inhibitions bourgeoises de la grande
reine Victoria, dont le portrait officiel, rengorgé et sévère, n'avait
jamais cessé de présider au respect des bonnes mœurs dans toute

L'examen du « petit lapin » : si Hefner dit oui, elle aura peut-être la
carrière de Marilyn Monroe qui débuta en posant pour « Play Boy ».

61

Avec Barbi,
sa compagne
qu'il n'épouse
pas pour ne
pas tuer le mythe
du play-boy :
Hugh Hefner
devant son
château sur la
côte Ouest
(Holmby Hills,
à Los Angeles.
Barbi,
découverte par
« Play-Boy », est
pour
les Américains
l'héroïne
d'un célèbre
feuilleton
télévisé
dominical.

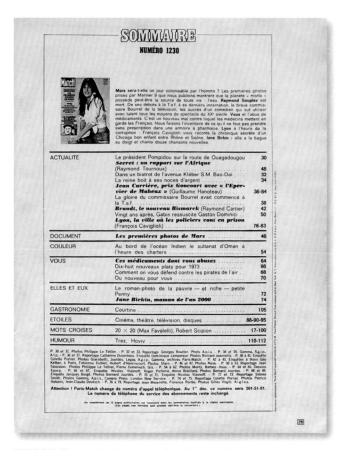

BEFORE: The contents page before the redesign.

AFTER: A more pictorial contents page in the new, smaller format.

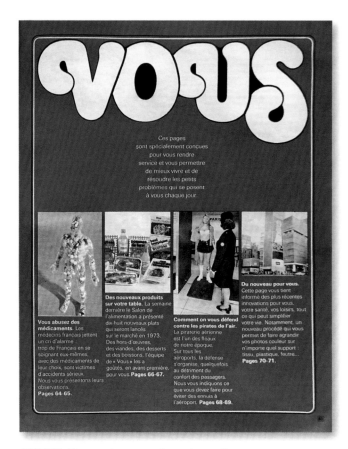

BEFORE: The opening page of a major section.

AFTER: Emphasizing the news content with a heavy serif type.

BEFORE: Two typical feature stories with type treatments that varied from page to page with no attempt at unity.

COUSTEAU CITOYEN DU MONDE

Le gouvernement mondial est une utopie. Il n'existera pas avant l'an 2000. Mais il a déjà son ministre de l'Environnement, Jacques-Yves Cousteau. Celui qui prend une loutre de mer avec une bonne tête d'animal en voie de disparition en train de crever à cause du mazout et la projette sur les consciences de cent millions de spectateurs dans les pays industriels riches pour leur dire : vous êtes en train d'assassiner la vie. Pour mener cette guerre contre la société, le « capitaine Nemo » surgit avec ses hommes, caméra au poing, au milieu des baleines de Patagonie à bord d'un « Nautilus » qui s'appelle « Calypso » et qui a maintenant son hélicoptère. Ils sont partis pour trois mois dans les mers australes. Ils rapporteront des films qui écraseront à nouveau les records aux Etats-Unis et nos reporters sont avec eux en exclusivité. Voici les' premières images de notre photographe Pierre Vals et le récit de la vie à bord de la « Calypso » et de la rencontre avec la première baleine.

AFTER: These two features demonstrate the new, bold style throughout the magazine.

Time to Move On

Nudging the venerable newsweekly into a new era

I was approached by *Time* magazine just weeks after I decided to leave *New York*. The idea of working on another weekly, after seven grueling years at *New York,* did not sound so appealing, especially since *Time* was not particularly well designed.

Ray Cave, the newly appointed "color editor," invited me to meet with him. Over a long lunch, he asked me to critique the magazine. I told him that *Time* covers relied too frequently on cartoon images and that the magazine needed a complete overhaul. I said that I'd consider becoming the art director only if I could redesign the whole magazine. Ray seemed to agree with my critique and arranged for me to meet Henry Grunwald, the legendary managing editor of *Time*, who was rumored to be "moving upstairs" to the corporate offices.

I was given a budget and three months to finish the redesign. In order to prevent alarming its staff or tipping off rival publications, Henry asked that the project be carried out in secret. I was to report only to Ray Cave.

I rented the ground floor in Milton's building on East Thirty-Second Street where *New York* magazine was launched, a short walk from my apartment. Rudy Hoglund, art director of *[More]* magazine, joined me in the project.

I chose *Time*'s current issue of February 28, 1977, to redesign, page by page, including a new cover treatment. Linda Ronstadt graciously agreed to pose for the prototype, but I ended up selecting a photograph from the previous shoot for the cover.

When Milton moved back into the building a short time later, I found that he had been assigned to redesign *Newsweek*. So, on the first and second floors of the same building, the major rival newsweeklies were being secretly redesigned. We agreed not to show each other anything and to keep our mouths shut.

One of Henry's requests was to find an elegant solution for introducing a "second billing" on the cover without running type across the bottom as they often did. The answer came to me as

I thought about the word "inside." How can we give the reader a glimpse of what is inside the magazine? That led to the now-famous "corner fold," which became *Time*'s signature for the next decade. I briefly toyed with the idea of getting rid of the red border, but I realized that it was an important part of *Time*'s identity. So I introduced a white rule between the red border and the cover image to prevent color clashes, a minor detail.—WB

HENRY GRUNWALD (1922–2005) was managing editor of *Time* from 1968 to 1977. During this time he introduced new sections on the economy, the environment, behavior, and gender, and added color photography and writers' bylines. He became editor in chief of *Time* from 1979 to 1987. President Reagan appointed him ambassador to Austria in 1988.

RAY CAVE Former executive editor of *Sports Illustrated*, Ray was managing editor of *Time* from 1977 to 1985. He brought his enthusiasm for graphic design and nontraditional stories to the magazine as well as his sharp eye for writing talent. He was editorial director of Time Inc. from 1985 to 1988.
Photo: Ray Cave

RUDY HOGLUND worked with me on the redesign of *Time*. He came on staff as assistant art director, and in 1980, he succeeded me as art director and remained there for fifteen years.
Photo by Tobey Sanford

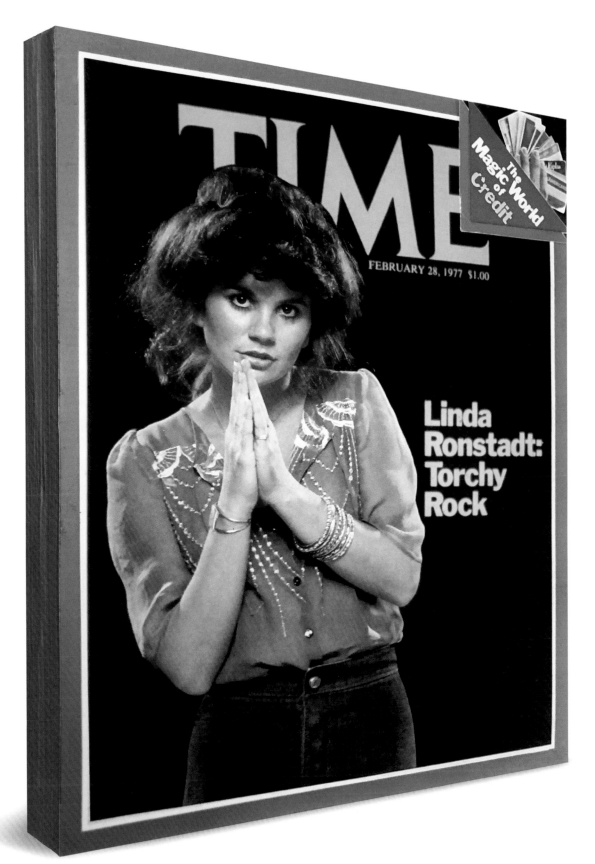

THE CORNER FOLD was inspired by two sources: a cover I had designed for the *Journal of The American Institute of Graphic Arts* (above) in 1970 with several folded corners on the page, and the cover of *Paris Match*, which Milton redesigned in 1973, with the corner of the logo frame folded to proclaim its "Nouveau" look.

THE *TIME* DUMMY The ninety-six-page hand-bound presentation (left) of the new design was based on the issue of February 28, 1977, far left, on newsstands the week I started the project.

TIME

FEBRUARY 28, 1977 $1.00

The Magic World of Credit

Linda Ronstadt: Torchy Rock

COVER STUDIES
My presentation to editors included twelve cover designs, five of which are shown above.

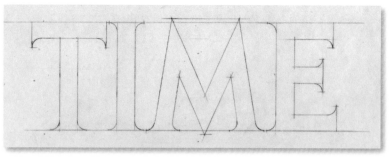

THE NEW LOGO, shown in Gerard Huerta's pencil tissue sketch (left), was designed to accommodate the proposed corner flap.

GERARD HUERTA began his career at CBS Records, creating iconic logos for many bands, magazines, media companies, and various products. His work is in the permanent collection of the Museum of Modern Art.

Photo: Gerard Huerta

To produce a magazine of this size every week, a clear page grid with strict parameters is needed. I hoped to create a format unique to *Time* and flexible enough for staff designers to occasionally violate (with permission).

On May 26, I presented the hand-bound dummy to the top editors. The meeting went well, with everyone in good spirits. I accepted the position, reporting to work on June 6, 1977.

My first week was relatively easy. I got to know the large design staff and watched them work. The redesign was not due to be launched until October. That Friday, as I was leaving, I stopped at Grunwald's office to say good night. "Wait a minute," he said. A report came over the wires that James Earl Ray, convicted of killing Martin Luther King, Jr., had escaped from prison. The lead story had to be changed and a new cover prepared.

Time's staff kicked into high gear. Reporters and editors worked furiously to produce the story, hoping Ray would be recaptured quickly so we could all go home. A diagram of the prison was the only visual material on hand. I somehow persuaded Harvey Dinnerstein, a superb and swift draftsman, to spend the weekend in our offices creating drawings based on field reports.

When we finally finished on Sunday night, I was exhausted and excited. At home, my wife, Bina, a writer at *People* magazine and a veteran of late closing nights, greeted me with a smile. "Welcome to the world of *Time*."

Having been trained at *Esquire* and *New York*, I was taught that the art director was the equivalent of a senior editor in charge of the look of a magazine. The art director at *Time* was supervised by editors who dictated layouts, photography, illustration, and covers. My most important challenge initially was to change the magazine's attitude toward art directors. It was very important to have the editorial staff accept a new style of art direction.

When presenting the new format to the senior editors, I didn't use the word "design." I used terms like "editorial intent" and "clarity" to convince them that as art director I was interested in more than making a visual splash.

The fact that during the redesign process I reported only to Ray Cave was a signal to me that he was more than the "color editor." He became Grunwald's successor later that year. It was a wise choice. I enjoyed my three years working with him. He not only supported our ideas but even urged me to openly express my disagreement with him. That was rarely done to the managing editor of *Time* by an art director.—WB

The new format made use of hairline rules around the pages and between the columns to distinguish a *Time* page from other newsweeklies.

BEFORE: The conventional approach: showing credit card use in each section of the country. Three photographs with no visual impact.

AFTER: The world's largest credit card collector, Walter Cavanagh, could run up bills totalling $9.3 million in a single month. I thought this photograph would dramatize the story more effectively.

BEFORE: This cover story was filled with random photographs of Linda Ronstadt.

AFTER: These photographs, from a David Alexander photo session, provided a more intimate and cohesive portrait of Ronstadt.

A NOTE ABOUT TYPE:
Franklin Gothic, used mostly in advertising, was my choice as the new typographic voice of *Time*. All headlines, captions, and section heads would be set in this typeface in various sizes. Along with Times Roman for text, these would comprise the typographic vocabulary. *Time* would speak with one voice.

A SHOWING
Editors gathered in the conference room for a "showing" every time a section layout was ready. In this photo, managing editor Ray Cave (left) and executive editor Jason MacManus (right) are reviewing the pages for a cover story about Cheryl Tiegs, *Sports Illustrated*'s favorite swimsuit model at that time. Ray was a former editor at *SI* and was a big fan of hers. Unlike Ray and Jason, I didn't often wear white shirts and ties to work. Before computer desktop publishing, art direction was a hands-on job. We were messing with rubber cement, X-Acto knives, and T-squares.—WB

Waking up Charts and Graphs

Nigel Holmes miraculously appeared in my office in the nick of time.

In September 1977, I was still agonizing over how to improve *Time*'s bland information graphics. A far cry from the 1930s and '40s, when the magazine presented numbers in surprising graphic formats, charts and graphs at that time were treated as space filler material that could be cut if an article ran long.

It was around that time that Nigel Holmes, an affable British graphic designer who always wore blue, knocked on my door. Poring through his portfolio was a breath of fresh air. His work was clever and extremely well executed. What's more, he was willing to move his family from London to New York City and lead our information graphics department.

Time's redesign encouraged more space for illustration and photography, so we unleashed Nigel to deploy his illustration skills and fine sense of humor to energize the infographics, which he did brilliantly.

At first, Nigel's unconventional data presentation—bar graphs on horseback, droopy charts on hospital beds—ruffled several editors, especially those in the business section. (*Time*'s business section was largely devoted to head shots of mostly white, male CEOs.) They accused him of trivializing the data.

It was the readers who helped change their minds. Many sent fan mail to applaud Nigel's work and to declare that they were now reading the business articles and grasping complicated financial content with the help of his lively charts. Nigel recalls:

> From time to time I overstepped the mark and illustration got in the way of the numbers. All I wanted to do was help people become interested in the subject of the articles. I spent a lot of time talking to the writers, who helpfully fed me metaphors that I could work into the charts. If I could get readers to smile, I was at least halfway to helping them understand.
>
> After a few years, I felt that perhaps some of the charts had gone too far, so I calmed the illustration down a bit. That led to another round of critical mail: 'So now we are back to boring charts again?'
>
> A funny thing: after many years of changes in style, I still get requests for the lighter touch I'd used at *Time* (I'm happy to oblige). The point is the same as it always was—to engage readers.

Nigel revolutionized information graphics at *Time* for the next sixteen years. —WB

BEFORE: A typical chart.   **AFTER:** One of Nigel's first charts.

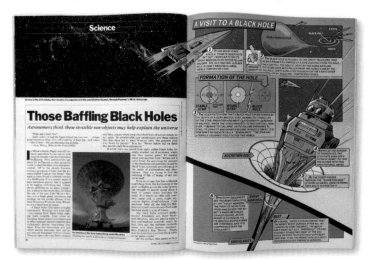

FULL PAGE The first time Nigel's graphics commanded the entire page.

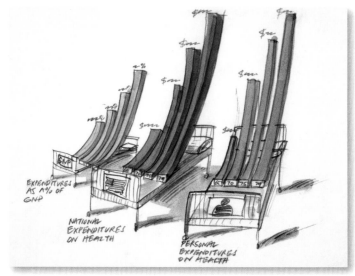

SKETCH for the chart (opposite), which I enthusiastically approved.

NIGEL HOLMES

Born in Britain, Nigel moved to the United States to become the graphics director of *Time,* where his skill and humor made understanding complex information fun. He taught at the Stanford Professional Publishing Course for thirty years.

NIGEL HOLMES ON CHARTS AND DIAGRAMS

[They] "had to be drawn at twice the reproduction size [to minimize any flubs and imperfections when reduced]. That made for some large (and heavy) artwork, with as many as 16 overlays on top of the key drawing, mounted on a thick cardboard base. There had to be three versions of each piece: one for |the American edition (usually in full color), and two for the international editions (printed in two colors in Europe; monochrome elsewhere)."

"I used Rotring pens and had a huge collection of plastic templates—ovals, circles and French curves—which meant that no line was ever drawn truly freehand. This was all pre-computer."

—*Eye Magazine,* Winter 2012

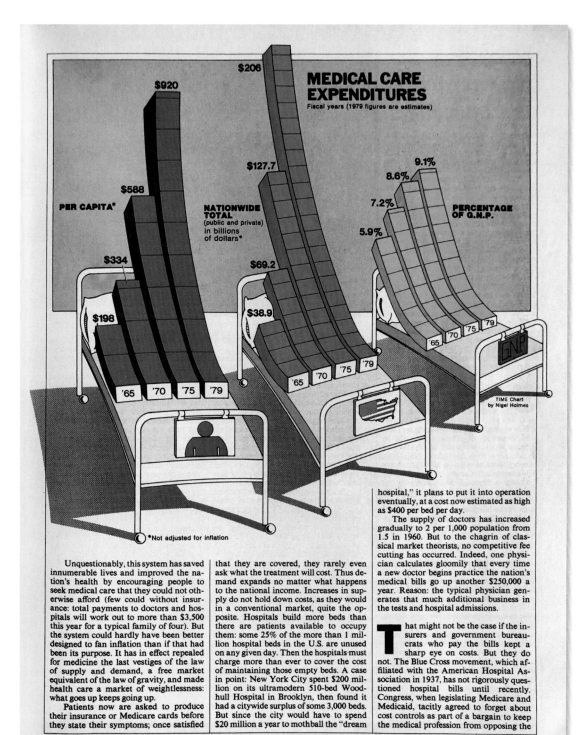

MEDICAL CARE EXPENDITURES
Fiscal years (1979 figures are estimates)

PER CAPITA*
$920
$588
$334
$198

NATIONWIDE TOTAL
(public and private)
in billions
of dollars*
$206
$127.7
$69.2
$38.9

PERCENTAGE OF G.N.P.
9.1%
8.6%
7.2%
5.9%

'65 '70 '75 '79

*Not adjusted for inflation

TIME Chart by Nigel Holmes

Unquestionably, this system has saved innumerable lives and improved the nation's health by encouraging people to seek medical care that they could not otherwise afford (few could without insurance: total payments to doctors and hospitals will work out to more than $3,500 this year for a typical family of four). But the system could hardly have been better designed to fan inflation than if that had been its purpose. It has in effect repealed for medicine the last vestiges of the law of supply and demand, a free market equivalent of the law of gravity, and made health care a market of weightlessness: what goes up keeps going up.

Patients now are asked to produce their insurance or Medicare cards before they state their symptoms; once satisfied that they are covered, they rarely even ask what the treatment will cost. Thus demand expands no matter what happens to the national income. Increases in supply do not hold down costs, as they would in a conventional market, quite the opposite. Hospitals build more beds than there are patients available to occupy them: some 25% of the more than 1 million hospital beds in the U.S. are unused on any given day. Then the hospitals must charge more than ever to cover the cost of maintaining those empty beds. A case in point: New York City spent $200 million on its ultramodern 510-bed Woodhull Hospital in Brooklyn, then found it had a citywide surplus of some 3,000 beds. But since the city would have to spend $20 million a year to mothball the "dream

hospital," it plans to put it into operation eventually, at a cost now estimated as high as $400 per bed per day.

The supply of doctors has increased gradually to 2 per 1,000 population from 1.5 in 1960. But to the chagrin of classical market theorists, no competitive fee cutting has occurred. Indeed, one physician calculates gloomily that every time a new doctor begins practice the nation's medical bills go up another $250,000 a year. Reason: the typical physician generates that much additional business in the tests and hospital admissions.

That might not be the case if the insurers and government bureaucrats who pay the bills kept a sharp eye on costs. But they do not. The Blue Cross movement, which affiliated with the American Hospital Association in 1937, has not rigorously questioned hospital bills until recently. Congress, when legislating Medicare and Medicaid, tacitly agreed to forget about cost controls as part of a bargain to keep the medical profession from opposing the

OVER THE TOP?

This graphic chart (above) made us laugh and was thought of, in hindsight, as one in which we may have pushed too far. Purist fans of information graphics criticized it as trivializing serious data.

Saturday Night Fever
The movie *Saturday Night Fever* opened nationally on December 16, 1977. Directed by John Badham, it was based on "The Tribal Rites of the New Saturday Night," a 1976 article by Nik Cohn, in *New York* magazine. The movie defined the disco craze of the 1970s, made John Travolta a mega star and his white suit a fashion hit, and the Bee Gees' music soar.

"The Little Tramp" Dies
Charlie Chaplin, the first international movie star as the Little Tramp, died in his sleep on December 25, 1977. He was eighty-eight years old. Chaplin had survived poverty and the ire of J. Edgar Hoover and been knighted by Queen Elizabeth in 1975.

Audrey's Dream of Anwar

Audrey Flack, a pioneer of photorealism, proved to be the perfect choice to paint our "Man of the Year" portrait in 1977.

Since the tradition of naming the year's top newsmaker began in 1927, prominent artists and illustrators such as Boris Artzybasheff, Robert Rauschenberg, Bernard Buffett, Robert Vickrey, David Levine, Aaron Shikler, and George Segal had created portraits for the cover. Following that tradition, I asked Audrey Flack, a well-known artist and pioneer of photorealism in the 1970s, to paint Egyptian President Anwar Sadat, whose negotiations with Israel cumulated in the Egypt–Israel Peace Treaty. I thought it was appropriate to have a woman do "Man of the Year," which was only renamed "Person of the Year" in 1999.

Not only were we pleased with the portrait of Sadat, I was impressed by the huge painting (3' x 4') she delivered to me. I learned later that Audrey greatly admired Sadat and had dreamed about painting his portrait. "There was something about him that reached me," she said. "If that man creates peace in the Middle East, I will paint his portrait. I loved his face."

Although Audrey had wanted to keep her original painting so she could present it to Sadat herself, *Time* finally bought the portrait as the magazine's gift to him. This was just three years before his assassination.

Having David Hume Kennerly photograph Sadat in Giza for the feature was a great bonus. The stately portrait was one of the largest photographs that the magazine had ever published until that time. Standing between two pyramids, Sadat was presented as the visionary "Architect of a New Mideast."—WB

AUDREY FLACK (above left) is shown at work painting the Sadat portrait for the cover (opposite). Audrey is an internationally recognized painter and sculptor. She enjoys the distinction of being the first photorealist painter whose work was purchased by the Museum of Modern Art for its permanent collection.
Photo: Audrey Flack

AUDREY REMEMBERS:
"During a trip to Egypt just before the Arab Spring, my husband and I made small talk with two brothers who ran a convenience shop near our hotel. I mentioned Anwar Sadat's name and said that I had painted his portrait for the magazine. After a moment of intense silence they pulled a heavy maroon drape aside, and there it was: Sadat's *Time* Man of the Year cover—over three decades after the issue came out—framed and hanging. I was incredibly proud."

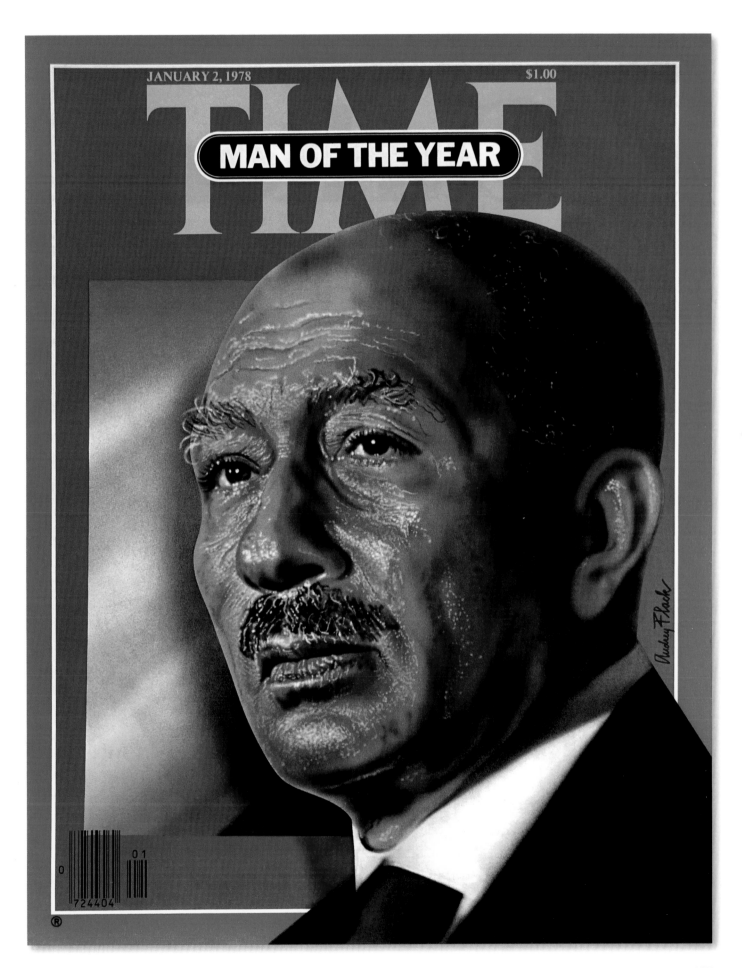

Man of the Year

TIME/JAN. 2, 1978

Anwar Sadat: Architect of a New Mideast

With one stunning stroke he designed a daring approach to peace

He called it "a sacred mission," and history may judge it so. By the trajectory of his 28-minute flight from a base in the Canal Zone to Tel Aviv's Ben Gurion Airport, Egyptian President Anwar Sadat changed the course of Middle Eastern events for generations to come. More emphatically than anything that has happened there since the birth of Israel in 1948, his extraordinary pilgrimage transformed the political realities of a region blackened and embittered by impermeable hatreds and chronic war. In one stroke, the old rules of the Arab-Israeli blood feud no longer applied. Many of the endless hurdles to negotiation seemed to dissolve like Saharan mirages. Not in three decades had the dream of a real peace seemed more probable. For his willingness to seize upon a fresh approach, for his display of personal and political courage, for his unshakable resolve to restore a momentum for peace in the Middle East, Anwar Sadat is TIME's Man of the Year.

"What I want from this visit," Sadat had told TIME Cairo Bureau Chief Wilton Wynn during the historic flight that took him to Jerusalem, "is that the wall created between us and Israel, the psychological wall, be knocked down." The wall fell. The astonishing spectacle was global theater—the images caromed off television satellites to viewers around the world. In a wash of klieg lights, the Egyptian who had hurled his armies across the Suez Canal in 1973 stood at attention next to the old Irgun guerrilla whose name has been a dark legend to Palestinian Arabs for 30 years. An Israeli military band played first the Egyptian national anthem, *By God of Old, Who Is My Weapon,* and then the Israeli *Hatikvah.* In a hushed, deeply moving tableau, Sadat walked along the receiving line with Israeli Premier Menachem Begin to greet the old and resolute enemies: former Premiers Yitzhak Rabin and Golda Meir, Foreign Minister Moshe Dayan, Ariel Sharon, "Israel's Patton," who thrust Israeli armor deep into Egypt in the October War of 1973.

Next day, fulfilling a vow he had made to himself *(see interview),* Sadat prayed in Al Aqsa mosque in the Old City of Jerusalem, one of Islam's holiest places. Then the son of Ishmael stood before the sons of Isaac in the Israeli Knesset and formally declared that the deep, violent enmity between them had somehow passed.

Sadat's demands on Israel, in exchange for peace, were tough and familiar: the return to Arab sovereignty of all territory (including East Jerusalem) conquered during the 1967 Six-Day War; a homeland for Palestinians on the West Bank and in Gaza. Yet far more important were the generous words of acceptance that few Israelis ever expected to hear from an

Egyptian President Sadat standing before the Pyramids of Giza
The old rules of the Arab-Israeli blood feud no longer applied.

David Hume Kennerly

11

ANWAR SADAT (left), described as "Architect of a New Mideast," standing before some amazing Egyptian architecture. Photograph by David Hume Kennerly

DAVID HUME KENNERLY was named "One of the 100 Most Important People in Photography" by *American Photo Magazine.* He won the Pulitzer Prize in Journalism in 1972 and became President Gerald R. Ford's chief White House photographer in 1974. He was a contributing photographer for *Time* and *Life* and contributing editor at *Newsweek.* Kennerly has published several books of his work, and received the prestigious Lucie Award for achievement in photojournalism in 2015.

Photo: Ansel Adams/Kennerly Archive

DAVID BURNETT'S photograph of David Hume Kennerly photographing Anwar Sadat at the Giza pyramid site. Both were on assignment for *Time*'s Man of the Year issue, Kennerly to cover only Anwar Sadat and Burnett everything else.

As Burnett said, "I was doing the pyramids, the goats, and folks in the street. It was after Sadat had gone to Jerusalem, and it's hard to explain in this day and age what a big deal that was."

Photo © 2018 David Burnett/ Contact Press Images

Harvey Milk Celebrates
"If a bullet should enter my brain, let that bullet destroy every closet door," Harvey Milk said when he became the first openly gay elected official of a major U.S. city, having been elected to the San Francisco Board of Supervisors on November 8, 1977.

A Scientific Find
Microbiologist Carl Woese and University of Illinois scientists proudly announced on November 2, 1977, the identification of methanogens, a form of microbial life dating back 3.5 billion years.

The Find of a Lifetime

ON SITE IN KENYA (left) Carl Fischer, standing, and Richard Leakey, crouching, supervise the model maker as he adjusts the mask of our subject. The cover photograph (opposite) was taken on the site where Leakey made his discovery.
Photo: Carl Fischer

A profile of Richard Leakey celebrated his great discovery and led to the creation of a whole new magazine.

I n November 1977, *Time* published a major cover story by Leon Jaroff about Richard Leakey, the charismatic Kenyan paleoanthropologist. Leakey had discovered the bones of a two-million-year-old hominid, believed to be the oldest direct predecessor of humans.

Leakey had agreed to be photographed by Carl Fischer during his scheduled visit to New York. Carl asked Hollywood makeup artist Bob O'Bradovich to create a mask portraying the likeness of the *Homo habilis* that could be worn by a model for the shoot. My idea was to pose Leakey next to his discovery in the spirit of Irving Penn's evocative portraits of indigenous peoples.

Several days before the shoot, I learned that Leakey's trip to New York was abruptly canceled. I was at a loss at how to rescue the cover. When I told managing editor Henry Grunwald about the conundrum, he looked at me as if I were an idiot and said simply, "Go to Africa!"

Of course! Unlike our lean operations at *New York* magazine, *Time* had a big budget that allowed us to fly Carl and his crew to Kenya. This was a much better idea, and Carl's photograph of *Homo habilis* on the exact site where Leakey made his discovery was certainly worth the trip.

This issue was a hit with our readers. Leon Jaroff, *Time*'s science editor, had been proposing a science-oriented magazine to Time Inc.'s management for several years with no success. The spectacular newsstand sales of the Leakey issue were proof that there was an audience for such a publication. Three years later, Leon became the founding editor of his dream magazine, *Discover.*—WB

CARL FISCHER REMEMBERS:
"No family snapshots of *Homo habilis* exist, so when we arrived in Kenya, Leakey was fixated on trying to get the image as correct as possible, and he and the model maker changed the mask again and again until Leakey was satisfied, sort of. Eventually we did two versions of the cover, one [below], and one on location in the nearby Rift Valley, with the now accurate, or so Leakey believed, reconstructed head of early man. I wish I had asked Leakey why *Homo habilis* was clean-shaven."

TIME

NOVEMBER 7, 1977 $1.00

How Man Became Man

CLOSE ENCOUNTERS
A Dazzling New
Movie

Anthropologist
Richard Leakey
with Homo habilis

724404

STEVE CAUTHEN was a hot topic in horse racing. He was about to ride Affirmed in the second leg of the Triple Crown. The race started at 5:41 p.m. on Saturday, May 20, 1978, past our normal press time. Editor Ray Cave's idea was to prepare two cover stories. If Cauthen won, his cover would immediately go to press and be on newsstands Monday, beating *Newsweek*. If he lost, another cover would run. I assigned illustrator

James McMullan to do a portrait of Cauthen (above, left) and had it ready to go. A relentless Neil Leifer desperately wanted to shoot Cauthen for the cover. I said, "Fine, but he has to look like he's already won the race." Neil's photograph of Cauthen holding a victory cigar was irresistible. When *Time* appeared on the following Monday, *Newsweek* canceled its own Cauthen story, which would have run a week later.

NEIL LEIFER'S career as a photojournalist has spanned almost sixty years. He was a staff photographer for *Sports Illustrated*, *Time*, and *Life* magazines. His photographs have appeared on over 200 *Sports Illustrated*, *Time*, and *People* covers. In 2008 Neil was honored with The Britton Hadden Lifetime Achievement Award for outstanding contribution to Time Inc. journalism. Now a full-time filmmaker, producer, and director, he has made documentaries for both HBO and ESPN. He photographed Muhammad Ali on almost sixty different occasions, covering all of his biggest fights.

Photo: Neil Leifer

RUSSIA AND CHINA were at odds in 1979. *Time* requested interviews with each country's leader, Leonid Brezhnev, General Secretary of the Communist Party, and Deng Xiaoping, leader of China's Communist Party, but both refused. Finally in January Brezhnev relented and agreed to an exclusive interview, for which

I commissioned a portrait by Burt Silverman. Deng, admiring the Brezhnev cover, said he would only agree to an interview if he was assured equal treatment. We sent word to Deng that if he gave *Time* an exclusive interview and indeed became the cover subject, the same artist would paint his portrait.

BURT SILVERMAN'S classical realist portraits were an asset to *Time*, which still considered the portrait as a key element of its personality. His work has appeared on the covers of *Time*, *Newsweek*, and *New York* magazines. He was elected to the National Academy of Design as a full Academician in 1974 as well as to the prestigious Society of Illustrators Hall of Fame in 1990. Silverman has been painting and exhibiting as a fine artist for over sixty years. He has had numerous gallery and international exhibitions, and his work is in over thirty museum collections, including the Smithsonian National Portrait Gallery, the Brooklyn Museum, and the Metropolitan Museum.

Photo: Burt Silverman

Illustration by Robert Giusti

Illustration by Edward Sorel

Illustration by Marshall Arisman

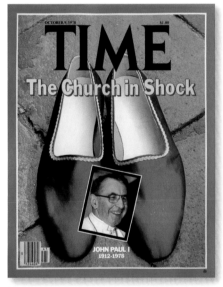

Photograph by Enrico Ferorelli

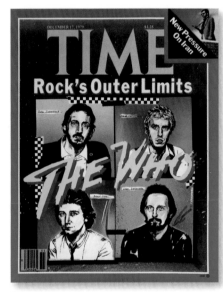

Illustration by Gary Panter

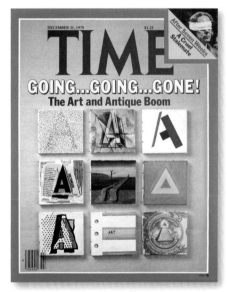

Illustration by Eugene Mihaesco

Photograph by Pete Turner

Illustration by Alan Magee

Illustration by Marvin Mattelson

It began at 6:30 a.m. on November 4, 1979, with 300 students demonstrating in front of the U.S. embassy in Tehran. The students left when security guards appeared with weapons. Busloads of supporters that followed ultimately stormed the embassy gate. (In spite of warnings from diplomats, President Carter had allowed the shah into the United States for medical treatment on October 22.) The fifty-two hostages, held for 444 days, were released on January 20, 1981, once President Reagan was inaugurated.

President Carter Acts
Instead of yielding to the "unacceptable demands" of those holding the hostages to return the shah to Tehran, President Carter ordered oil imports from Iran stopped on November 12, 1979. In a TV speech, he asked Americans to conserve energy to offset the loss of Iranian crude oil.

Khomeini Revolutionizes "Man of the Year"

1979 marked an unforeseen turning point in the history of *Time*'s iconic issue.

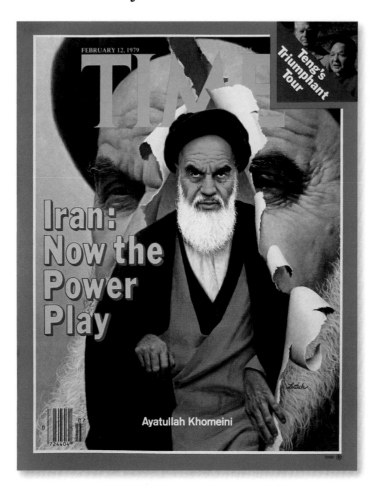

FEBRUARY 12, 1979

Teng's Triumphant Tour

Iran: Now the Power Play

Ayatullah Khomeini

KHOMEINI'S ARRIVAL
Birney Lettick's image of the Ayatollah breaking through a street poster (left) announcing Khomeini's takeover of Iran aroused no reader protest, unlike Brad Holland's "Man of the Year" cover (opposite).

BIRNEY LETTICK
(1919–1986): A painter and illustrator, Lettick served in the U.S. Army Corps of Engineers during World War II, and designed the first American landing strip in Europe. He illustrated covers for *Time* magazine, as well as for *The Saturday Evening Post*, *Collier's*, and *National Geographic*. Lettick also created posters for movie studios, for films such as *Heaven Can Wait* and *Escape from Alcatraz*.
Photo: the Lettick family

U ntil 1979, the title of "Man of the Year" was bestowed on the personality who made the most news headlines—for good or evil. Controversial leaders such as Adolf Hitler (1938), Joseph Stalin (1939 and 1942), and Nikita Khrushchev (1957) garnered the position. But Ayatollah Khomeini was different. The radical anti-American cleric was considered the messianic leader of violent extremist groups in Iran. When this issue was published with Brad Holland's provocative portrait, many newsstands around the country refused to display it—especially after Americans had been taken hostage by Khomeini acolytes in Tehran. *Time* received many angry letters protesting this choice.

It was the last time a so-called "villain" was on the cover. This choice was so upsetting to readers that *Time* never did it again. We quickly learned that readers interpreted "Man of the Year" as an honor, despite the magazine's definition. Think of 9/11: "Person of the Year" in 2001 could have been Osama Bin Laden, but *Time* selected Rudy Giuliani, the mayor of New York City during the attacks. It has been seen as an honor and celebration to this day.—WB

BRAD HOLLAND is a self-taught artist and writer whose work has appeared in major national and international publications. His art has been exhibited in museums around the world, including one-man exhibitions at the Musée des Beaux-Arts, Clermont-Ferrand, France, and the Museum of American Illustration in New York. In 2005 he was inducted into the Society of Illustrators Hall of Fame.
Photo: Brad Holland

JANUARY 7, 1980 $1.25

TIME

MAN OF THE YEAR

Ayatullah Khomeini

King Hussein of Jordan Marries Lisa Halaby
After a whirlwind courtship, twenty-six-year-old Lisa Halaby married forty-two-year-old King Hussein of Jordan on June 15, 1978, in Amman, Jordan. He named her Queen Noor al-Hussein, meaning "Light of Hussein." She was the only woman at the Zahran Palace ceremony. The newlyweds honeymooned at a Red Sea resort in Aqaba and in Scotland.

One Is Much Better Than Three

A new national advertising magazine emerges from three small regional publications.

In 1977, Jack Thomas and Ken Fadner joined with Pen Tudor to acquire three regional advertising news journals: *ANNY* (*Advertising News of New York*), *MAC* (*Media Agents and Clients*), and *SAM* (*Serving Advertising in the Midwest*). Thomas was previously the publisher and Fadner the vice president of finance of *New York* magazine. Both left when Rupert Murdoch took over. Tudor was a former sales executive with *Life* magazine.

Their idea was to create additional regional journals for the thriving U.S. advertising industry at that time. When they asked me to redesign these journals, I suggested they unify their brand under one name rather than relaunch each separately. I proposed "Adweek" as the umbrella for all three, which would contain regional advertising news, along with national stories, which they enthusiastically adopted.

Since *Adweek* would be principally delivered by mail, a large address label had to be placed on the cover. To accommodate the mailing label without blocking the name, I set the word "ADWEEK" large enough in an all-caps Anzeigen Grotesk typeface running across the top of the page in bright red.

A simple typographic template was needed to produce the issues without an art director. Valentine Cardinale, the magazine's editor, along with Jeff Precourt and Marty Beiser, had to make up the pages for each issue. The cover format (opposite) gradually evolved, still featuring the contents of each issue while emphasizing two major stories with larger headlines and text.

It wasn't all smooth sailing. Initially, each of the three journals displayed a paid ad on the cover. The new team decided to stop that practice. After hearing the reasons for scrapping front-page ads, their largest advertiser, *Barron's*, the financial newspaper, announced that "*Adweek* would not see another dime from *Barron's* for a long time." *Barron's* stayed away for two years. But *Adweek* went on to becoming a major force in advertising news.—WB

ANNY, MAC, AND SAM
The three regional journals (above) that we turned into *Adweek* (opposite), the name that prepared the new company for expansion.

Jack Thomas

Ken Fadner

Pen Tudor

THE FOUNDERS
Thomas, Fadner, and Tudor founded *Adweek* in 1978. Jack Thomas died in 2015, Pen Tudor in 2019. Ken Fadner is the chairman and publisher of *MediaPost*.
Photo: Ken Fadner

ADWEEK

Vol. XXXIV No. 44   EASTERN EDITION   November 1, 1993 • $2.50, £1.95

GREY SPINS OFF A BOUTIQUE

Grey Advertising is expected to set up a division of itself to deal with a special account. The offshoot, which may be called G2, will be based in Orange County, Calif., and tend to the needs of Mitsubishi.
(See page 3)

PIZZA HUT OFFERS A SLICE

Pizza Hut is putting a $10-million bit of business, for kids and select projects, into review. The work will go to an agency other than BBDO, the chain's AOR.
(See page 4)

QUINTESSENCE SHIFT PRESAGES REVIEW

German conglomerate Benckiser has shifted the marketing of its Quintessence fragrances to its sibling Coty, the top seller of mass market perfumes. The shift will take some $15 million in billings away from Foote, Cone & Belding/Chicago, and prompt a flurry of positioning by a number of New York agencies.
(See page 2)

MYSTERY CAR: TOYOTA

Management Change Prompts Agency Evaluation

By David Kiley—Toyota Motor Sales could open up a portion of its huge account—which bills nearly $500 million with Saatchi & Saatchi agencies in the U.S.—to a third shop, a number of well-placed sources close to the automaker's management said last week.

The evaluation, believed to have been demanded by R. Chikuma, a high-ranking Japanese official who arrived   *(Continued on page 8)*

Think Big Media Here

Saatchi Sees U.S. Buying Hub à la Zenith

By Alison Fahey and Michael McCarthy—Executives of Saatchi & Saatchi Co. PLC and its domestic agencies are in the midst of what are thought to be the most serious discussions to date about how a media buying operation along the lines of Saatchi's European media consortium called Zenith Media Worldwide could be   *(Continued on page 5)*

THE POST OFFICE MAILS RFPs

This month the U.S. Postal Service will be contacting agencies regarding the mandated review of its $60-million account. The incumbent in the business is Young & Rubicam. About 100 agencies will be getting RFPs, the client said. If you don't get one, drop the client a line.
(See page 44)

DATA HIGHWAY

The information superhighway will be built on technology and programming but maintained by advertising. Michael Schrage surveys the road.
(See page 27)

CREATIVES

Noreen O'Leary profiles ex-bullfighter Neil French, and more.
(See page 34)

O&M's Neil French

ADWEEK'S 10 HOTTEST OF 1980

1 **TexasMonthly**
ADWEEK PERFORMANCE INDEX
529
Revenue Up $2,800,000 (46%)
Ad Pages Up 13.9%

2 Smithsonian
ADWEEK PERFORMANCE INDEX
460
Revenue Up $5,400,000 (37%)
Ad Pages Up 18.3%

3 Parents
ADWEEK PERFORMANCE INDEX
457
Revenue Up $3,800,000 (33%)
Ad Pages Up 20.3%

4 TOWN & COUNTRY
ADWEEK PERFORMANCE INDEX
433
Revenue Up $2,600,000 (37%)
Ad Pages Up 25.4%

5 BAZAAR
ADWEEK PERFORMANCE INDEX
404
Revenue Up $2,900,000 (35%)
Ad Pages Up 19.3%

6 Money
ADWEEK PERFORMANCE INDEX
402
Revenue Up $3,900,000 (33%)
Ad Pages Up 13%

7 People weekly
ADWEEK PERFORMANCE INDEX
395
Revenue Up $17,200,000 (19%)
Ad Pages Down 2.5%

8 BRIDE'S
ADWEEK PERFORMANCE INDEX
341
Revenue Up $2,700,000 (29%)
Ad Pages Up 17.9%

9 ARCHITECTURAL DIGEST
ADWEEK PERFORMANCE INDEX
326
Revenue Up $2,800,000 (27%)
Ad Pages Up 15.9%

10 SPORTS AFIELD
ADWEEK PERFORMANCE INDEX
324
Revenue Up $1,500,000 (28%)
Ad Pages Up 7.7%

THE 10 HOTTEST
Adweek's annual ranking of magazines (the *Adweek* performance index according to revenue and total ad pages) became such a popular feature (left) that the magazines listed gleefully promoted their achievement.

SPECIAL ISSUES
Throughout the 1980s, *Adweek* produced many special issues on various industry topics (opposite). My favorite is Ed Sorel's take on creativity (bottom left), which is both funny and true.—WB

Illustration by Seymour Chwast

Sculpture by Robert Grossman

Illustration by Ed Sorel

Illustration by Milton Glaser

President Ronald Reagan Shot in D.C.
To impress actress Jodie Foster, John Hinckley, Jr., shot President Ronald Reagan, Press Secretary James Brady, Tim McCarthy, a Secret Service officer, and Thomas Delahanty, a police officer, outside the Hilton Hotel in Washington, D.C., on March 30, 1981, Hinckley was tried and found not guilty by reason of insanity, and committed to St. Elizabeth Hospital in D.C. He was released on September 10, 2016.

Zuckerman Unbound

One of the oldest U.S. magazines reinvented with a real estate developer as the new owner.

Mort Zuckerman, CEO of Boston Properties, one of the largest real estate investment trusts in the United States, invited me to meet with him shortly after he acquired *The Atlantic* in 1980. In a surprise hiring coup, he managed to lure Bill Whitworth, editor-in-waiting at *The New Yorker*, to run the magazine. Mort, an avid reader of magazines himself, envisioned a new look to signal the new era under Bill. After thirteen years at the text-driven *New Yorker*, Bill had little experience dealing with magazine design but strongly felt that the design should convey the seriousness of the iconic periodical founded by prominent writers such as Francis Underwood, Ralph Waldo Emerson, Harriet Beecher Stowe, and Henry Wadsworth Longfellow.

After I left on good terms, *Time* generously gave me an office in the Time & Life building, where I redesigned *The Atlantic* with Tom Bentkowski, my former assistant at *New York*. *The Atlantic*'s articles tended to be quite lengthy, at times running to sixteen pages. We had to find the proper balance between text and images, so we devised a system where we used large illustrations or photographs every three or four pages to interrupt the density. We also tried to create more arresting covers by eliminating multiple cover lines and using more inventive illustrations. We tweaked the logo slightly as well, making it smaller and slimmer.

The first redesigned issue featured a cover story about Philip Roth's new novel *Zuckerman Unbound*. This presented a curious challenge: If we had simply used the novel's title on the cover, it would have seemed like a pun on Mort's ownership of *The Atlantic*. So I asked Milton, who was a friend of Roth's, to create a portrait for the cover. This was an unusual assignment for Milton because he always maintained that capturing likenesses wasn't his strength. His solution was clever. We announced Roth's novel without showing his face or the title of the book.

It was clear to me that Bill needed an exceptional art director as he began to reshape *The Atlantic*. I chose Judy Garlan, a former

art director of *Cue* magazine and a designer at *Time*. I'm happy to say they collaborated brilliantly for twenty years. "Judy was endlessly creative, and thank goodness for that," Bill says. "It wasn't easy to illustrate so many abstract policy pieces, but she had good ideas and worked well with the artists. Judy was a careful, deep reader of the pieces we were publishing and was not afraid to argue with me, not just about the art but about the text."—WB

WILLIAM WHITWORTH
was a staff writer (1966-1972) and associate editor (1973-1979) at *The New Yorker* before joining *The Atlantic* in 1980. He lives in Little Rock, where he has been a book editor for twenty years. He recalls Mort Zuckerman as a good boss. "He let me hire new people and give raises. He gave me a budget, but he said, 'Don't ever let money stand in the way of a great story.'"

MORT ZUCKERMAN
cofounded the real estate firm Boston Properties, one of the largest developers of office properties in the United States. He purchased *The Atlantic* in 1980, *U.S. News & World Report* in 1984, and the *New York Daily News* in 1994. Zuckerman was a regular member of *The McLaughlin Group*, a popular Sunday news show, until 2015.
Photo by Tobey Sanford

THE REDESIGNED COVER
(opposite), illustrated by Milton Glaser, featured a thinner logo with modest cover lines highlighting writers' names. I also designed a border to be reimagined from issue to issue to signal a big change from the previous look (left).

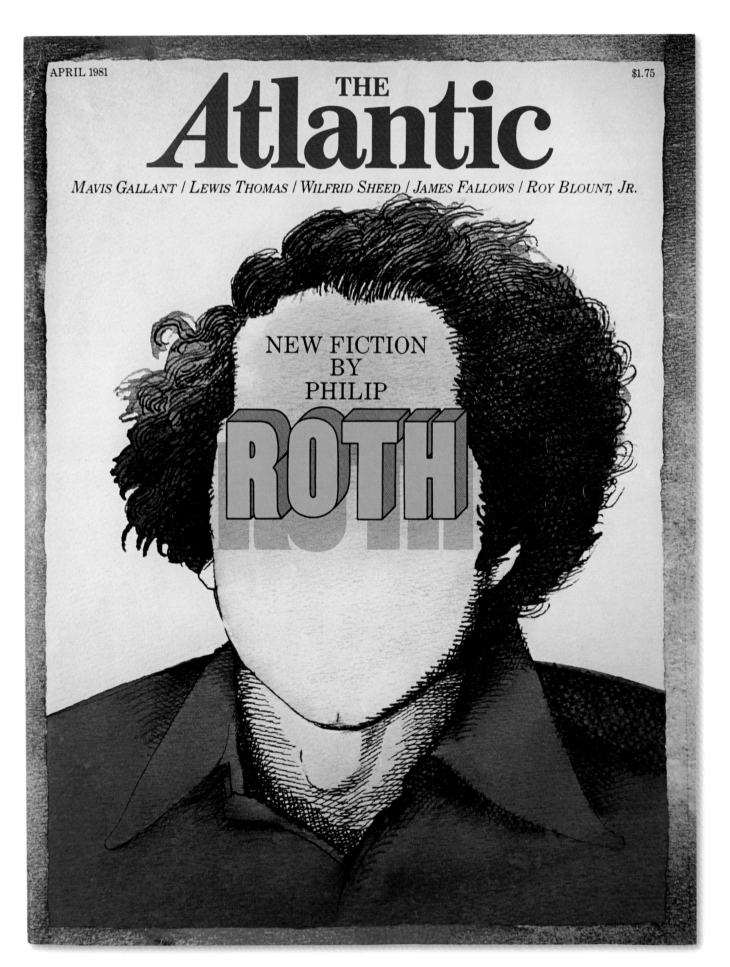

APRIL 1981 $1.75

THE
Atlantic

Mavis Gallant / Lewis Thomas / Wilfrid Sheed / James Fallows / Roy Blount, Jr.

NEW FICTION
BY
PHILIP
ROTH

BEFORE

AFTER

JUDY GARLAN was the art director of *The Atlantic* from 1981 to 2001 and made it one of the best designed magazines in the United States. Previously, she had designed five others including *Cue*, *Crawdaddy*, and *Art News*. She served as a special design consultant for *Time* magazine and as publications designer for Sarah Lawrence College. Her illustrations have appeared in *The New York Times*, *Psychology Today*, and *The Atlantic*. Winner of numerous design awards, Garlan lectures at corporations, museums, design schools, and universities.

Photo by Martin Cornel

BEFORE

AFTER

UPFRONT MATTER
For the contents page (above left) and the "Reports & Comment" section (left), we resurrected two old iconic colophons of the magazine's illustrious past.

CONSERVATIVE TYPE
and modest headlines typified the approach to the lengthy feature articles (opposite top).

OUR COLUMN format in the back of the book was distinguished by a drawing in the outer margin (opposite bottom left).

INTERRUPTIONS
Ed Sorel's one-page comic strip (opposite bottom right), used to interrupt the heavy text, was the forerunner of other stand-alone features by Guy Billout and Nancy and Ed Sorel.

Illustration by Eugene Mihaesco

Illustrations by Mel Furukawa

Illustration by Edward Sorel

TOM BENTKOWSKI
was assistant art director at *New York* magazine for four years. He was *Time* magazine's special projects art director in 1983, then director of design at *Life* magazine from 1987 to 1998. He was also director of design at *National Geographic Adventure* from 1999 to 2002.

Photo by Tobey Sanford

TOM REMEMBERS that "the editor's office in Boston faced the park, had high ceilings and deep-set windows with light pouring in. There was an Oriental carpet and an enormous fireplace. That office was the domain of the newly hired editor William Whitworth. He would sit down with a manuscript and pore over it for hours. On his desk was a box of Ritz Crackers, and every so often he would reach for one without lifting his eyes. He was a writer's editor, as he should well have been. The result of his long, careful examinations was sometimes the elimination of a single superfluous word or the changing of a semicolon to a comma. Down the hall, somewhat more extensive modifications were in the works."

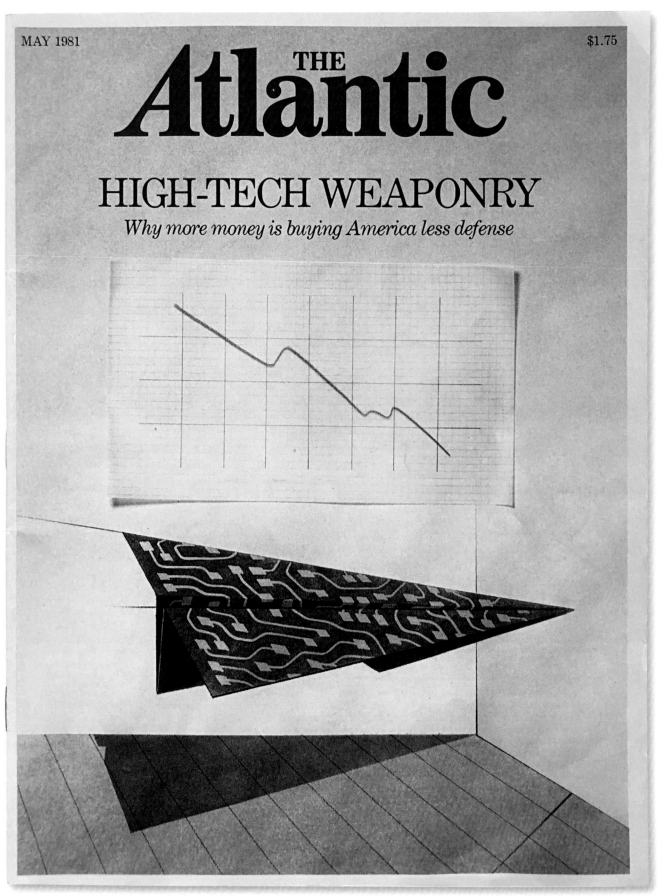

MAY 1981

$1.75

THE
Atlantic

HIGH-TECH WEAPONRY

Why more money is buying America less defense

Illustration by André Thijssen

JUNE 1981

$1.75

THE Atlantic

MOSHE DAYAN / JAMES FALLOWS / BOBBIE ANN MASON / ROY BLOUNT, JR. / SANFORD UNGAR

RAW MATERIALS: A CHALLENGE TO THE CONVENTIONAL WISDOM

BY JULIAN L. SIMON

Illustration by J. C. Suarez

NOTE: After all these years, I noticed these two consecutive covers each have elements with cast shadows enclosed in a room. This was not an intentional theme!—WB

185

Travel and Literature

Celebrated authors and correspondents on the pleasures of their favorite places

Responding to the surge in international travel in the early eighties, the *New York Times* launched *The Sophisticated Traveler* as part 2 of the Sunday magazine in 1983. Louis Silverstein, the paper's esteemed art director, invited me to work with travel editor Michael Leahy on the first issue. For this task, I hired Genevieve Williams, a graphic designer whose patience and talent helped us close the magazine on time.

Advertisers responded well to the idea of *The Sophisticated Traveler*, and the number of ads kept increasing until we reached 148 pages. This meant a large but complicated editorial well, causing us to wrap text around many half-page and quarter-page ads. But it also provided us with several large uninterrupted sections to display the fine photographs provided by picture editor Nina Subin.

Magazine designers typically have no control over the look of ads, and we would sometimes be unhappy if an ugly one ran in the front of the book. But I've been working in magazines long enough to know that "if you don't have ads, you die."

What made the issue distinctive was the many celebrated authors enlisted as travel writers, for example, "My Paris" by Saul Bellow, "My London" by V. S. Pritchett, "My Rome" by Muriel Spark, "Joie de Vivre of Montreal" by Margaret Atwood as well as an essay by the Australian American novelist Shirley Hazzard.

There was some initial resistance to Seymour Chwast's cover image, which some thought was too retro. But somehow, I convinced managing editor Arthur Gelb that retro was cool.—WB

MICHAEL J. LEAHY,
editor of *The Sophisticated Traveler*, began at *The New York Times* in 1961. He edited various sections, including "Travel," "Arts & Leisure," and "Real Estate."
Photo by Grace Glueck

SEYMOUR CHWAST
is a graphic designer and illustrator. In 1954 he cofounded Push Pin Studios. His monograph, *SEYMOUR: The Obsessive Images of Seymour Chwast,* was published in 2009 by Chronicle Books. He has lectured and exhibited worldwide with posters and paintings. Chwast is in the Art Director Hall of Fame and has designed and illustrated over sixty books for adults and children.
Photo by Tobey Sanford

THE RETRO LOOK
Chwast's cover (opposite) reflects the golden age of travel in the 1920s. Travel was associated with luxury and adventure, and people were proud to show the stickers on their suitcases. His cover couple appear to start their journey on the contents page (above).

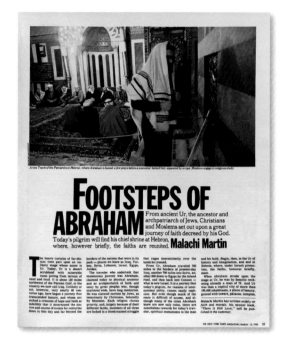

SHIRLEY HAZZARD, in her introduction to this issue, wrote, "Many a traveler departs in the hope of defining an elusive self or mislaying a burdensome one: of being, literally, carried away. Literature has prepared us to expect the release of new aspects of ourselves in the presence of the fabled and unfamiliar. Simply looking on given scenes and monuments, human beings have been known to become happier and wiser."

THE EDITORIAL WELL (above, below, and opposite) with photographs by *Time*'s skilled photographers, featured large Franklin Gothic Extra Condensed headline type, often interlocked with the subhead and byline. The bylines were always set in bold type, highlighting the prestigious writers.

E. GENEVIEVE WILLIAMS was assistant art director of *The Sophisticated Traveler* and later became an art director at *The New York Times* (1985–1998). She taught at the School of Visual Arts (1988–2012), was a visiting professor at Yeungnam University in Korea (2015–2018), and is a teacher at Marymount Manhattan College.

Photo: Genevieve Williams

Photographs: ("Footsteps of Abraham") Micha Bar-Am/Magnum; ("My Rome") Cotton Coulson/Woodfin Camp; ("My Paris") Martine Franck/Magnum and Thomas Victor; ("My London") Elisabeth Zeschin

O, GREECE!

Here one is caught by the beauty, the simple food, the melancholy zest for life — by a sense of homecoming both immediate and absolute: This is where we belong. This is where we began. **Hugh Leonard**

Hugh Leonard's newest play, "Moving," will have its premiere at the Dublin Theater Festival in October.

There are two sights the traveler in Europe never forgets. One is that first glimpse of Chartres Cathedral from five miles away, solitary and seeming to sail the wheat fields like a leviathan. The other is the Parthenon just after sunrise. Athens is slate gray with dusk and smog; high above it, pricked by first light, the columns soar, dwarfing even the Acropolis itself. No photograph can prepare the visitor for the actuality; it sandbags the senses. The heart is seized. And far off behind the temple and beyond Piraeus, the Aegean is molten silver.

I love Greece for many reasons: for its good manners, for the melancholy that masks its zest for life, for its climate and its islands, each one different from the next. But most of all I love it for the immediacy of the past. To arrive there is a homecoming; at once, and with a certainty as serene as it is absolute, the mystery is solved: This is where one began.

Athens, for all its size, yields its pleasures quickly. And you need no guide for the 96-minute drive to Cape Sounion, no one to tell you where the land ends, that the sea has blues and violets that never knew an artist's palette, that Byron carved his name into the marble of the Temple of Poseidon. Elsewhere, however, it is good to travel with a Greek as mentor; inevitably, he will treat myth as history, time as an impertinence and antiquity as last week.

On my own first visit to Greece, my guide was the venerable and gaunt Manos Katrakis, an actor who is to Greek theater as Olivier is to British. We drove on a January morning to the

Caption (top right): *A column of the Temple of Poseidon, overlooking the sea at Cape Sounion. Inset: Just after sunrise, the Parthenon rises above the smog of Athens.*

Caption (middle right): *The monumental hillside tomb of Agamemnon at Mycenae, entered through a rock-cut passageway, recalls the tragedy of the House of Atreus and the Trojan War.*

Photographs by Mitch Epstein

PASSAGE TO MALABAR

South of Bombay, the coast of India holds places whose very names — Calicut and Mangalore, Goa, Cochin and Trivandrum — are scented by the history of the spice trade, when the West first realized its great dream of finding a sea route to the fabled riches of the Orient. **Santha Rama Rau**

For any traveler, certain journeys hold a remembered enchantment that bears little relation to the particular monuments visited or beauty spots enjoyed. Some other quality seems to inform such voyages, coloring even the most prosaic details of everyday life with its peculiar magic.

I myself have made many journeys to Malabar, in the state of Kerala on the southwest coast of the Indian peninsula. I have traveled there sometimes by plane, sometimes by road and even on one occasion by oxcart. I have always been refreshed by the extraordinary and lovely things that the region holds. But the truly magical journey to Malabar started for me many years ago with an invitation from an old friend to stay with her on a farm she owned and managed.

I decided to travel south from Bombay on a small trading steamer largely because it called at ports whose names alone evoked a chapter of romantic and bloody history that had always stirred my fancy. Goa, Mangalore, Calicut, Cochin, Trivandrum — all centers of the spice trade between India and Europe that began at the end of the 15th century, when the West realized its great dream of an ocean route to the riches of the Orient.

We left the superb harbor of Bombay at sundown, passed the scattered islands with their ruined forts, lighthouses and ancient Hindu temples, and arrived in Panjim, the Goan capital, at dawn. At that time Goa was still a Portuguese colony, and Panjim (now Panaji) was a charming, somnolent settlement built on the lines of a southern European provincial town, with stuccoed arcades and formal government buildings, flying the Portuguese flag, surrounding a central plaza. It is set on the bank of the wide Mandavi River, and on the hill behind it the piercing pinks and purples of bougainvillea cas-

Santha Rama Rau has recently completed adapting E. M. Forster's "Passage to India" for the screen.

caded over the walls enclosing private villas and compounds.

In the busy harbor traffic, freighters of a dozen nationalities steamed to their moorings, tugs and ferries fussed between the ships and shores. It seemed incredible that Affonso de Albuquerque had navigated precisely this same route up the Mandavi with his fleet of 23 ships in 1510, to wrest the tiny, luxuriant state from its Moslem rulers. At the end of desperate hand-to-hand fighting, he rode into the capital bearing the Portuguese standard and a gold cross. Kneeling in the public square, he dedicated the city to St. Catherine, in honor of her feast day, and claimed Goa as a possession of the King of Portugal and of the Catholic Church — which later sparked one of the most brutal and wholesale forced conversions recorded in Asia. All in the search for spices.

I spent my day in Velha Goa, the deserted old Portuguese capital built in the 16th century to rival Rome. It was a hushed, mysterious place, about six miles from Panjim. All the original houses, shops, offices and bazaars of an active city had crumbled away, and only the fantastic baroque churches, the Archbishops' Palace, the great ceremonial Arch of the Viceroys, the extraordinarily beautiful convents and their chapels rose out of the encroaching jungle. Nobody stopped me from exploring the vast, empty monuments. The elderly caretakers, when I could find them, seemed, if anything, mildly surprised at any display of interest. Only the Basilica of Bom Jesus was more closely guarded, for the "incorruptible body" of St. Francis Xavier is enshrined there and pilgrims were occasionally allowed, on his feast day, to pass by and kiss his toe. (This practice is no longer permitted, since a zealot bit the toe off a few years ago.)

Now, of course, Velha Goa has been expensively cleaned up for the tourists. Wilderness and scrub trees have been cleared to make roads and gardens; walls and facades are newly whitewashed;

(Continued on Page 60)

Caption: *The port of Cochin is one of the oldest in India, visited, traded with and fought over by foreigners for at least 2,000 years.*

Photograph by Mitch Epstein

IN THE NEWS

British Sub Torpedoes Argentine Cruiser
The most controversial event of the Falklands war was the sinking of the Argentine cruiser *General Belgrano* by a British nuclear submarine, the H.M.S. *Conqueror*, on May 2, 1982. Members of Parliament accused Prime Minister Margaret Thatcher of ordering the attack to stop a Peruvian-brokered peace plan.

Refreshing a Fading Franchise

The Redesign Team: Carol March, Walter Bernard, Paul Richer, and Margery Peters
Photo by Matthew Klein

Fortune's new format challenged feature writers to get to the point quicker.

Starting with founding art director T. M. Cleland, illustrious art directors Eleanor Tracy, Peter Piening, Will Burtin, Leo Lionni, and Walter Allner had shaped the look of this elegant business journal over the years. *Fortune* launched with a cover price of $1 in 1930 (the equivalent of $14 today), when other newsstand publications were selling for ten to twenty-five cents. With a healthy budget for commissioning the best photographers and illustrators, they lavished a rich visual mix on subscribers.

In 1982, soon after it became a biweekly publication, Time Inc.'s editor-in-chief, Henry Grunwald asked me to redesign *Fortune*. It had been a monthly for fifty-three years, so this was a big change that posed a challenge to its staff. For example, *Fortune*'s writers were used to long-form articles that were not suited for the new frequency. Managing Editor William Rukeyser had to coax writers to produce shorter articles that engaged readers more quickly. My solution was to eliminate subheads and enlarge the first paragraph of every article, forcing writers to make the most of their first few words. Many writers weren't too happy about this new format, but I believe it accomplished the desired editorial goal.

Once the redesign was in place, my next assignment was to hire an art director to carry on. I convinced a reluctant Margery Peters, who worked with me on the redesign, to come on board. She remained for the next fifteen years, thus joining the long line of excellent *Fortune* art directors.—WB

1929-1982

BEFORE

AFTER

THE *FORTUNE* LOGO
Art directors of *Fortune* frequently redesigned the logo as they updated the format over the years. The logo in 1982 (before) looked generic to me—like the brand name on the front of a refrigerator. We were entering the computer age, and I wanted *Fortune* to look tougher and more modern. I designed a new nameplate using Futura Black, which was versatile and bold.

BEFORE

AFTER

BEFORE

AFTER

NEW FEATURE HEADLINES SET IN FUTURA EXTRA BOLD ALL CAPS

THE NEW FORMAT included bold headlines and the enlarged first paragraph of every feature. It also encouraged a more prominent use of photography and illustration.

■ The first paragraph of the text, enlarged to 14 point on 18 point Century Old Style, eliminated the usual subhead and brought the reader into the story more quickly. It forced feature writers to grab the reader's attention with a compelling opening paragraph.

191

Photograph by Diana Walker

Illustration by Michael Doret

VERSATILITY
The heavy Futura typeface used for the logo along with the box rules surrounding each letter gave us options to configure the logo in many different ways depending on the cover image (left). Whether it was positive or negative, dropping out of or overprinting its background, the logo retained its identity.

Construction and photograph by André Thijssen

Illustration by Guy Billout

MARGERY'S COVER
(opposite). Way back before smart phones—when mobile phones resembled bricks— it was enormous news when telecom monolith AT&T was mandated to break up into a series of "Baby Bells." Monumental pop artist James Rosenquist had just shown an exciting series of new paintings that featured a "pulling apart" motif. Margery Peters, now art director (I was design director) thought this would be the perfect metaphor for the story. She met with Rosenquist in New York, and he agreed to create an entirely new work for *Fortune*. After he showed her a sketch, he began the piece in his Aripeka, Florida, studio. When the work was finished, we dispatched a photographer to shoot it for reproduction. When the stunning photograph arrived, Margery made a mock-up of the cover. It was not well received by Managing Editor William Rukeyser. He thought it both radical and a non sequitur. Peters and Rukeyser went to the thirty-fourth floor to show the cover to Editor-in-Chief Henry Grunwald, where— it turned out—the cover was very warmly endorsed.

Photo: Margery Peters

Illustration by Melinda Bordelon

Photograph by Roberto Brosan

JUNE 27, 1983

$3.00

FORTUNE

SPECIAL REPORT

BREAKING UP
THE PHONE COMPANY

Painting by James Rosenquist

In 1982, two big projects, *The Washington Post* and *Lire*, led us to form WBMG, an editorial design and development company in the very same building where we first produced *New York* magazine. Getting back together, we were able to pick right up where we left off.

Lire

The Washington Post Magazine

U.S. News & World Report

Designing with Women: Jardin des Modes, Alma, Plum

Adweek Portfolios

U&lc

Magazine Week

Failure to Launch: Globe, Inspired, The New York Film Review

Time Special Issue

Modern Maturity

Fortune 1996

ESPN Magazine

The Nation

CHAPTER

Together Again

As I was finishing up at *Fortune* magazine in 1982, Ben Bradlee, executive editor of *The Washington Post*, called asking if I might consider redesigning the paper. I had never worked on newspapers before, but the opportunity to reshape one of the country's major news dailies was an irresistible new challenge. This would be a big job, and I would need a studio and a staff.

Around the same time, Sir James Goldsmith asked Milton if he would redesign *Lire*, a French literary magazine that he had just acquired. Milton asked if I wanted to join him on this project and I asked him if he wanted to be my partner on the redesign of the *Post*. It became obvious that we should get back to working together.

Now that I had the experience of working on my own, I felt confident that we could enter into a partnership and collaborate once again. We formed WBMG to concentrate on editorial projects: magazines, newspapers, and books. We didn't agonize over the business name too much: WBMG, a combination of our initials that sounded good when said aloud. It sounded so smooth, in fact, that we got calls from people who thought we were a radio station.

Suddenly we had a real business! We set up the office in the original *New York* magazine headquarters at 207 East Thirty-Second Street, and our first clients were in Paris and Washington, D.C. Among WBMG's first and finest hires was Killian Jordan, our managing editor, who had a knack for witty correspondence that delighted our clients.

Milton maintained his studio, Milton Glaser, Inc., on the second floor while I was on the floor above, along with seven or so employees. As in our *New York* magazine days, we collaborated on the principle of interruption. We would pop in and out on each other throughout the day without having to make appointments. Milton once said to me, "The trick is to operate by interruption. Don't fight it; don't be annoyed by it. Welcome it. You will get more accomplished each time and your capacity for dealing with problems will increase."

All in all, we have designed over 100 publications. WBMG offered us many fascinating adventures and a chance to interact with editors and newsrooms around the world.—WB

Apart from its functional purpose, some believe that a graphic designer's business card or letterhead is a distillation of their sensibility. Walter and I didn't spend much time mulling over WBMG's stationery, but there are a few elements that could be instructional.

On the back of our letterhead is a lesson about the value of white space via the sixth-century B.C. sage Lao Tzu:

We put thirty spokes together and call it a wheel;
But it is on the space where there is nothing that the
usefulness of the wheel depends.

We turn clay to make a vessel;
But it is on the space where there is nothing that the
usefulness of the vessel depends.

We pierce doors and windows to make a house;
And it is on these spaces where there is nothing that
the usefulness of the house depends.

Therefore, just as we take advantage of what is,
we should recognize the usefulness of what is not.

We thought to include this passage because it was provocative and signaled that we were not an ordinary design office. It also contained information about the nature of what is and what is not, which could be significant for someone paying attention.

Chinese philosophy has been fundamental to the way I think about things. In the *I Ching* and in the *Tao Te Ching*, from where the passage is derived, one sees the interconnectedness of seemingly disparate ideas and objects. Not only that, the ancient oracle is also really helpful when you have to make a life decision. I would trust the *I Ching* more than many friends I have. There was even a time when I used it every day. Shall I get hot coffee or iced coffee?

On the back of our business card is a quote from the extraordinary Marxist thinker Frantz Fanon: "If the building of a bridge does not enrich the awareness of those who work on it, then that bridge ought not to be built."

The white letters against the yellow bars are nearly imperceptible, but they say something about the mutual satisfaction of a client and a designer. This principle could also describe how we determined what projects to take on. Designing a magazine, like building a bridge, is collective work.—MG

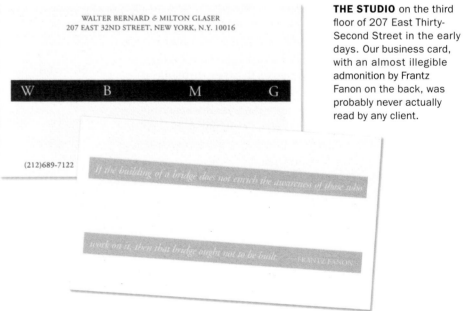

WALTER BERNARD & MILTON GLASER
207 EAST 32ND STREET, NEW YORK, N.Y. 10016

W   B   M   G

(212)689-7122

If the building of a bridge does not enrich the awareness of those who

work on it, then that bridge ought not to be built. —FRANTZ FANON

THE STUDIO on the third floor of 207 East Thirty-Second Street in the early days. Our business card, with an almost illegible admonition by Frantz Fanon on the back, was probably never actually read by any client.

Our French Connection

Sir James Goldsmith gave WBMG its first project.

A COLLABORATION
Working in the Paris office of *Lire*, from left: Jimmy Goldsmith, Milton Glaser, Bernard Pivot, and Walter Bernard. Photograph by Jean-Régis Roustan

THE COVER REDESIGN
First, we eliminated the *Time* magazine-like border, which did nothing to help *Lire*'s identity (above). Next, we designed the logo for *Lire* to signify a new direction. With only four letters, one is tempted to emulate *Life* magazine, with a simple sans serif typeface in the upper left corner, but we decided to spread the new logo across the top of the cover. The close-up photograph of the statue of Victor Hugo with a red scarf at the Sorbonne (opposite) was an appropriate cover image for the fifteenth anniversary of the May 1968 student protests.

Sir Jimmy Goldsmith asked us to rethink *Lire*, the seven-year-old French literary journal that he had just acquired along with *L'Express*. Newsstand sales were down, its readership a little too old; it was stagnant and needed something but didn't know what it was. Working with its editorial staff led by Bernard Pivot, Pierre Boncenne, and art director Jean-Pierre Cliquet, we repositioned the magazine. Apart from giving *Lire* a more engaging character, we offered the staff a new set of operating principles: talk about ideas through people and personalities; be broader, be more accessible, be more lively.

Lire's staff constantly delighted us with how, working with our template, their own graphic inventiveness blossomed. Pierre says that the new formula encouraged them to consider the visuals seriously from the conception of each issue.

Lire's circulation doubled almost instantly. There was no marketing, no nothing. It just took off. *Lire* is among the best magazine redesigns we've worked on. Not only did it represent a totally new graphic positioning, but also it changed the staff's ideological stance and their editorial viewpoint.

Le magazine des livres

N° 93 / Mai 1983 / 20 F

ISSN 0338-5019 BELGIQUE : 150 FB - CANADA : $ 3.25 - ESPAGNE : 325 PTAS - SUISSE : 8 FS

M-1974-93-20 F

LIRE

15 ans après
Mai 68
Qui tient le haut du pavé ?

Graham Greene
Semprun
et Montand
Emmanuel Bove
Cavanna
Maurice Rheims

INTERVIEW
Claude
Lévi-Strauss

Photograph by Manuel Bidermanas

THE CONTENTS PAGE
(above) was redesigned as
a two-page spread (right)
to make it easier to navigate
the new sections and to
have more visual variety.

THE MAIN FEATURES
contained both an introduction to ("Le Livre") and an
excerpt ("L'Extrait") of a
book. While we designed
a fairly strict typographic
format using Caslon almost
exclusively, our idea was to
use different thematic initial
caps within each excerpt
(right and opposite), giving
Jean-Pierre Cliquet an
opportunity to have some
fun within the format.

Photograph: Cahiers du Cinéma

Portrait of Machiavelli by Santi di Tito/Photoscala

Illustration by Jean-Pierre Cliquet

BERNARD PIVOT is a journalist and the host of several celebrated television programs such as *Apostrophes* and *Bouillon de culture*. An ardent champion of language, he cofounded the national spelling competition *Dicos d'or* in 1985 and is currently the chairman of the prestigious French literary association Académie Goncourt. Pivot's passion for literature is only rivaled by his love of wine. He owns a vineyard in the Beaujolais region and is the author of *French Wine: An Illustrated Miscellany*.

JEAN-PIERRE CLIQUET was the art director of *Lire* and *L'Express*, and an editor at French publishing house Les Éditions Cercle d'Art.

PIERRE BONCENNE is an award-winning writer and journalist. Apart from serving as *Lire*'s editor-in-chief for fifteen years, he published his own literary magazine titled *ecrivain*. Based in Paris, Pierre has written nine books, including *Le parapluie de Simon Leys,* which was awarded the Émile Faguet Prize and the International Association of Literary Critics' 2015 Grand Prize for Literary Criticism.

Photographs by Photo Michaud

Photograph by Gilbert Nencioli

"AU PEIGNE FIN" (With a fine-tooth comb), a new interview section (far left) that examines an author's work in detail. The design is based on the idea of mug shots.

"THE *LIRE* GUIDE" was an unillustrated listing of newly published books in the front of the magazine. We redesigned the guide with its own table of contents (left) and inserted a rating system. We also moved it to the back of the magazine.

"LE BUREAU DE . . ." (The desk of . . .) A new quiz in which a photograph of an author's desk is shown and readers are given clues before the author's identity is revealed on the next page (below left).

MIRKO ILIĆ is an illustrator and graphic designer who was the art director of *Time* magazine's international edition (1991) and later the art director of the "Op-Ed" page of *The New York Times* (1992–1993). He established Mirko Ilić Corp in 1995. His work is in the collections of the Smithsonian Museum, MoMA, and SFMoMA. Mirko is the coauthor of ten books with Steve Heller and cowrote *The Design of Dissent* with Milton Glaser.

Photo: Mirko Ilić

MIRKO'S INSPIRATION "For *Lire*'s primer to second-hand books [opposite], the first thing that came to mind was Bibendum, the iconic French mascot of the Michelin guides. I drew my version of the Michelin Man using books instead of tires."

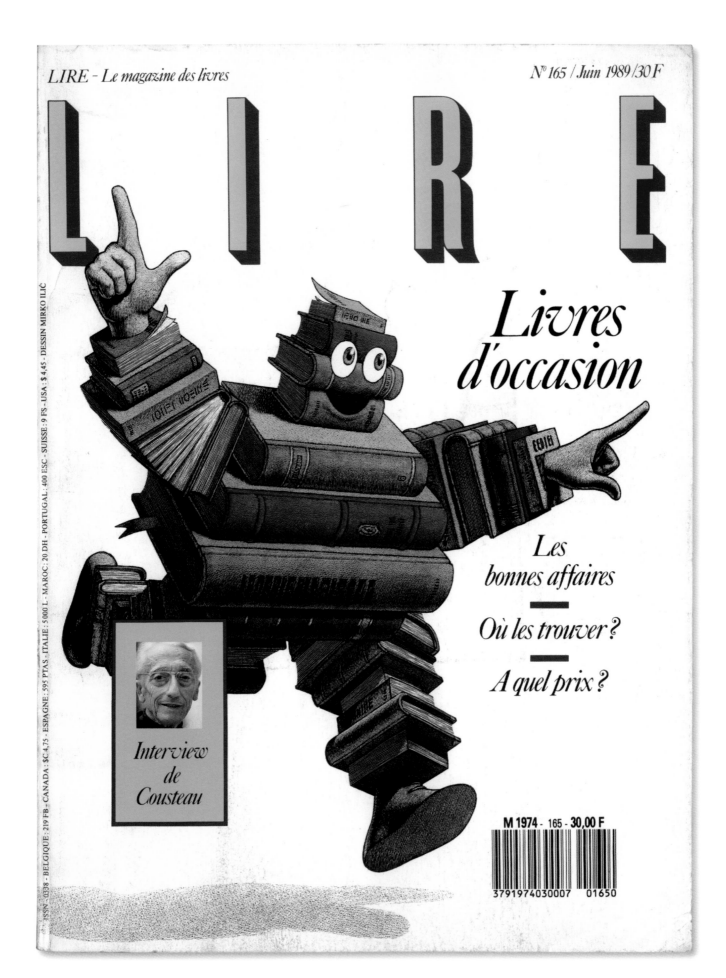

LIRE - Le magazine des livres

N° 165 / Juin 1989 / 30 F

LIRE

Livres d'occasion

Les bonnes affaires
—
Où les trouver ?
—
A quel prix ?

Interview de Cousteau

ISSN - 0338 - BELGIQUE : 219 FB - CANADA : $C 4,75 - ESPAGNE : 595 PTAS - ITALIE : 5000 L - MAROC : 20 DH - PORTUGAL : 400 ESC - SUISSE : 9 FS - USA : $ 4,45 - DESSIN MIRKO ILIĆ

M 1974 - 165 - 30,00 F

3791974030007 01650

A Self-Inflicted Perfect Storm

When a new design and good writing finally didn't matter

THE POST'S Sunday magazine was the same size as *The New York Times* Sunday magazine (far left). The plan was to reduce it to *Time* magazine's size in the hopes of attracting national advertisers. We rearranged the logo to signal the change and emphasize the word "magazine" (left). Photograph by Harry Benson

In 1984, we completed an extensive redesign of *The Washington Post*, a complex project that taught us a lot about its culture and operations. Executive editor Ben Bradlee asked us to turn our attention to the paper's rather lackluster Sunday magazine. The idea was to make it smaller—"*Time* size"—to energize the advertising sales staff and attract national ads.

Working with editor Jay Lovinger, we designed a zero issue to show *Post* executives, potential advertisers, and influential subscribers. With better paper, full-color printing throughout, and a Century Old Style typeface, one of our favorites, we provided a format for a new art director to follow. Our aim was to elevate it into the same league with *The New York Times* Sunday magazine.

But *The Post*'s brand-new magazine was cursed by a perfect storm. The first article in the September 7, 1996, issue was a column by Richard Cohen taking the side of store owners who discriminated against young black males. A cover story about the murder conviction of rapper Joseph "Just Ice" Williams added to the problem. (An article about Vice President George Bush was originally planned as the cover story, but editors had to scramble when the VP postponed the interview.) Washington, D.C.'s African American community was so enraged that protesters showed up outside *The Post*'s headquarters. Black radio condemned the magazine and urged advertisers to withdraw, which they did.

In retrospect, Cohen describes the debacle as damning proof of how disconnected the paper was from the African American community in D.C. then. Ben Bradlee later wrote an apology and reflected on the miscalculation. "In the context of that highly promoted first issue, many blacks felt that *The Post* prints stories about the problems of our community, and not about its achievements; that *The Post Magazine* is full of words about black failures and has none about the many successful blacks in the community." This was an unforeseen, self-inflicted wound that even a bright new editor and a new design could not overcome.

JAY LOVINGER, a writer and journalist, was the editor of *The Washington Post Magazine* from 1985 to 1989. Previously, he was an editor at *Inside Sports* (1979–1981) and *People* magazine (1981–1985). He became the managing editor of *Life* magazine in 1996. Lovinger worked for ESPN until 2017, winning an Emmy award for outstanding sports programming.
Photo: Jay Lovinger

Photograph by Harry Benson

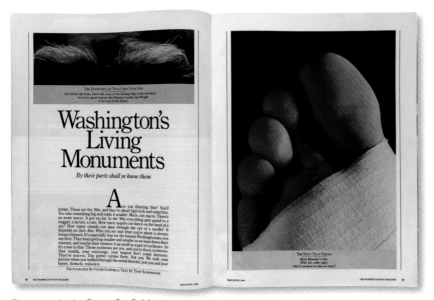

Photographs by Peter Garfield

Photographs by Andrea Blanch

THE FIRST ISSUE COVER

Photo illustration by Matt Mahurin

RICHARD COHEN'S COLUMN

RICHARD COHEN RECALLS:

"This was the most consequential—and certainly, the most controversial—column of my career. Given the lead time for the brand-new magazine, weeks went by from writing to publication. In the interim, the column was read by inside the paper—and praised. So it came as substantially more than a shock to have the published piece denounced as racist. I continue to insist it wasn't, but I cannot defend my and the paper's naïveté and insensitivity. Along with the cover article, It showed how alienated we were from important elements in the black community."

Reagan Sworn in Again
For his second term, President Ronald Reagan was officially sworn in on Sunday, January 20, 1985, in the Grand Foyer of the White House. His public swearing-in ceremony was held at the U.S. Capitol in Washington, D.C., on January 21, 1985, not outside as is customary, but inside the Capitol Rotunda because of the seven-degree temperature. Chief Justice Warren E. Burger administered the oath of office.

Too Many Cooks?

Designing covers during a rapid turnover of editors

Mortimer Zuckerman

Sir Harold Evans

Shelby Coffey III

David Gergen

MORT'S TEAM
Editor-in-Chief of *U.S. News* Mort Zuckerman assembled an experienced and talented team, including:

SIR HAROLD EVANS, a British-born journalist and writer, was editor of both *The Sunday Times* and *The Times* of London. He was the founding editor of *Condé Nast Traveler*. Evans was president and publisher of Random House trade group (1990-1997). He has written several books on history and journalism. He was knighted for services to journalism in 2004.
Photo: Condé Nast

SHELBY COFFEY III was a deputy managing editor at *The Washington Post*. After leaving the editorship of *U.S. News*, he became editor of the *Dallas Times Herald* and later the *Los Angeles Times*. He was executive vice president at ABC News and is vice chair of the Newseum.
Photo: Shelby Coffey III

DAVID GERGEN is a former presidential adviser to four presidents: Richard Nixon, Gerald Ford, Ronald Reagan, and Bill Clinton. Gergen served as editor of *U.S. News* from 1986 to 1988. He is the author of *The New York Times* best-seller *Eyewitness to Power: The Essence of Leadership, Nixon to Clinton* (2000), and is also senior political analyst for CNN.
Photos of Gergen and Zuckerman: Richard Ellis/Alamy Stock Photo

After his successful purchase of the *Atlantic Monthly*, real estate mogul Mort Zuckerman bought *U.S. News & World Report* in 1984. The weekly news magazine was competing in a cutthroat field with *Time* and *Newsweek*, and Mort was determined to climb out of third place.

Unlike *The Atlantic,* which he entrusted to Bill Whitworth, Mort decided to appoint himself as chairman and editor-in-chief of *U.S. News*. He enlisted Harold Evans, the longtime editor of the *London Sunday Times*, as editorial director, and Edwin Taylor, the venerated design director of *The Times*, and *New York* magazine's cofounder Clay Felker as consultants. And in 1985 he hired Shelby Coffey III, with whom we worked on the redesign of *The Washington Post*, as the editor to oversee day-to-day operations.

We were invited to consult as well, but quickly realized that a redesign of the magazine was impractical without a clear editorial direction. There were many informed opinions on where and how to steer the publication. There were just too many cooks. We did, however, agree to design the covers which we did from 1984 to 1987. Shelby Coffey left after eight months and was replaced by David Gergen, former White House director of communications. Through it all we produced covers every week from New York City, working with the editors in D.C. and away from the internal turmoil. Our only actual redesign work was the subtle tweaking of the logo, completed in stages by 1986.

Illustration by Marvin Mattelson

Photograph by Matthew Klein

Illustration by David Suter

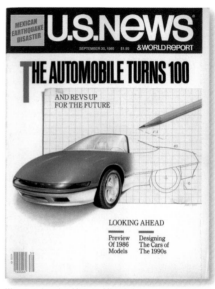

Illustration by Karen Kluglein

Illustration by Brian Bailey

Design by WBMG

Photograph by Carl Fischer

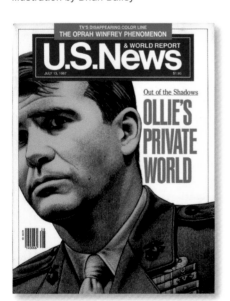

Illustration by Mirko Ilić

Photograph by Matthew Klein

THE LOGO
We gradually redesigned the nameplate of *U.S. News & World Report* over the years, from 1984 to 1988, changing "U.S. News" to an upper- and lowercase version that we felt was more assertive and neatly accommodated the rest of the title. Our designs covered a variety of topics, but the cover (opposite) seems particularly relevant in these times.

Good Stocks To Buy Now

U.S.news
&WORLD REPORT

AUGUST 19, 1985 $1.95

Will the Mexican Migration Create a New Nation?

THE DISAPPEARING BORDER

Illustration by Juan Suarez Botas

DESIGNING WITH WOMEN: 1

Sizing up French Fashion

How could we, who were ambivalent toward the fashion world, redesign a successful women's fashion magazine?

THE NEW FORMAT
(near left) was a dramatic change. It was much taller and wider than previous issues (far left), and the use of a high-quality newsprint paper gave it a completely different texture. The redesigned cover format and logo gave *Jardin des Modes* a new strength.

In many ways, working with *New York* magazine's strong female contributors prepared us for this job. Never would they toler-ate the condescending tone of most ladies' journals, which at that time were mostly edited by men. Working alongside these remarkable women trained us to reject the clichés of femininity. When designing for any audience, the readers' education, income, and geography were much more relevant considerations.

Jardin des Modes was the first women's magazine I designed. Founded in 1922, it was conceived as a fashion-illustration journal with sewing patterns and sketches by fashion designers. Invited by *Jardin des Modes*' editor-in-chief Alice Morgaine, I worked on its 1979 relaunch with the intent of giving it a more journalistic quality. I proposed two operating principles for the magazine's new era: balance and common sense.

We made the size dramatically larger (approximately 11" x 15"), and I designed a new nameplate to make it more distinctive on news-stands. I introduced a frame that served as an organizing element on the cover. Now there was a place for the main image and cover lines that tend to junk up the page. With the new large format we had room for more ambitious visual treatments. We presented the sewing patterns like architectural blueprints and made them fold-out inserts.

With the efforts of *Jardin des Modes*' inventive staff, who did wonders with the template, their readership grew dramatically and soon spawned a Swiss edition.

In 1986, Alice commissioned Walter and me to design *Jardin des Modes*' 100th issue. It was wonderful to see that many of the major graphic elements from 1979 were still intact.—MG

ALICE MORGAINE was the editor-in-chief at *Jardin des Modes* from 1979 to 1997. She was the artistic director of the Verrière-Hermès gallery in Brussels from 1999 to 2012, and is an adviser to the artistic director of Hermès.
Photo: Alice Morgaine

The centennial issue of *Jardin des Modes*. Photograph by Peter Winfield

JARDIN DES MODES had a strong fashion and graphic staff whose photographs and layouts worked well in the redesigned template that introduced the bold Gill sans serif as well as a Goudy Old Style into the mix. What we did in the 1986 issue was to emphasize the service aspect, as shown in the pages of the "L'atout-prix" section (left and opposite) that focused on price and value.

"Sommaire" photo by Eric Feinblatt
"Redingotes" photo by Véronique Roux-Voloir
"L'atout-prix" photos by Serge Guérand

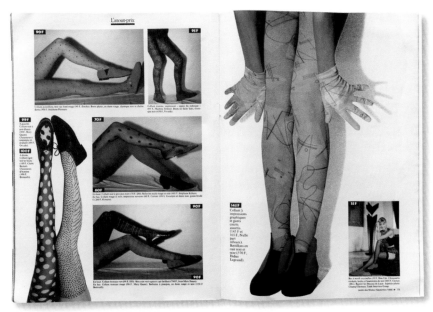

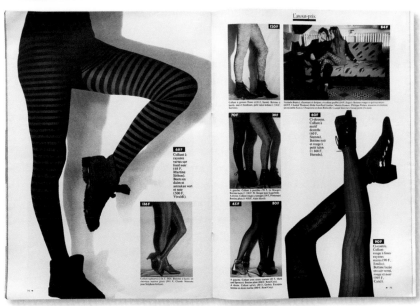

213

IN THE NEWS

The UK and France Announce Tunnel Plans
In a joint press conference, on January 21, 1986, French President François Mitterrand and British Prime Minister Margaret Thatcher unveiled a plan to build a privately financed rail-only Channel Tunnel between the villages of Cheriton in England and Frethun in France. Construction took six years and cost 80 percent more than expected. It was officially opened by Queen Elizabeth II and President Mitterrand on May 6, 1994.

DESIGNING WITH WOMEN: 2
A Brief but Beautiful Run

Geneviève Jurgensen created a sophisticated service magazine that she hoped would appeal to working mothers in France.

The publisher Bayard Presse already had around 300,000 loyal subscribers to their high-end children's journals, so it seemed natural to develop a magazine focused on women who were juggling professional and domestic domains.

Alma's founding editor Geneviève Jurgensen envisioned a multifaceted publication that was "meant for educated, active women with one or two young children," as she puts it. Following her lead, we created three major sections: "Le Journal," a summary of pertinent current events; "Alma Plus," for shopping guides and DIY articles about home and family; and "Ramdam" (from *faire du ramdam,* or create a buzz), with short clips about cinema, books, and museums.

Building on the wonderful symmetry in the letters of the name, we drew a logo based on the font Rainbow, originally created for the Rainbow Room in New York. The letters had a lively quality that seemed fitting for *Alma*.

Though they achieved half of their readership goal in a few months, *Alma* folded after eight issues. Geneviève recalls, "One subscriber said: 'I am always happy when I find *Alma* in the mailbox. I put it on my bedside and say to myself that I will read it as soon as possible.' This was terrible to hear because we all know that when our favorite magazine has a new issue, we open it right away, and start reading it on the spot."

GENEVIÈVE JURGENSEN is a journalist and a speech therapist. A leading road-safety advocate, she cofounded *Ligue contre la violence routière* after her two young daughters died in a car crash. Geneviève was awarded the Chevalier de la Légion d'honneur in 2003 and was included in *Time* magazine's list of European heroes in 2005.
Photo: Geneviève Jurgensen

THE FIRST ISSUE
Jurgensen remembers, "We wanted the reader to be proud of her magazine, and also to instantly build an affective link with it. This is why my own child is on the cover of the first issue [opposite], and the picture of me on the introductory page [left] is also very casual. I wanted to convey the atmosphere of getting together after school and kindergarten, a happy, intimate time of the day. It was important, also, to show that we were not targeting women about to give birth to a first baby; these magazines already existed."
Photo by Valérie Winckler

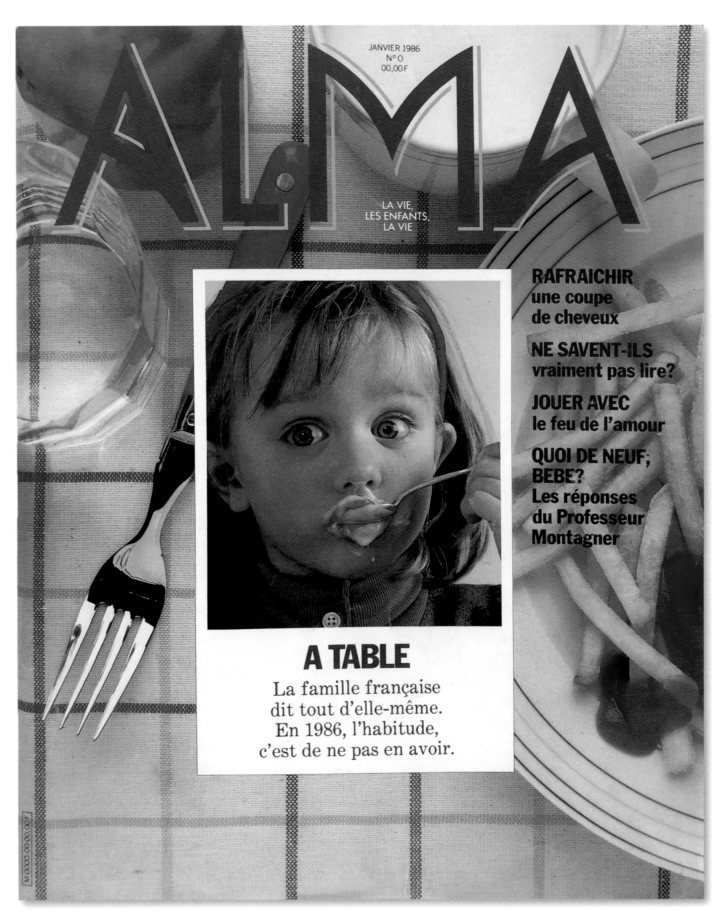

JANVIER 1986
N° 0
00,00 F

ALMA

LA VIE,
LES ENFANTS,
LA VIE

RAFRAICHIR
une coupe
de cheveux

NE SAVENT-ILS
vraiment pas lire?

JOUER AVEC
le feu de l'amour

**QUOI DE NEUF;
BEBE?**
Les réponses
du Professeur
Montagner

A TABLE

La famille française
dit tout d'elle-même.
En 1986, l'habitude,
c'est de ne pas en avoir.

Background photograph by Matthew Klein; portrait photograph by Valérie Clément

"LE JOURNAL" The opening section was designed to look somewhat like a news magazine, in a four-column format with yellow markers highlighting certain paragraphs for a quicker read.

"RAMDAM" The entertainment and cultural section opened with a contents page containing excerpts from each article, marked by large quote marks. The following pages of this section were designed with a more open format.

"ALMA PLUS" opened with its own contents page, followed by pages with practical information about the home.

"A TABLE" (At the Table). Kids give their opinions about food, cooking and table manners. Photograph by Steve Murez

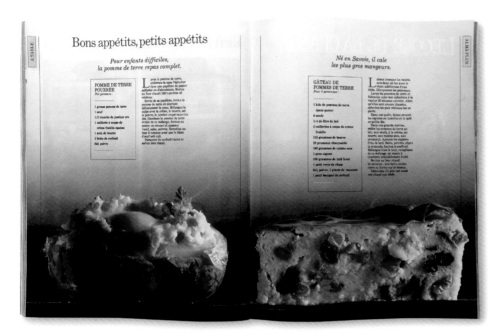

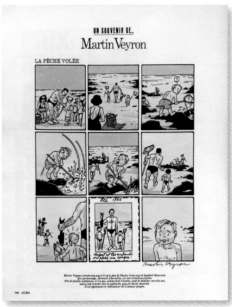

"A TABLE" Recipes with potatoes for kids. Photograph by Pierre Hussenot

"UN SOUVENIR DE . . ." (A Memory of . . .) A comic strip of family life on the last page. Illustration by Marin Veyron

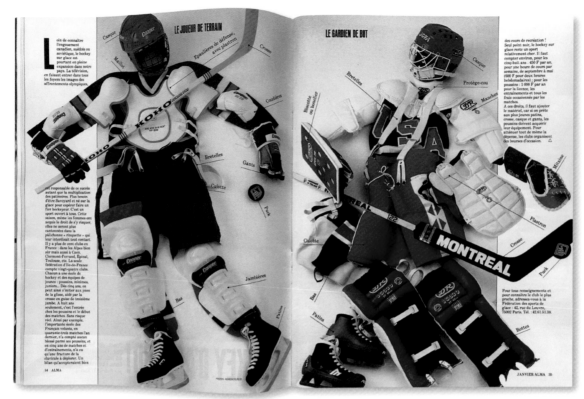

"HOCKEY D'ACCORD!" (Hockey, All Right!)
The anatomy of a list of kids' hockey equipment
with prices. Photograph by Bénédicte Petit

"QUOI DE NEUF BÉBÉ?" (What's Up Baby?) An
interview with Professor Hubert Montagner of
the University of Besançon about communicating
with children. Photograph by J. Guichard/Sygma

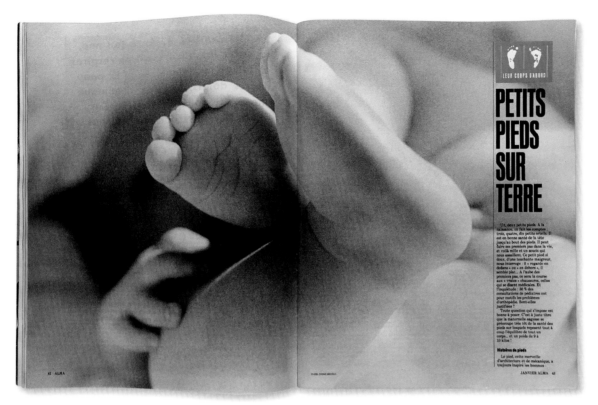

"LEUR CORPS D'ABORD" (Their Bodies First)
All about childrens' foot development and care.
Photograph by Sydnie Michele

"VIENS, JE T'EMMÈNE" (Come, I'll Take You)
Family travel to the Château Raray north of Paris.
Photographs by François Halard

DESIGNING WITH WOMEN: 3

Rebooting the Picture of Parenthood

The first-ever pregnancy magazine for women over thirty-five, started by "Rebekah from the block"

LIGHTHEARTED
The humorous format of this feature (above, left) and on the following pages is typical of the style throughout *Plum*. The cover (opposite) always pictured a happily pregnant woman. We made the *Plum* logo, originally designed by Matthew Egan, slightly thicker.

A design job arrives at your door in many mysterious ways. In the case of *Plum*, the words engraved in the window above our building entrance—"Art is Work"—was one reason founding editor Rebekah Meola approached us when she was looking to redesign the magazine in 2006.

"I contemplated the phrase often as pushing a rock up a hill," she says. "I saw the sign every day walking down Thirty-Second Street, where I lived in the early dream days of launching *Plum*. It was a reassuring mantra."

Born during a time when attitudes about pregnancy were changing, *Plum* was a bimonthly designed for women who were experiencing motherhood in their thirties and forties. Rebekah had a clear vision for the magazine, which is always key to getting a good design: "*Plum* was based on the idea that our readers were pregnant, but they weren't just pregnant. We set out to create a stylish, sophisticated, well-designed, yet fun magazine."

The five young women on our staff—Aurora Danon, Alicia Hallet, Molly Kromhout, Rebecca Marshall, and Patricia Rengifo— particularly liked the idea of a magazine that challenged the image of "geriatric pregnancies."

Plum got a stamp of approval from the American College of Obstetricians and Gynecologists and attracted 400,000 subscribers from the United States, Europe, South America, and the Middle East at its peak. The magazine ended its run in 2009 with a big scoop: an exclusive interview with soon-to-be-First Lady Michelle Obama, a personality who embodied the ideas that shaped its founding. Rebekah says, "I'm pretty sure that *Plum* was the only pregnancy magazine with a photographer on the campaign trail."

"ART IS WORK," the words engraved above the entrance to our building, inspired *Plum* magazine founder Rebekah Meola to approach WBMG for the redesign of her magazine.

REBEKAH MEOLA was the founder and publisher of *Plum* magazine from 2003 to 2009. She works in a management role at Internet Brands, an online media and software-as-a-service company.
Photo by Dalmiro Quiroga

THE COMPLETE PREGNANCY GUIDE FOR **WOMEN 35+**

FALL/WINTER 2006
$7.95

plum
something especially prized

MIND & BODY
How to Relax, Eat Well,
Exercise Right and
Take Good Care of Yourself

PRENATAL TESTING
A Comprehensive Review

Sustainable Chic Eco-Fashion Arrives
Designer **Linda Loudermilk**
creates a world of
environmentally friendly
luxury

SIX POINTS OF VIEW
How does having a
child change you?
A real-mom roundtable

YOU AND YOUR OB-GYN
PARTNERS IN HEALTH

Photograph by David Harry Stewart

Photographs by David Harry Stewart

The New Fertility Gods

BY KATHERINE STEWART

WITH ADDITIONAL

REPORTING

BY DEBRA GORDON

The ART and Science of Making Babies

*Above: Sheila Na Gig,
the goddess of fertility in
British-Celtic mythology.*

*Left: Akua'ba doll, carried by
infertile women of the Ashanti
tribe in Ghana.*

Leaving fertility up to nature, it turns out, has never been part of human nature. For thousands of years, our species has done everything in its power to sway the fickle winds of reproductive fortune. Fertility rites have been widely practiced in every culture, on every continent. From the 25,000-year-old carved fertility figures of the Paleolithic era, to the Sheila Na Gig, the goddess of fertility in British-Celtic mythology, to the Akua'ba doll, carried by barren women of the Ashanti tribe in Ghana, fertility symbols abound. Throughout history and around the world, men and women yearning for babies have made every effort to influence fate.

Today, instead of relying on myth and superstition, we look increasingly to science. Rapid advancements in reproductive technologies have altered the landscape of possibilities. In some instances, science simply gives nature a nudge, stimulating a woman's ovaries to produce greater numbers of eggs or uniting a sperm and egg with a greater degree of certainty. For others, science can correct a catalogue of genetic, age or disease-related problems.

Just a few decades ago, at a time when reproductive medicine was in its comparative infancy, the outlook was different. Many assisted reproductive techniques were poorly understood, and success rates were perhaps no better than those for praying to the rain gods.

ART AND SCIENCE TO THE RESCUE
Fast-forward to the present. The revolution in fertility treatments is only now gaining momentum, giving rise to new possibilities. Fertility clinics have proliferated—there are currently more than 428 registered with the Centers for Disease Control and Prevention (CDC) in Atlanta. Success rates are improving. In 2002, a total of 115,392 attempts at assisted reproduction resulted in 33,141 live birth deliveries and 45,751 infants. That's up from the 2001 figures of 107,587 attempts, 29,344 live birth deliveries and 40,687 infants.

People are even investing huge sums of money in research on new technologies and techniques, with spotty success rates, with the hope that those success rates will improve, too.

The growing numbers are indicative of widespread demand. According to a 2002 CDC report, 7.3 million American women and their partners—more than 10 percent of the reproductive-age population—have experienced infertility. As increasing numbers of couples delay childbearing into their 30s and 40s, that number is sure to rise. During

Photographs by Molly Kromhout

Photo illustration by Milton Glaser, Inc.

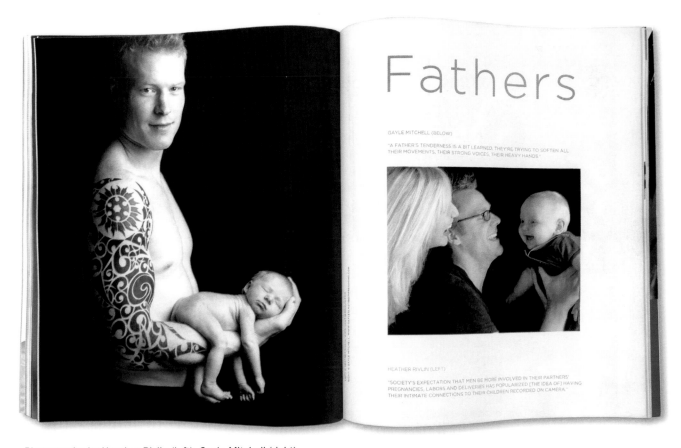

Photographs by Heather Rivlin (left), Gayle Mitchell (right)

223

Pre-internet Portfolios

THE ADWEEK PORTFOLIO OF
GRAPHIC DESIGN

Agencies once found creative talent on the pages of a special directory.

Conceived as a high-quality phone book, *Adweek Portfolios* showcased illustrators, graphic designers, photographers, and vendors working in the United States. The full-color volumes were distributed free to buyers in the advertising, television, and magazine industries. The production was paid for by professionals and firms who bought pages to show off their work.

Because *Adweek Portfolios* had virtually no editorial content, our primary task involved coming up with a unique cover for each edition. We had fun working on these because there were fewer constraints than with conventional magazines. With no cover lines or newsstand competition to worry about, the job was like designing a poster. We even had recurring jokes: For instance, the graphic design directory always had a telephone element, and the recurring cat-themed covers were puns on "cat-a-logue." Not to upset canine lovers, photographer Matthew Klein also managed to cast his beautiful bull terriers on several covers.

The internet eventually eliminated the need for *Adweek Portfolios*, but back issues, featuring outstanding artists and photographers, are now sold as collectibles.

PHONE CALLS The creative professionals who were listed in the *Adweek Portfolios* were waiting for one thing: the phone call from a potential client. The telephone became our theme on many of the covers, including the ones for graphic design (left) and photography (opposite), both photographed by Matthew Klein.

MATTHEW KLEIN is a photographer who has taught at Parsons and Pratt Institute. For the last twenty-five years he has specialized in food and still-life photography for advertising and packaging. His commercial photographs, he jokes, are currently in a group show in your local supermarket.
Photo: Matthew Klein

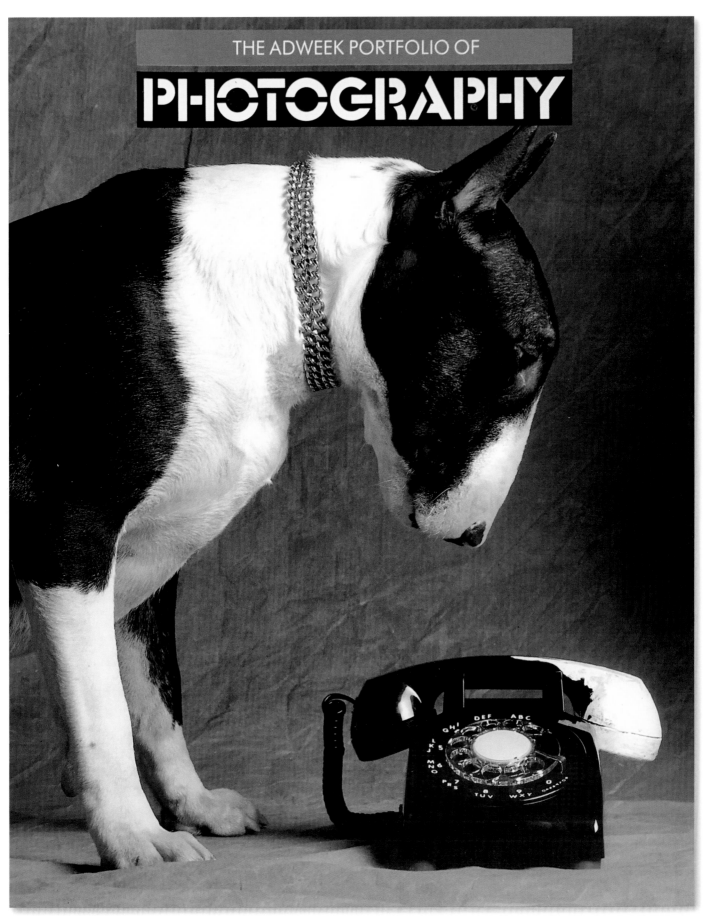

THE ADWEEK PORTFOLIO OF
PHOTOGRAPHY

Photograph by Matthew Klein

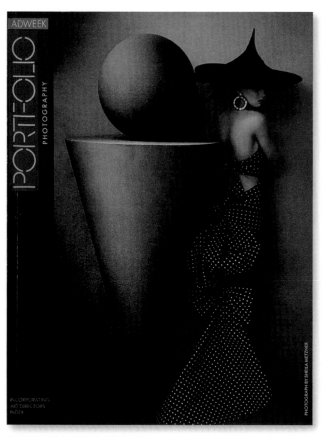

Photograph by Sheila Metzner

Illustration by James McMullan

Illustration by Elwood Smith

Photograph by Matthew Klein

Photograph by Giraldi-Suarez Productions

Photograph by Matthew Klein

Photograph by Matthew Klein

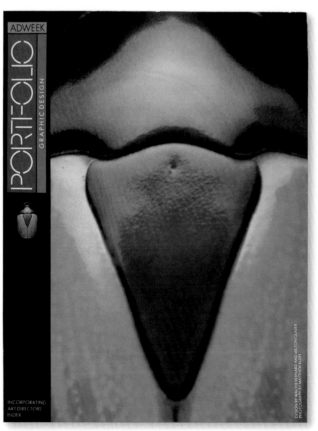

Photograph by Matthew Klein

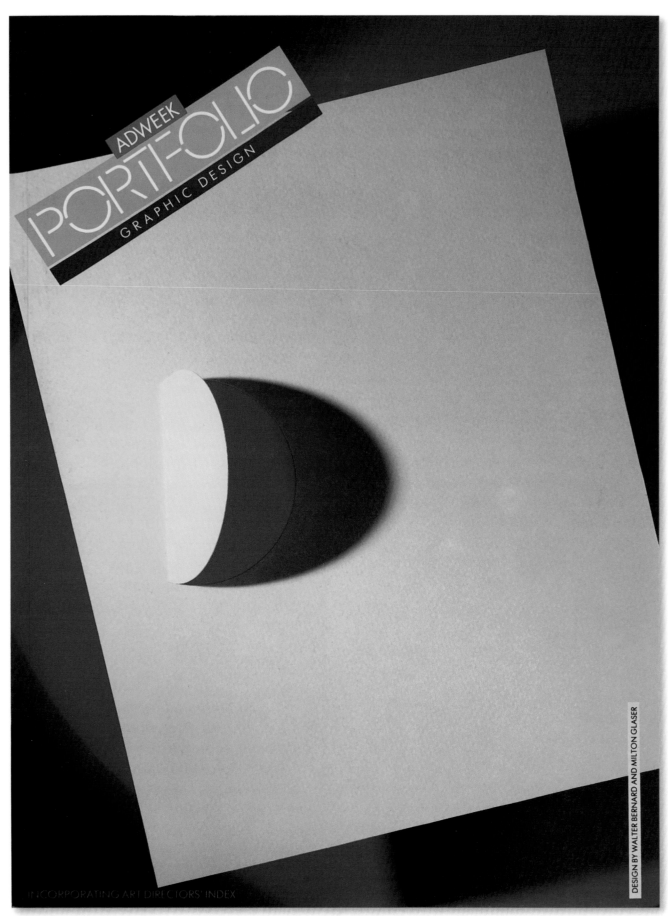

ADWEEK

PORTFOLIO

GRAPHIC DESIGN

INCORPORATING ART DIRECTORS' INDEX

DESIGN BY WALTER BERNARD AND MILTON GLASER

Photograph by Matthew Klein

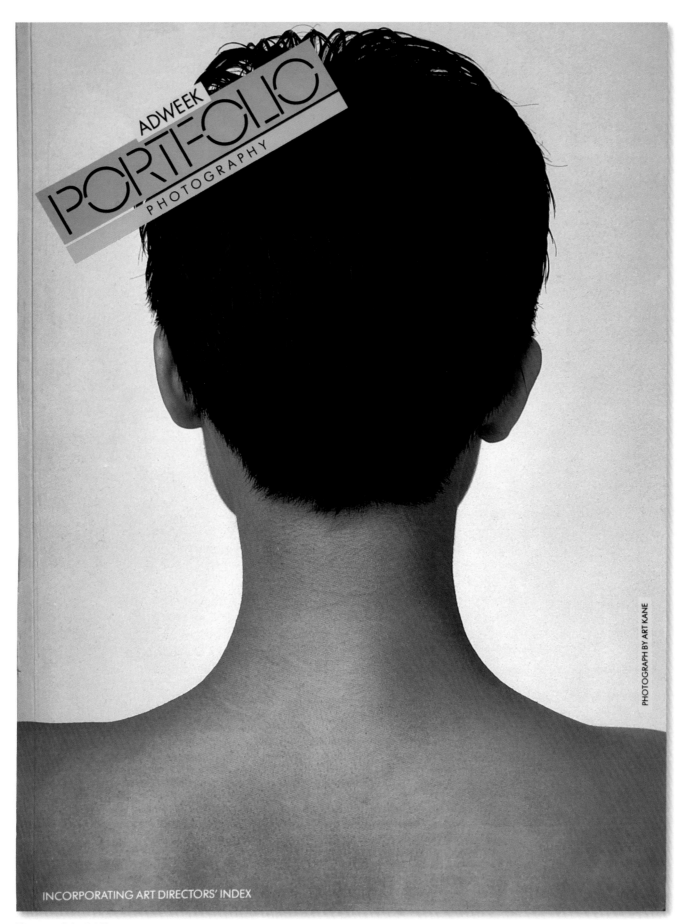

ADWEEK
PORTFOLIO
PHOTOGRAPHY

PHOTOGRAPH BY ART KANE

INCORPORATING ART DIRECTORS' INDEX

Photograph by Art Kane

229

Typecasting: Designer Eye Candy

The battle between clarity and expressive typography

Photo by H. Brooks Walker/Arts Counsel

Launched in 1970, *U&lc* was a journal conceived to showcase fonts produced by the International Typeface Corporation. Beloved by graphic designers and type fanatics, *U&lc* was a forum for experimenting with type compositions and unusual page layouts. Its purpose was simply to "show off typography and break boundaries."

We were given free rein to design two successive issues in 1991 with the condition that we use typefaces from ITC's collection. Though we had some good articles to pore over—a feature about printed ephemera, a profile of Ed Benguiat, and a cover profile of painter Brookie Maxwell by Joyce Rutter Kaye—we had a hunch that the graphic designers who composed most of *U&lc*'s audience were more interested in the drama that came out of the visuals than in the literary content.

The kind of expressive experimental typography championed by *U&lc* has often made it into mainstream magazines today. Many general interest publications rely on artistic treatments, often to the brink of incomprehensibility. But ultimately, doing something for effect without understanding its narrative is an art school trick. Being interesting and being understood don't necessarily need to be in opposition. It's always a balance between how much you can transgress tradition and how far you can take an audience before totally losing them.

The designers' tendency to favor visual acrobatics over legibility may be due to the fact that attentive reading isn't more formally encouraged in most design schools. Perhaps this is why it's so hard to convince graphic designers that words are their partners.

THE COVER IMAGE with artist Brookie Maxwell (left) was unusual because it didn't emphasize type. It purposely looked like a mainstream magazine meant to pique the curiosity of the typical *U&lc* reader. For the cover about ephemera (opposite), our collage used a large typographic *E* to announce the theme.

THE COLLECTORS

Open an issue of *Spy* magazine, or scan recent ads for the Brooklyn Academy of Music, and you'll likely see the typographic influence of the antique books and magazines graphic designer Stephen Doyle keeps by his side at Drenttel Doyle Partners, New York. Though their cultural lineage ranges from a classically elegant 16th century bible to the crude, cacophonous *National Enquirer*, Doyle maintains that they all have something in common: "Each has a quality that draws you closer to the printed page," he says. "There is always an element that delights." He points to an Italian magazine page which appears to be a flower pressed directly on top of type; as well as a title page with curved lettering that looks "more like farmland than type." Both have inspired Doyle's work: The flower, for example, prompted a *Spy* cover featuring writer/actor Chris Elliot "standing" on cover lines. And the title page influenced the curvy, playful type used in World Financial Center ads. All of Doyle's historical references bring to mind this credo he once shared in a talk at the Art Directors Club of New York: "Look backward, look forward, but never look sideways."—J.R.K. (Page 14)

On any particular day, Seattle-based designer Art Chantry can be seen adding to his ever-growing collection of ephemera: handbills, play money, party invitations, fortune-telling fish, whatever catches his eye and ends up in his pocket or on his desk. When he was asked to contribute to this survey, he admits that he "just grabbed a fistful of stuff" and sent it to *U&lc*. Like many collectors, Chantry began as a child. He explains, "I come from a long line of obsessive/compulsive behavior disorders. I collected everything as a kid, including bottle caps. I just discovered some of the collections in my mother's attic. I was really excited to find the monster trading cards I collected when I was six." Today as a professional designer, he views his collection of ephemera as having a serious purpose: "It's part of my personal esthetic. It's how I look at the world. I'm in the business of producing ephemera." He venerates what he describes as the "by-product of shared culture, anything from packages to billboards to scraps of paper I pick up off the street. There is something about the quality of something that is badly printed on cheap paper, thrown in the gutter, that you can't reproduce. We're not capable of reproducing this quality; it's the product of time and of our culture. I wanted to be an archaeologist at one time; I look at ephemera as contemporary archaeology."—K.C. (Page 15)

On an extended stay in Paris in 1977, the New York artist Bascove began to collect soap wrappers. Although she does not know when they were printed, her collection has the grace of a by-gone era. They also remind her of that time in her life when she was living and painting there. Attracted by their design, color and typography, she does not rely on them for inspiration in her work as an illustrator and book cover designer: "You could use this type on a book cover, but I don't do anything that has that kind of feeling."—K.C. (Page 18)

Other than matchbox labels, Lanny Sommese of Sommese Design also collects printed game boards, ceramic water pitchers, whirligigs and wind-up toys. This only proves the point that true collectors are rarely exclusive. They love their collections, but are rarely faithful to only one attraction. The matchbox covers featured in this issue interest Sommese "from a graphics and typography point of view. The designer is replying to the realities of production techniques and like other ephemera, they mirror society. In all my collections I like the way the pieces related to the times they were created in." Although about a third of Sommese's game boards are framed and hanging in his living room, his matchbox labels still reside in envelopes in a drawer, but he has considered framing them. Living in Pennsylvania where he is head of graphic design at Penn State University, Sommese is located in an area ripe with antiques and collectibles. He admits that when he doesn't see what he is looking for at the junk stores and flea markets he frequents, he will buy something else that interests him. "I see it. I buy it. I have a big house, but it's filling up."—K.C. (Page 19)

Our house is crammed with so many collections," admits Kristen Breslin, assistant professor of graphic design at Penn State University, echoing the sentiments of her husband, Lanny Sommese, whose matchbox covers are represented on page 19. Of all the collections of antique whirligigs, labels, board games and wind-up toys, Breslin most cherishes her collection of antique perfume and toiletry bottles and labels found in Reading, Pennsylvania antique stores. Many of the elaborate creations were designed during the Art Nouveau and Art Deco periods, but she says she is "not limited to those eras" when searching for new additions. One particular find was a collection of toiletry labels that a manufacturer had apparently never affixed to the intended bottles. Breslin realizes the irony of her collection: "I'm collecting them and preserving them. In a sense, they are being used for the opposite of what they were intended."—J.R.K. (Page 18)

Once Paul Davis, illustrator and designer of Paul Davis Design, New York, acquires something, he never throws it away. "I maintain the illusion that all this stuff is going to turn out to be useful, but I do not collect in any organized way," he says. In fact, Davis says that he "accumulates" rather than collects, and the things he tends to accumulate are man-made and natural objects: pots and sticks, for example, as well as printed ephemera, which he defines as "everyday graphics meant to be seen and discarded: temporary." These Davis sometimes incorporates into his collages, but often he relates to them as "found art" which can have an indirect influence on his typographic solutions. Davis is attracted to color and design and interesting letterforms. "I like everyday working type," he says.—M.R. (Page 17)

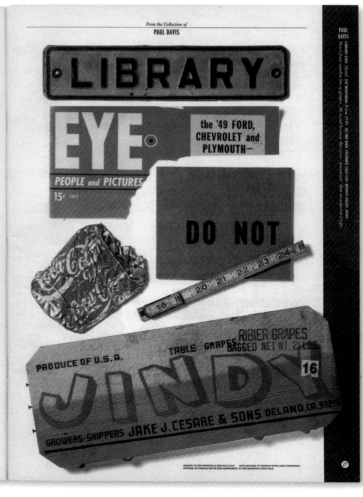

THE COLLECTORS of ephemera were numerous. Many well-known designers and illustrators are avid collectors and were happy to show us their treasures and write about them. Some supplied photographs, but most lent us items to be photographed by Matthew Klein. We ran a black bar alongside each photograph with captions describing the contents.

THE TEXT contained each collector's statement set in a variety of ITC typefaces. Sometimes rectangular, sometimes angular, but always in interlocking blocks, each text began with the same letter and was violated by a black bar containing the collector's name. These bars obscured words, but the message was surprisingly easy to read. It was our spoof on the art of typesetting.

Photograph by Matthew Klein

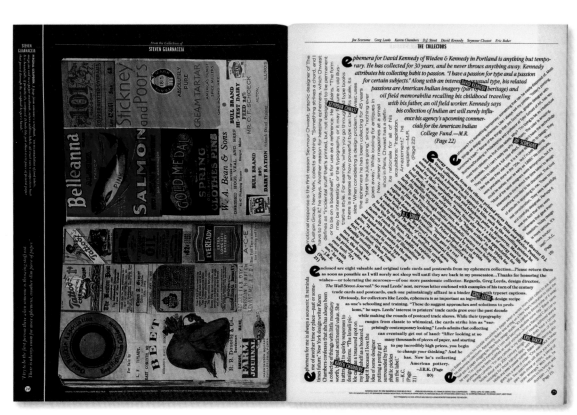

CRAZY CAPTION CHALLENGE: "The editorial team writing the captions—editor Margaret Richardson, writer Karen Chambers, and me, as managing editor—couldn't have possibly been prepared for the designers' eleventh-inning decision to further 'Marie Kondo' our text after much of it had finalized. . . . So the three of us dutifully returned to our Macintosh Classics to rewrite each of our captions to start with, in some cases, the letter O, or I or E or M, all the while laughing and occasionally horse trading (If I can take your 'On,' I'll give you my 'Once'). Somehow we even managed to avoid using the same opening word twice."—Joyce Rutter Kaye

Photograph by Matthew Klein

EACH ISSUE contained a major feature on a new ITC typeface series. This one celebrated Franklin Gothic Book Condensed, so we used a "book" motif to demonstrate designs using varieties of the Franklin Gothic fonts (left and below).

Photograph by Matthew Klein

THE LETTER R
Every issue also celebrated one letter of the alphabet, showing it in various typefaces and explaining a bit of its history. But illustrating the letterform in a graphic way was the challenge. Mirko Ilić's *R* (opposite) dissects the components of this Egyptian hieroglyph.

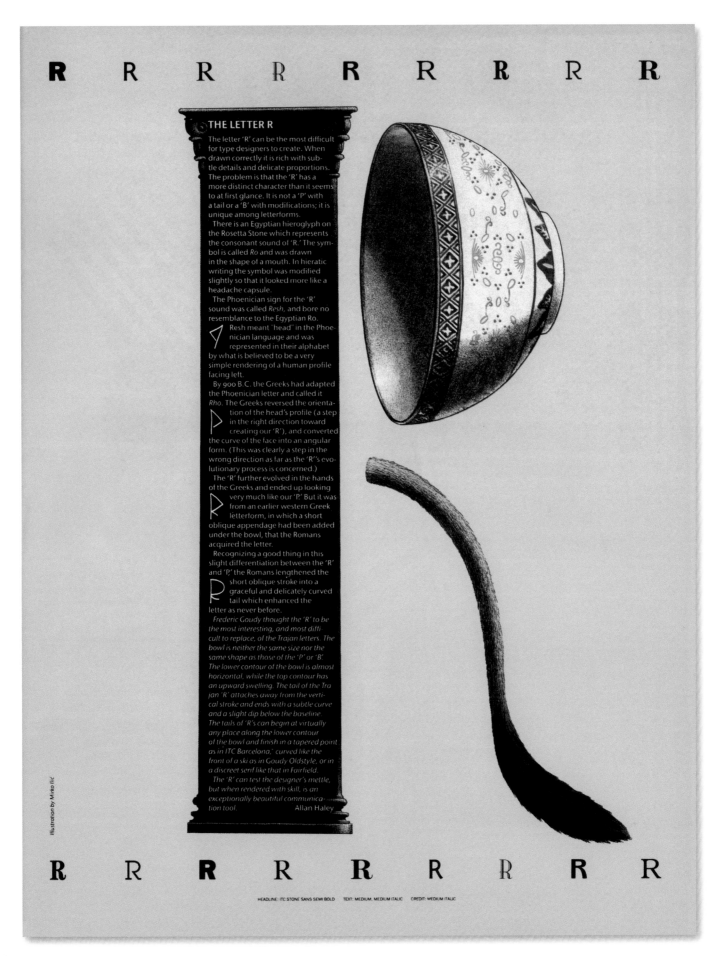

THE LETTER R

The letter 'R' can be the most difficult for type designers to create. When drawn correctly it is rich with subtle details and delicate proportions. The problem is that the 'R' has a more distinct character than it seems to at first glance. It is not a 'P' with a tail or a 'B' with modifications; it is unique among letterforms.

There is an Egyptian hieroglyph on the Rosetta Stone which represents the consonant sound of 'R.' The symbol is called *Ro* and was drawn in the shape of a mouth. In hieratic writing the symbol was modified slightly so that it looked more like a headache capsule.

The Phoenician sign for the 'R' sound was called *Resh*, and bore no resemblance to the Egyptian Ro. Resh meant "head" in the Phoenician language and was represented in their alphabet by what is believed to be a very simple rendering of a human profile facing left.

By 900 B.C. the Greeks had adapted the Phoenician letter and called it *Rho*. The Greeks reversed the orientation of the head's profile (a step in the right direction toward creating our 'R'), and converted the curve of the face into an angular form. (This was clearly a step in the wrong direction as far as the 'R''s evolutionary process is concerned.)

The 'R' further evolved in the hands of the Greeks and ended up looking very much like our 'P.' But it was from an earlier western Greek letterform, in which a short oblique appendage had been added under the bowl, that the Romans acquired the letter.

Recognizing a good thing in this slight differentiation between the 'R' and 'P,' the Romans lengthened the short oblique stroke into a graceful and delicately curved tail which enhanced the letter as never before.

Frederic Goudy thought the 'R' to be the most interesting, and most difficult to replace, of the Trajan letters. The bowl is neither the same size nor the same shape as those of the 'P' or 'B.' The lower contour of the bowl is almost horizontal, while the top contour has an upward swelling. The tail of the Trajan 'R' attaches away from the vertical stroke and ends with a subtle curve and a slight dip below the baseline. The tails of 'R's can begin at virtually any place along the lower contour of the bowl and finish in a tapered point as in ITC Barcelona, curved like the front of a ski as in Goudy Oldstyle, or in a discreet serif like that in Fairfield.*

The 'R' can test the designer's mettle, but when rendered with skill, is an exceptionally beautiful communication tool.   Allan Haley

Illustration by Mirko Ilić

HEADLINE: ITC STONE SANS SEMI BOLD   TEXT: MEDIUM, MEDIUM ITALIC   CREDIT: MEDIUM ITALIC

A WBMG MEETING in our conference room with editors from *L'Expansion*. We are shown with Killian Jordan, our studio manager, taking notes next to Jean-Pierre Montagne, art director of *L'Expansion*.
Photo by Matthew Klein

A Magazine About Magazines

Satisfying the hunger for news and gossip about the magazine industry

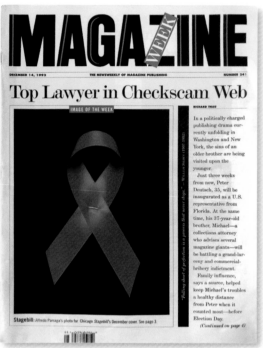

Against the backdrop of the last golden age in magazine publishing, *Adweek*'s owners asked us to redesign *Magazine Week* when they bought the four-year-old trade publication in 1992. The creative brief: Transform *Magazine Week* into a lively, must-read periodical befitting the fast-paced, still flourishing print industry.

As a tabloid-sized weekly, it had neither a big budget nor a big staff. But its editor-in-chief, Gary Hoenig, was inventive. He recruited talented contributors and created sections that delighted readers. They included "Out There," a roundup of wacky periodicals; "Hello and Goodbye," about job transitions; "Stats," an infographic of amusing magazine-related trivia; and "Dr. Magazine," a kind of Dr. Phil for magazine wonks.

Our greatest contribution was devising a way for the magazine to get free images for its covers. We suggested that they choose a striking image from a magazine or advertisement and celebrate it as "Image of the Week." To help with the research, we also suggested they invite readers to nominate images they found worthy of the honor. It worked pretty well. We designed a new logo, emphasizing the word "magazine," to signal *Magazine Week*'s new attitude.

After over 250 issues, *Magazine Week*'s run ended when electronic publishing emerged in mainstream media. In 1993, *Adweek* sold the magazine to Cowles Media Company, which decided to combine it with *Folio* magazine.

NEWS DRIVEN
Wanting to discard the look of every other trade newspaper, *Magazine Week* drastically changed its format (above left) to a more graphic announcement (right) featuring one major story on the cover.

GARY HOENIG became editor of *Magazine Week* in 1992. He was editor of the *ESPN* magazine prototype and later became the editor-in-chief of *ESPN The Magazine* in 2003. Since 2014, he has been the editorial director of *The Player's Tribune*.
Photo: Gary Hoenig

MAGAZINE WEEK

OCTOBER 19, 1992 · THE NEWSWEEKLY OF MAGAZINE PUBLISHING · NUMBER 234

FIRST PICK

Rolling Stone October 29: The dread Sinead sans props by Albert Watson. See page 3.

"A reporter is a primitive being who would go after his own mother if that was a good story." — COLUMNIST RICHARD COHEN

An Old Feud Heats Up...

IRIS COHEN SELINGER

No one would ever say Steve Florio is shy. Adjacent to his handsome, very cherry wood office at *The New Yorker*, is his shrine — a private bathroom lined with photographs and framed newspaper articles of his successes. In fact, within the corridors of Conde Nast, Florio's self-promotion is sometimes jokingly compared to Don King's.

But the *New Yorker* president hardly corners the prima donna market at Conde Nast.

(Continued on page 21)

239

On May 18, 1980, a magnitude 5.1 earthquake struck Washington state, below Mount St. Helens, and triggered a landslide that exposed the core of the volcano. A major volcanic eruption followed, with ash falling as far away as Minnesota. The blast removed 1,300 feet of the mountain's summit, sending forth shockwaves, mudslides, and pyroclastic flows, destroying the surrounding landscape for hundreds of miles. Fifty-seven people were killed.

FAILURE TO LAUNCH: 1
Imitating a Literary Success

READABLE This interview with Robert Benton by Bina Bernard (left) was the only real article in our prototype, apart from the Cinemacrostic. The illustration by David Levine includes characters from Benton's films *The Late Show* and *Kramer vs. Kramer*. Opposite, Levine's cover of John Travolta in *Urban Cowboy*.

Like the man who invented the shoelace, we couldn't understand why no one had thought of this before.

Inspired by our shared love of movies, Ed Sorel, David Levine, and I had a concept for a different kind of film magazine. A departure from breezy celebrity-focused periodicals, of which there were plenty, ours was to be a serious publication modeled after *The New York Review of Books*.

We envisioned a publication where major writers, journalists, and historians would review films and conduct in-depth interviews. The tone would be stereophonic—light and serious, learned and impassioned, scholarly and vernacular. David and Ed—both masters of caricature—would supply "sight gags." *The New York Film Review* would spur satisfying conversations about films, filmmakers, and their audiences. It would bring you everything but the popcorn.

We produced a prototype issue in a large (11" x 14") format. The simple design, set in an elegant Bodoni typeface, featured substantial essays, large illustrations, opinion columns, and a thematic puzzle section called "Cinemacrostic."

Since we had a long list of established writers eager to write for us, we thought we could raise the money for our venture and attract advertisers. Ultimately, our efforts proved inadequate. We realized that even with seventy-five years of combined professional editorial experience, we were amateurs at the business side of publishing. Even Joe Armstrong, a former publisher of *New York* and *Rolling Stone*, who raised $2.5 million for *The Movies* magazine, called it quits after five issues. In 1980, we believed there was a sizable audience of movie buffs like ourselves, avidly seeking insightful things to read about films. We were wrong.—WB

EDWARD SOREL, a caricaturist, cartoonist, designer and author, cofounded Push Pin Studios with Milton Glaser, Seymour Chwast, and Reynold Ruffins in 1953. His work has appeared in all major magazines and many children's books. Sorel is also the author of several books, including *Mary Astor's Purple Diary: The Great American Sex Scandal of 1936*, published in 2016.
Photo by Tobey Sanford

FOLLOWING PAGE
Ed Sorel's illustration of "The Warner Mob," an example of a proposed regular double-page series by Sorel and Levine.

A Conversation with Robert Benton

The New York Film Review

Tom Wolfe on
'Urban Cowboy'

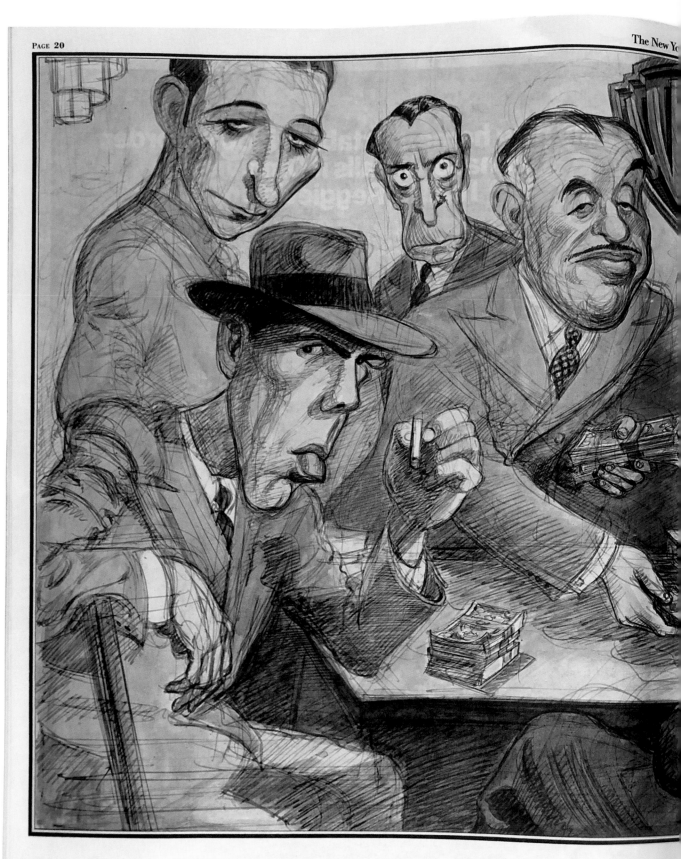

THE WARNER MOB

CIRCA 1938

CLOCKWISE FROM LEFT:
HUMPHREY BOGART, GEORGE RAFT, EDUARDO CIANNELLI, JACK L. WARNER, BARTON MACLANE,
JOHN GARFIELD, EDWARD G. ROBINSON, JAMES CAGNEY

FAILURE TO LAUNCH: 2

Going Global, but Going Nowhere

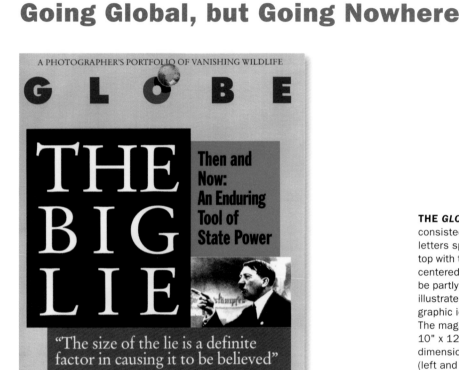

A PHOTOGRAPHER'S PORTFOLIO OF VANISHING WILDLIFE

G L O B E

THE BIG LIE

Then and Now: An Enduring Tool of State Power

"The size of the lie is a definite factor in causing it to be believed"

THE *GLOBE* LOGO consisted of Futura Black letters spaced across the top with the idea that the centered *O* would always be partly eclipsed by an illustrated globe or another graphic idea (opposite). The magazine's size was 10" x 12", unusual dimensions. These covers (left and opposite) demonstrate our emphasis on words as visual imagery.

Globe was based on a single, unifying concept: the connectedness across national and even regional boundaries.

Years before "globalization" became an established media buzzword, *Time*'s foreign affairs columnist Strobe Talbott had the foresight to create a magazine that would tackle the fascinating cross-pollination of ideas across geographic borders. Simply named "Globe," it would be a first-of-its-kind publication to interpret and synthesize international events in the broadest perspective. Strobe was also keen about hiring non-American writers at *Globe*: "The world as a whole will not only be our subject, but our talent pool as well."

Over the course of three years, we worked with Strobe to gain the support of Time Inc. for his venture. We created sections like "World Watch," a graphic summary of current events plotted on a map, and an extended contributors section highlighting the diversity of voices.

Despite our best efforts, *Globe* flunked reader tests and was never published. "I'm obviously deeply disappointed, as I know you guys are too," wrote Strobe in a note to us in December 1992. "I haven't given up. I'm convinced that there is a great and successful magazine to be done there."

But Strobe had to put his dream magazine aside when Bill Clinton (his roommate from Oxford University) appointed him to the U.S. State Department in 1993.

STROBE TALBOTT is a journalist, diplomat, and academic. He is among the most distinguished foreign policy experts in the United States. During his twenty-one years at *Time* magazine, he covered Eastern Europe, the State Department, and the White House, then became Washington bureau chief, editor-at-large, and foreign affairs columnist. He served as the Deputy Secretary of State for seven years. He is the founding director of the Yale Center for the Study of Globalization and was president of the Brookings Institution until 2017.

THE FIRE NEXT TIME

On May 28th, 1990, the world came closer than ever to nuclear war. The antagonists? India and Pakistan. A report on this and other conflicts that could reach critical mass in the next decade.

Clay model by Robert Grossman

Illustration by James McMullan

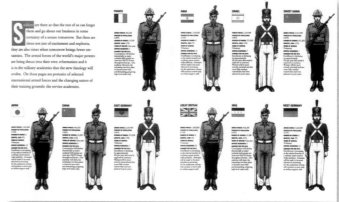

Illustration by Mirko Ilić

Illustration by Julian Allen

WORLD WATCH (top)
World maps pinpointing events of interest would be presented in a different graphic style in each issue.

VANISHING CADET (middle)
A feature about the reduced ranks of military cadets around the world included illustrations of each country's uniforms.

THE FALL OF KUWAIT (left)
The amir of Kuwait fleeing Kuwait City during the Iranian invasion.

DEBATE While we were developing the magazine, the issue of the name kept surfacing. Should it be *Globe* or *Globe Review*? As shown in the studies (opposite), we were exploring both options. In the end, we were leaning toward *Globe Review*, but it was never resolved.

Design by WBMG

Photograph by Matthew Klein

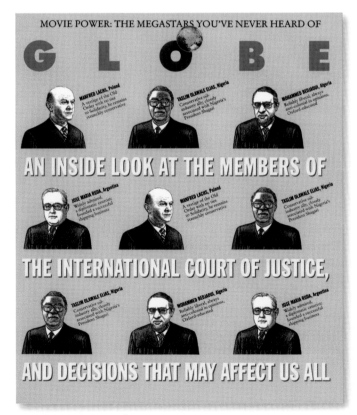

Illustration by Mirko Ilić

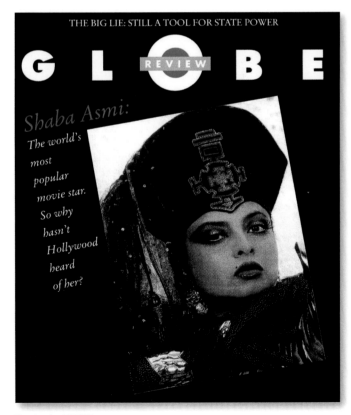

Design by WBMG

FAILURE TO LAUNCH: 3
Motivating Creativity

JUMP-STARTING the issue on the contents page was Herb Ritt's photograph of Jackie Joyner-Kersee, Olympic track and field medalist.

An open-ended concept that seemed like a good idea at the time.

While celebrating human invention and creativity, *Inspired*, as its name suggests, aimed to document how successful people find their creative spark. With the inaugural issue, the editors wanted to get people fired up. "We hope you'll feel the drive and energy that drives our subjects to create." The magazine was commissioned by Knowledge Universe, an educational company led by financier Michael Milken. We were given a free hand in the graphic design and editorial makeup of *Inspired*. This was an unusual arrangement. We were used to working shoulder-to-shoulder with editors to get a new magazine off the ground.

We designed a prototype with three variations of the cover. The quirky calligraphic logo was meant to evoke the magazine's unorthodox sensibility and set the stage for an "inspiring read." The issue contained articles about Dale Chihuly, Junot Diaz, Lauryn Hill, and Cirque du Soleil. It was completely photo-driven because of the subject matter, but in future editions, we anticipated featuring art and illustrations. Text and headlines were set in Galliard, a font based on the sixteenth-century typeface by French type designer Robert Granjon.

It was a promising magazine concept, but *Inspired* never saw the light of day. Soon after we completed the issue, Milken decided to divert his attention and resources to cancer care and canceled the project.

No.0

$5.00

An Encounter
With Cirque
du Soleil

Catching
Lauryn Hill

The Starry
Nights of
Wu Xia Liu

DALE CHIHULY
The Glass Alchemist

Photograph by Herb Ritts

Portrait of Dale Chihuly by Herb Ritts

Photograph courtesy of Dale Chihuly

Photograph by Ellen Von Unwerth

Photographs of founders courtesy of Cirque du Soleil
Photograph on right by Véronique Vial

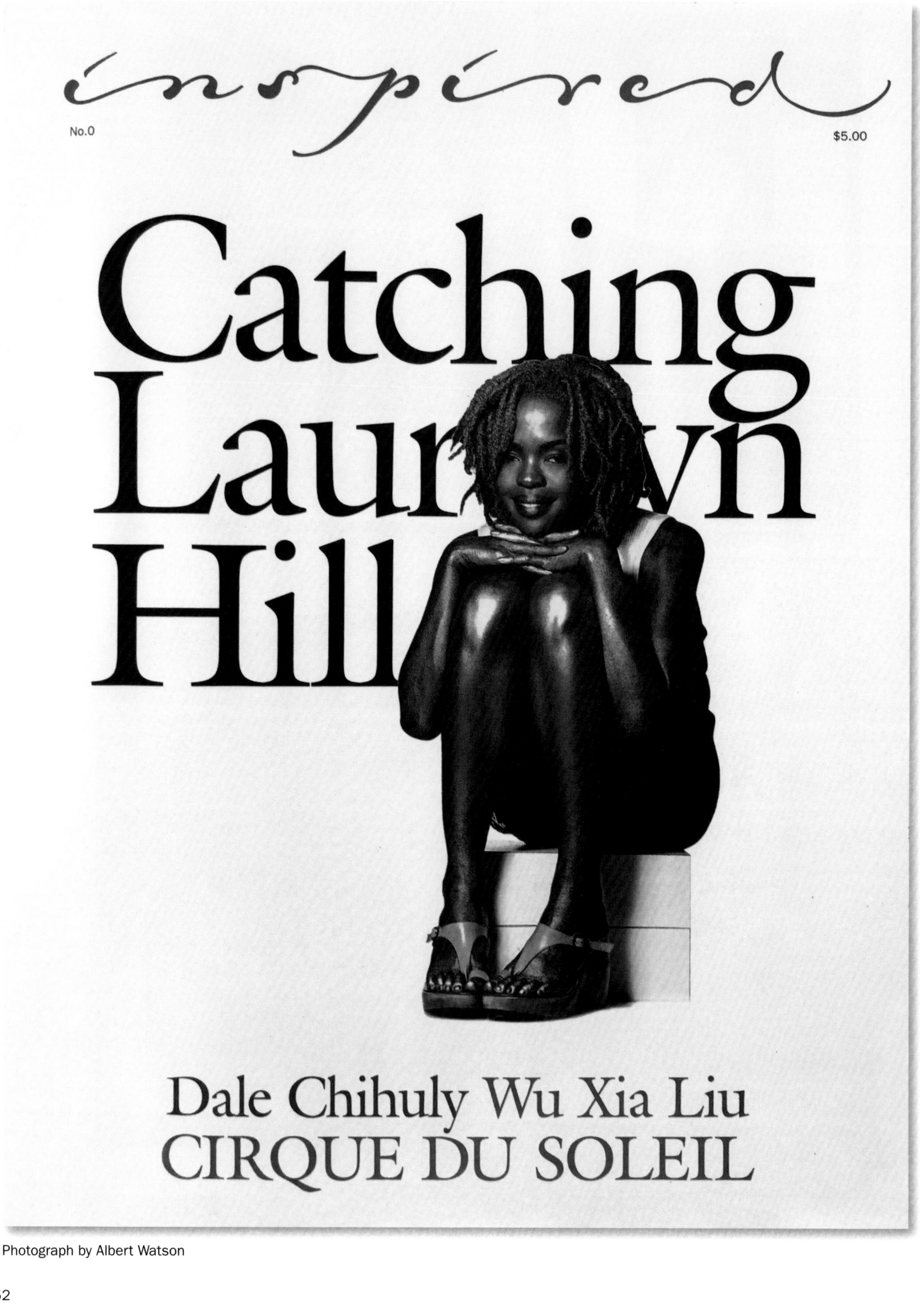

No.0

inspired

$5.00

Catching Lauryn Hill

Dale Chihuly Wu Xia Liu
CIRQUE DU SOLEIL

Photograph by Albert Watson

No.0

$5.00

An Encounter with Cirque du Soleil

Dale Chihuly:
The Glass
Alchemist

Starry Nights
of Wu Xia Liu

Catching
Lauryn Hill

Photograph courtesy of Cirque du Soleil

The Face of the Future

Hollywood CGI magic illustrated the changing complexion of America's identity.

FUTUREFACE
As a teenager in 1993,
Alex Wagner saw herself
on this *Time* cover. She
recalls: "In high school,
I wanted to belong—badly.
As the mixed-race, only
child of Burmese-Irish-
Luxembourgian stock,
finding the people whom
I could call my own was . . .
complicated. I wasn't
Burmese, I wasn't Europe-
an, I was something
else—but what was that?
In November of 1993,
Time magazine heralded
on its cover 'The New Face
of America,' a composite
image that kind of (if
you squinted or were legally
blind) looked like me.
It was a revelation: I was
a precursor, sent from
the future, to show my
fellow citizens what
they would all look like a
few generations hence.
I may not have found my
people, but I found myself.
Maybe that was even
better—I was futureface!"

ALEX WAGNER is a
journalist and author of
*FutureFace: A Family
Mystery, an Epic Quest,
and the Secret to Belonging.*
She is a contributor to
CBS News and a contribut-
ing editor to *The Atlantic.*
Wagner is the cohost of
The Circus on Showtime.
Photo: Alex Wagner

R ace and ethnicity were hot topics in the United States in
1993. Newly elected President Bill Clinton promised to
build an administration that "looks like America," alluding
to the diversity of immigrant populations in the country.

This was the subject of the first of four special issues we
designed for *Time*. Building on Jill Smolowe's cover story about
interracial marriages, we had the idea of combining the faces
of fourteen people from various ethnic backgrounds. The woman
on the cover is the result.

We worked with *Time*'s imaging whiz Kin Wah Lam, who clocked
sixty-five hours on a Macintosh Quadra 900 running a software
package called Morph 2.0 to produce the cover image and an illustrative chart (opposite). Morph was a version of the film industry's special-effects technology used to generate the memorable face-morphing sequence in Michael Jackson's "Black or White"
music video and the shape-shifting villain in the film *Terminator 2*.

Our cybergenetic experiment looks convincingly human—so
much so that a young Alex Wagner saw herself in this image.

REBIRTH OF A NATION, COMPUTER-STYLE

OW DO YOU GO ABOUT CREATING THE 49 COMBInations of progeny from the seven men and seven women featured in the TIME picture chart shown below? Doing so by the scientific rules of genetic engineering—themselves extremely complex and not yet fully understood—would be impossible. Instead, TIME chose a software package called Morph 2.0, produced by Gryphon, to run on a Macintosh Quadra 900. The Morph 2.0 is an offspring of Hollywood's sophisticated special-effects equipment used to produce such eye poppers as Michael Jackson's celebrated metamorphosis in his *Black or White* video and the evil robot that wreaks havoc in *Terminator 2*.

Morph 2.0 enabled TIME to pinpoint key facial features on the photos of the 14 people of various racial and ethnic backgrounds chosen for the chart. Electronic dots defined head size, skin color, hair color and texture, eyebrows, the contours of the lips, nose and eyes, even laugh lines around the mouth. The eyes in particular required many key points to make them as detailed as possible; otherwise the results would be very erratic. Similarly, miscalculating the dimensions of an upper lip only slightly, for example, could badly skew the resulting face.

Most of the images, or "morphies," on the chart are a straight 50-50 combination of the physical characteristics of their progenitors, though an entirely different image can

be created by using, say, 75% of the man's eyes, or 75% of the woman's lips. After the eyes, the most important parental feature is the neck, which often determines the gender of the morph offspring.

Sometimes pure volume counts. The more information extracted from a given feature, the more likely that feature is to dominate the cybernetic offspring. Even when the program is weighted 50-50, if an African man has more hair than a Vietnamese woman, his hair will dominate; the same thing applies to larger lips or a jutting jaw. One of our tentative unions produced a distinctly feminine face—sitting atop a muscular neck and hairy chest. Back to the mouse on that one. ∎

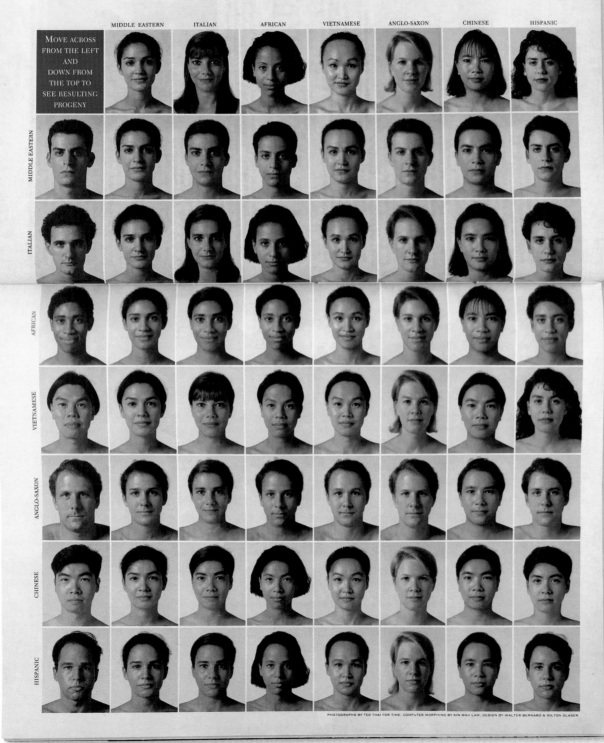

An Impossible Task?

AARP was eager to satisfy two audiences with one magazine.

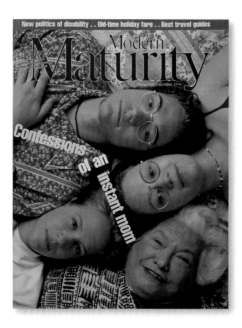

COVER CHANGE
Although there was a debate about changing the name, it was decided to keep *Modern Maturity*. We modified the old logo (left) to emphasize "Modern." Our first cover (opposite) was a symbolic reaction to "Black Rock," a nickname for CBS (referring to its new office building), canceling *Murder, She Wrote*, one of the network's most popular shows. That is not Angela Lansbury under the rock.

With a circulation of 23.5 million, *Modern Maturity* held the distinction of being America's most-read magazine. The bimonthly was sent to members of the American Association of Retired People (AARP) age fifty and over.

This large intergenerational spectrum posed a big editorial challenge and was confusing to advertisers. How can a car ad resonate with bedridden seniors? Or a wheelchair promo for healthy active adults traveling the world?

We both fell within this age range (Milton was sixty-six, Walter, fifty-eight) when we got the assignment and felt sympathetic to the editors' struggles. One of the first things we did was separate AARP's advocacy section called "Perspectives" from the rest of the book. This created a clearer distinction between the editorial content and their lobbying efforts.

Working with editor Henry Fenwick and executive editor Tom Dworetzky, we developed an eclectic editorial mix including photo essays and articles about world events. Henry, who had previously been at *Playboy* and the BBC, was especially eager to find ways to get fifty- and sixty-year-olds "to open the book and see something in there for them." We brought in cartoonist Stan Mack to inject humor with his comic page called "Stan Mack's True Tales" and proposed a "She Said He Said" column featuring a lighthearted dialogue about one topic. We also gave the magazine an overall clean-up and simplified the layout in many cases. When designing for aging readers, you have to inject clarity above all.

Ultimately, *Modern Maturity*'s biggest problem was its name. The word "maturity" was laden with deep-seated cultural stigma that a redesign can't undo. In 2003, AARP finally rebranded to "AARP: The Magazine"—a neutral and inoffensive name.

J. HENRY FENWICK
was the editor of *Modern Maturity* (now *AARP* magazine) in 1995. He was an academic and reviewer before working at *Playboy* magazine and BBC Publications.

TOM DWORETZKY was *Modern Maturity*'s executive editor (1991–1994). He was an associate editor, writer, and columnist at *Omni*, a writer and columnist at *Discover*, and founder of *ADAM* magazine, which launched with a WBMG cover and logo in 2002. Tom has since been an online editor for *IBT* and the *New York Daily News*.
Photo by Walter Hang

AARP PERSPECTIVES
WHAT WILL THE FUTURE BRING?

MODERN Maturity

The Plot to Murder 'Murder, She Wrote'

Photograph by Matthew Klein

"FRONT LINES," a new section opening with "ID," a personal account by a well-known figure.

"SHE SAID HE SAID" illustrates two people in a relationship with opposing views with interlocking text columns.

"ESSAY," a regular feature by Roger Rosenblatt, always illustrated by Guy Billout.

"TRUE TALES" Stan Mack's comic strip was based on actual dialogue overheard in the course of his travels.

"MM INTERVIEW" We introduced a new graphic treatment for this interview with Gerry Adams, leader of Sinn Fein, and British Prime Minister John Major on Northern Ireland's "Troubles."
Photographs: Jerry Adams by Andrew Moore/Katz/Saba, John Major by Annie Liebovitz/Contact Press

"CRIMSON HARVEST" The rich history and fascinating factoids of cranberry farming in New Jersey.
Photographs by Cameron Davidson

Photograph by Alen MacWeeney

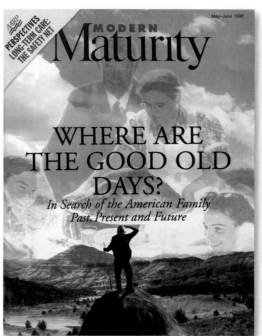

Photo collage by Mirko Ilić

Freedom from Want by Norman Rockwell © The Curtis Publishing Co.

Photographs: Roosevelt, South Dakota Tourism;
Moseley-Braun by Steven Rubin

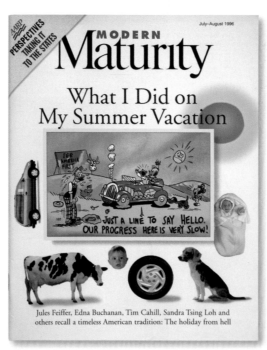

Postcard courtesy of Steven Guarnaccia

THE DIVERSITY of topics that the new *Modern Maturity* was trying to present are reflected in these covers. Top row: Etiquette with humor from the popular Miss Manners and nostalgia with a scene from *Freedom from Want* by Norman Rockwell. Bottom row: Celebrating the women of Washington, D.C., combining Theodore Roosevelt and Carol Moseley-Braun, and a humorous look at leisure fun for active seniors. Opposite: A play on words, as boomers face the fear of aging.

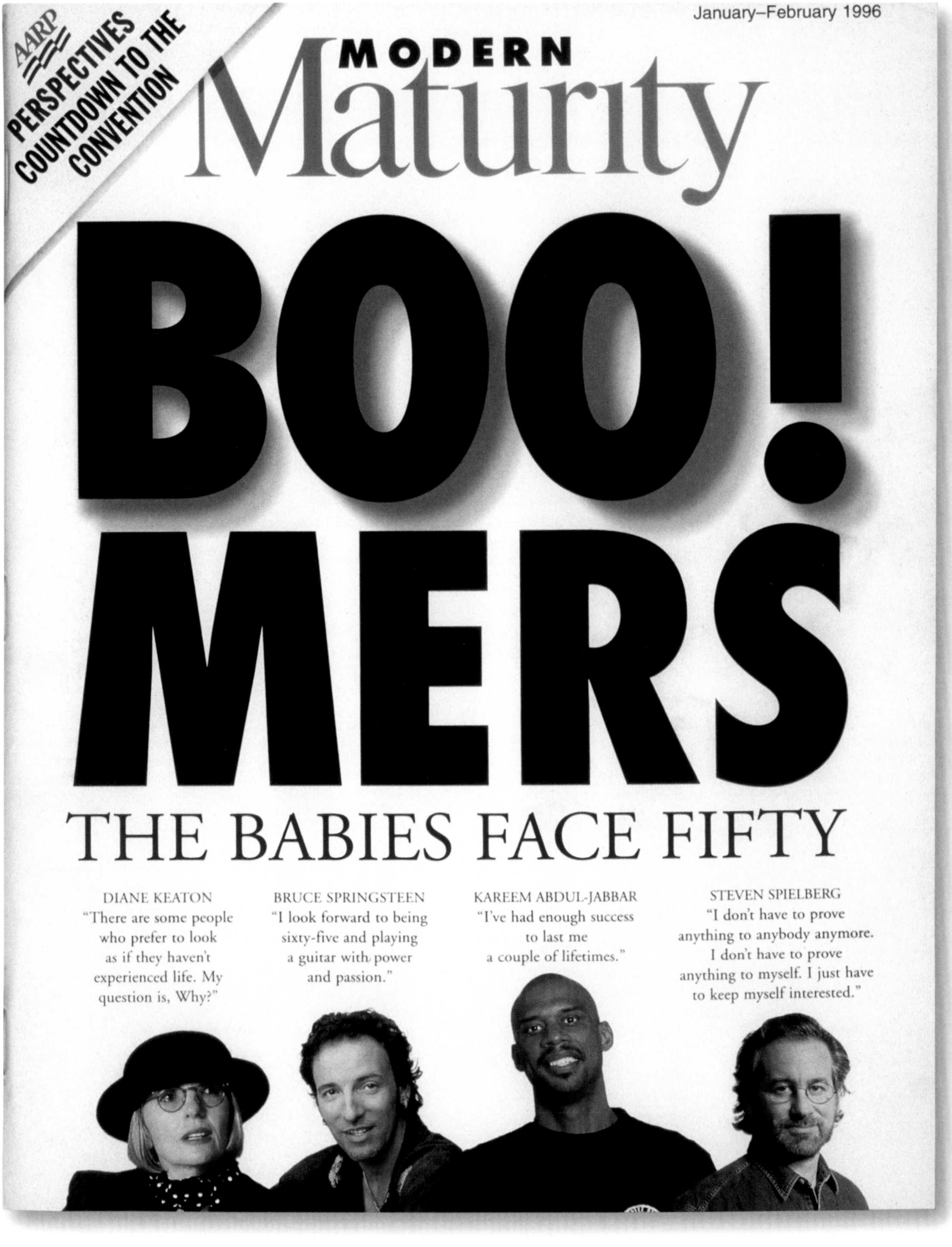

MODERN
Maturity

BOO!
MERS

THE BABIES FACE FIFTY

DIANE KEATON
"There are some people
who prefer to look
as if they haven't
experienced life. My
question is, Why?"

BRUCE SPRINGSTEEN
"I look forward to being
sixty-five and playing
a guitar with power
and passion."

KAREEM ABDUL-JABBAR
"I've had enough success
to last me
a couple of lifetimes."

STEVEN SPIELBERG
"I don't have to prove
anything to anybody anymore.
I don't have to prove
anything to myself. I just have
to keep myself interested."

Fortune, "Deboned"

A savory metaphor describes our approach to a redesign.

The Redesign Team: Margery Peters, Walter Bernard, Milton Glaser, Nancy Eising.
Photo for *Fortune* by Nina Barnett

BEFORE

AFTER (design study)

After his first year as managing editor, John Huey embarked on a wholesale rethink of the entire magazine, both visually and editorially. He was looking to change many things, except for *Fortune*'s art director. Margery Peters, the bright young woman who had guided the graphics for the past thirteen years, became his close partner in the process.

John and Margery decided that they needed an external team to evaluate the magazine with fresh eyes. Apparently, it was a metaphor about redesigning a magazine that won us the project. John says:

> We made the rounds of all the big design firms and took their pitches. WBMG was our last stop. The firm was so well known at Time Inc. On one hand, I was inclined to want to go that way, but on the other, I thought maybe we needed to branch out. I was excited to meet the legendary Milton Glaser. (I already knew Walter.) We sat down at the big table, and I laid out what I wanted the magazine to become.
>
> Milton mulled it over for a minute or two, then launched into an elaborate metaphor in which he related the restructuring of a magazine to the deboning of a chicken—in visceral detail.
>
> I had never been able to debone a chicken and I actually had no comprehension of what he was saying. I loved the metaphor so much, though, that I knew right then we were going to go with WBMG. It was a great decision. They gave us exactly what we wanted, and it worked exceptionally well. In the years to come I would occasionally lapse into my imitation of Milton's deboning theory just to confound the more literal-minded among us.

Working closely with the *Fortune* team, we cooked up a version that Kurt Andersen of *Studio 360* called "newsier, tougher, sexier, and funnier."

HOW MUCH CHANGE?
Since *Fortune* simply needed refreshing, we had to consider what to keep and what to discard. In a design study, we retained the current logo (top), which had been redesigned much too often, and tried to lighten up the overall design by injecting humor into the mix as well as adapting a lighter type style. The first issue of the redesign (opposite) displayed a new half-circle motif repeated on pages throughout the issue. This distinctly unbusinesslike cover was photographed by Louis Psihoyos/Matrix.

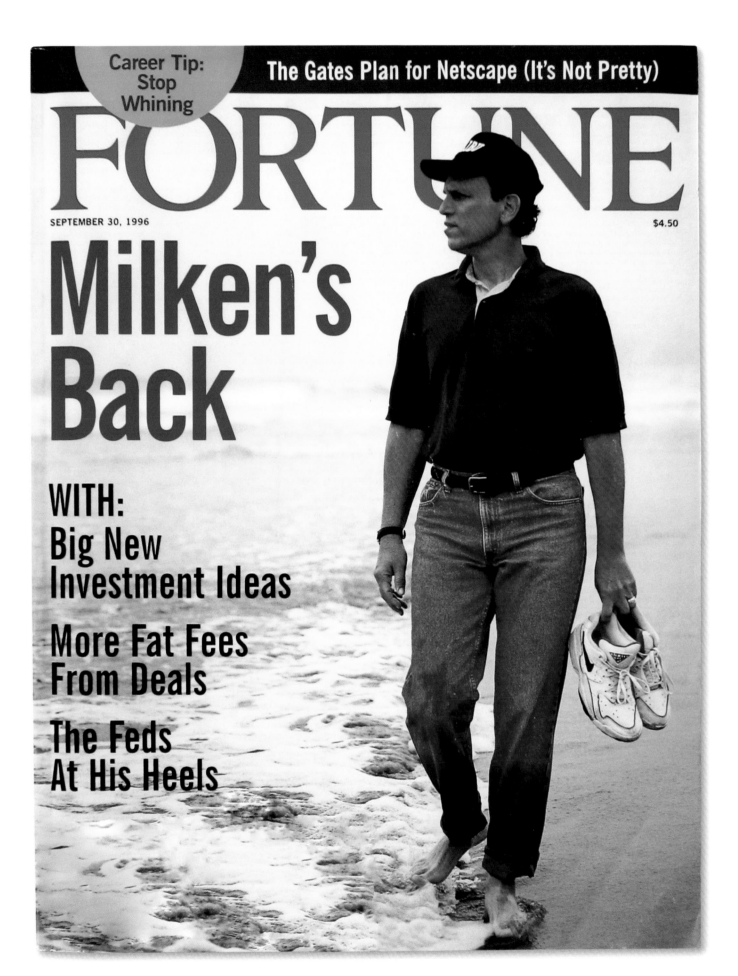

Career Tip:
Stop
Whining

The Gates Plan for Netscape (It's Not Pretty)

FORTUNE

SEPTEMBER 30, 1996

$4.50

Milken's Back

WITH:
**Big New
Investment Ideas**

**More Fat Fees
From Deals**

**The Feds
At His Heels**

BEFORE: "News Trends," the opening section of the front matter.

AFTER: "First," a new section label, with a simpler organization.

BEFORE: A classic *Fortune* layout for a profile of a major figure.

AFTER: In this study, we presented a more dramatic alternative.

BEFORE: At first glance, the reader might think that the two figures in the picture form the "alliance from hell." In fact, they are partners, and their rival in the alliance is not pictured.

AFTER: In this study, the "alliance" between KLM and Northwest Airlines is clearly demonstrated.

OUR GOAL was simple clarity. We made *Fortune*'s overall type style lighter and its pages more open, with large images where possible.

N

IN ORDER to lighten the look of the magazine, we chose to use the News Gothic family of weights from regular to condensed for headlines and subheads.

T

THE TEXT face is Times New Roman, an eminently readable typeface, which had been used in *Fortune* since our first design in 1983.

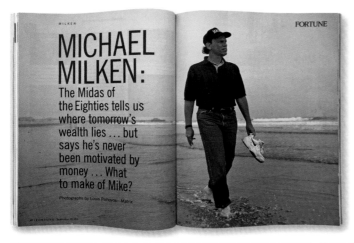

THE FIRST ISSUE: Above left, the cover story's opening spread. Above right, a feature on the control of the internet with humorous caricatures.

MAJOR DEPARTMENTS were reorganized and renamed "First," "Smart Managing," "Digital Watch," and "Personal Fortune." We created more dramatic opening pages and used a half circle to label all the pages in these sections.

How Many Ways Can You Say "500"?

Searching for a new look to announce *Fortune* magazine's celebrated annual issue.

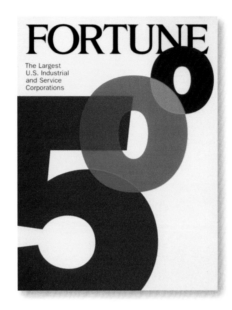

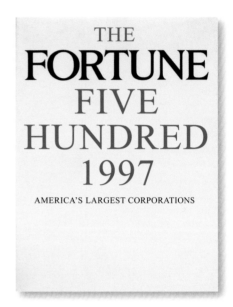

The annual ranking of America's largest corporations called "The Fortune 500" is the magazine's marquee issue and its annual best-seller. (Originally called "Fortune Industrial 500" when it began in 1955, it dropped "industrial" as the new service economy emerged.) After we completed the redesign of *Fortune* in 1996, Managing Editor John Huey asked us to take a crack at a new design for the Fortune 500 cover.

For the 1997 issue, we explored the idea of combining numbers with words in a dramatic new way. After we both made several sketches, we were still unsatisfied with the three best ideas we came up with, above. We tried one with a rather jokey statement, one with only large colorful numbers, and one using only words. Looking at all three mediocre solutions, Milton suggested combining both words and numbers. We finally proposed a white cover with a large red number 5 in the center alongside the word "hundred" in smaller type, with the intent of engaging the reader in figuring out the familiar title. This design was much simpler in concept than many of *Fortune*'s previous "500" issues, but the 1997 issue with this cover became one of the best-selling issues of the magazine. So much so that *Fortune* ran our cover design for ten years in a row.

STUDIES These three unsatisfactory sketches (above) led us to reconsider how to use words and numbers in the selected cover (opposite).

JOHN HUEY started his career as a reporter at *The Atlanta Constitution* before heading to *The Wall Street Journal* and in 1988 to *Fortune.* He was named managing editor of *Fortune* in 1995. In 2001, he was appointed Time Inc.'s editorial director, and he was editor-in-chief of Time Inc. from 2006 until December 2012.
Photo: John Huey

FORTUNE

DISPLAY UNTIL JUNE 9, 1997

1997

5 HUNDRED

Getting in the Game

A new kind of sports journal to challenge *Sports Illustrated.*

John Skipper

John Walsh

Gary Hoenig

John Papanek

THE CREATORS
Senior Vice President and General Manager John Skipper and Executive Editor John Walsh were the business and creative overseers of the project. Executive Editor Gary Hoenig was the editor of the prototype and the person we worked most closely with. John Papanek became the first editor of the magazine.

In 1996, we began working on the prototype of *ESPN Magazine*, the sports channel's new print venture that would complement its popular television broadcast and its new website. Working closely with Gary Hoenig, our editor at *Magazine Week*, we developed a full-scale seventy-four-page prototype in relative secrecy. We proposed an energetic (large bold type), visually driven layout (big images) making use of the oversized format (10" x 12").

Executives at ESPN and its parent company Disney were invested in the idea of a magazine that could rival *Sports Illustrated*. John Walsh, ESPN's executive editor, and John Skipper, the business manager, oversaw the project directly. As with most new publications, *ESPN Magazine*'s future would eventually be determined by focus groups. With great relief, the overall reaction across the country was an unequivocal "YES!" Impressed by the magazine's size, some even suggested that they would pay $12 an issue, which was more than double the price of a *Sports Illustrated* issue then.

Soon after we finished our assignment, we were disappointed to learn that ESPN's management had decided to appoint former *Sports Illustrated* Managing Editor John Papanek as editor-in-chief. Gary had nurtured the project until that point, and we assumed that he would get the position. But Papanek proved to have excellent instincts. Starting with the premier issue in March 1998, he produced striking issues that looked nothing like our prototype. With Darrin Perry as design director, *ESPN Magazine* was the first publication to receive the National Magazine Award for Design in its first year. Gary Hoenig did eventually become editor-in-chief in 2003. The magazine's last print edition was published in September 2019.

JOHN SKIPPER became vice president and general manager of *ESPN the Magazine* in 1997 and president of ESPN in 2012.
Photo by Steve Fenn ESPN

JOHN WALSH previously served as editor of *Inside Sports* and managing editor at *U.S. News & World Report* before becoming managing editor of *SportsCenter* and executive editor of ESPN.
Photo by Rich Arden ESPN

JOHN PAPANEK is a reporter, writer, and editor whose experience at *Sports Illustrated* brought him to ESPN. In 1992, he became Time Inc.'s first director of new media, and later he was editor-in-chief of Time Life Inc., for three years. He was named editor-in-chief of ESPN in 1997.
Photo by Simon Barnett

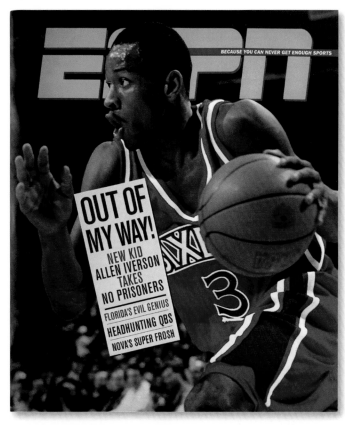

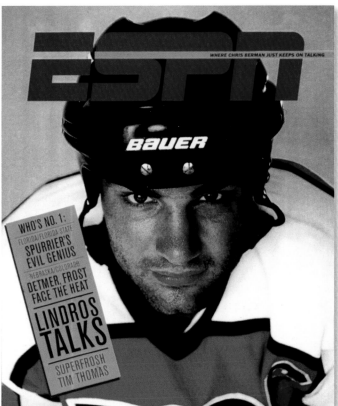

PROTOTYPES We produced four cover designs. They featured cover headlines in posterlike type within the shape of a ticket. That gave us flexibility to move it anywhere on the cover's surface.

OVERTURE

We decided to open the pages of the magazine with six dramatic photographs of recent sports events. We called it our "Overture." The idea was to inform and excite readers about the subject. In this case, the headlines "Snap," "Crackle," and "Pop" showed the fast-paced attitude toward this opening. We were all enthusiastic about the idea and thought it would be ours exclusively, but word somehow leaked to *Sports Illustrated*, and before *ESPN* was published, our "Overture" appeared in the pages of *SI*.

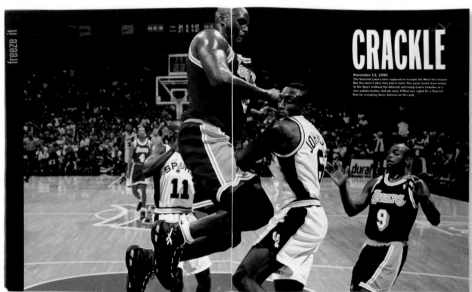

SKIPPER REMEMBERS

"The most important magazines for me growing up were *Rolling Stone* and *Sports Illustrated*. I started at *Rolling Stone* in 1979 as a secretary in the circulation department. For over ten years I cycled through departments and helped to transform *RS* from a biweekly newspaper to a biweekly magazine. That experience inspired me to publish *ESPN* at the same printer and on the same paper as *RS*, a saving for the printer and both publications. We created a hybrid of my two favorite boyhood magazines."

PROTOTYPE PAGES
The table of contents and "Red Zone," the front-of-the-book section (far left). Two examples of the bold feature section (center and bottom) that were typical of the prototype.

HOENIG REMEMBERS
"On a freezing cold night in December 1996, we went to a focus group in Chicago. There was a black construction foreman who emerged as the leader of the group. When he got to a page pitting heavyweight champion Evander Holyfield against Russian President Boris Yeltsin, he started laughing and proceeded to talk it up to the others in the room. That was the moment I knew that the magazine was going to happen. We had found a voice that was right for this audience."

PAPANEK REMEMBERS
"A key decision was that, unlike *SI*, this magazine would almost never look back. It would not be about 'last week' but about 'next week.' Part of this, of course, was forced by the financial choice to publish biweekly. ESPN fully expected that after a year or two the magazine would go weekly, both to capture twice the ad revenue and to more directly challenge *SI*. John Walsh shared that determination. But Skipper and I did not agree. We knew weekly publishing was dying—and we were right."

Redesigning and Redesigning "A Commie-Pinko Rag"

Our oldest and longest client, last but not least.

EVOLUTION
The Nation's logo has gone through many changes since 1865. A large "The" or a small "The," period or no period. The current logo (bottom) tips its hat to the original (top). The most significant improvement came as a result of putting "the" between the *n* and the *t*, making the logo larger and more authoritative.

W e end this book with *The Nation*, a progressive magazine we worked on for over the span of thirty-four years. As America's longest running weekly magazine, *The Nation* has published rousing political commentary and has been in the thick of controversy since 1865. Its views have always been left of center, but calling it a "commie pinko rag" is a stretch. Apparently, Calvin Trillin, the magazine's longtime "deadline poet," had something to do with it:

> A story I used to tell about an interchange I had with a reporter: He said, "For our readers who aren't familiar with *The Nation*, how would you describe it?" And I said, "Pinko. I would say that it's a pinko magazine." And he said, "Surely you have more to say about it than that," and I said, "It's a pinko magazine printed on very cheap paper—the sort of magazine that if you make a Xerox copy of your article the copy is a lot better than the original."

Our work began with a call from editor Victor Navasky. A believer in the efficacy of graphic arts and political cartoons, Victor wanted to give *The Nation* a more distinctive visual identity when he became editor-in-chief in 1978. Back then, the magazine had little money and no art department. We designed a tight, but simple type template that editors could manage without the help of a graphic designer. We restored the period at the end of the logo and created icons for the regular columns by Alexander Cockburn, Katha Pollitt, Christopher Hitchens, and others. Finally, in 1994 we agreed to design the covers for each issue, which we did every week until 2002.

Katrina vanden Heuvel became editor in 1995 and Navasky became publisher. Katrina hired Robert Best, formerly of *New York* magazine, as art director in 2013. As regular readers, we've enjoyed seeing *The Nation* evolve over the years and continue to cheer it on.

VICTOR NAVASKY was editor of *The Nation* (1978-1995) and is now publisher emeritus. Earlier, he was an editor at *The New York Times Magazine*. Navasky cofounded *Monocle*, a satirical magazine, in 1956. He was named chairman of the *Columbia Journalism Review* in 2005. Navasky's book *The Art of Controversy: Political Cartoons and Their Enduring Power*, was published in 2013.
Photo: Victor Navasky

KATRINA VANDEN HEUVEL, publisher of *The Nation*, had also been the editor from 1995 until 2019. She writes a weekly Web column for *The Washington Post* and is the author of several books, including *The Change I Believe In: Fighting for Progress in The Age of Obama*.
Photo by Sigrid Estrada

1978 A simple front-page template for editors to follow.

1994 An updated, all-typographic front-page template, with more color and a bolder emphasis on major stories.

2000 With a larger logo and full color, an example of our weekly art direction of the cover. Illustration by Mirko Ilić

2012 Ten years after we ended our engagement with *The Nation*, the covers had somehow lost their visual clarity and impact. I offered to design a few covers in the hope of getting them back on track.—MG

273

ALEXANDER COCKBURN

A Green Fall

In the first decade of its existence, after its founding in 1971, Greenpeace achieved a political impact and a measure of popular admiration and support that radical political groups can only dream of. The Greenpeace troops struck a chord precisely because they refused to compromise, stated their aims with theatrical flair and saw environmental causes as intimately linked to issues of social justice. This, remember, was a time when Richard Nixon was deftly exploiting the new environmental movement as a way of trying to isolate radical opponents of the war in Vietnam.

Greenpeace's first cause was one that linked the environment with jobs and the cause of peace. It tried to stop U.S. nuclear testing in the Aleutians by sending boats loaded with Greenpeace

newspaper is the vital link between leadership and mass base. But in the early nineties, to save $1 million out of a budget of more than $30 million, the Greenpeace high command shut down its publication, and later issued a pallid successor.

Another foolish decision was to bring in policy wonks like Cliff Curtis, who could just as easily have worked for the Wilderness Society or any other employer of the green bureaucrats in Washington, savoring their micro-brews at Jake's on M Street. It was Curtis who drove Greenpeace first to announce that it had no official position on the killing of marine mammals, and second—even more stupid—to help draft, and lobby for, the "dolphin death bill." This was the legislation (now passed in a somewhat adulterated form) promoted by the Clin-

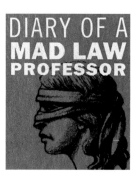

RUBRICS
The number of *Nation* columnists was growing, so we felt it necessary to design permanent recognizable rubrics for each, which were sunk into the text below the title (above and left).

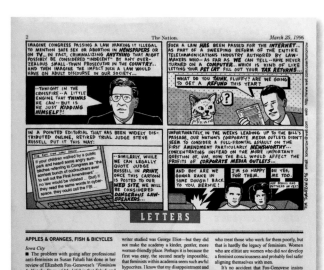

POLITICAL CARTOONS
In 1996 we instituted a regular weekly cartoon on page 2, including many by Tom Tomorrow (far left). Major contributors like Robert Grossman (left) often submitted full-page cartoons as well.

COVER STORIES
(opposite), which had not been visually different from other articles, were given full-page illustrated openings at the beginning of the feature section in 1996.

Illustration by Milton Glaser

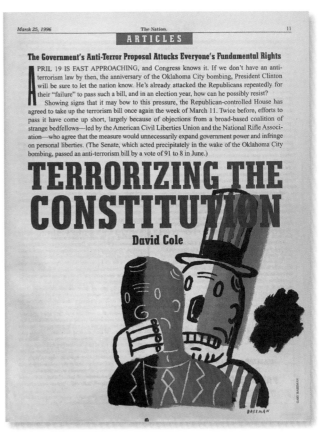

Illustration by Gary Baseman

Illustration by Peter Kuper

Illustration by Mirko Ilić

Design by WBMG

Illustration by Milton Glaser

Illustration by Milton Glaser

Design by WBMG

Design by WBMG

Photograph by Louie Psihoyos/Matrix

BUTTONS
I designed this series of buttons for *The Nation* during the George W. Bush administration in 2003. As someone involved in communications, I often find myself confused about whether I am an agent of propaganda. These buttons of dissent are the most obvious examples of my own interest in persuasion as well as left-wing convictions.—MG

Design by WBMG

Photograph by Matthew Klein

Photograph by Matthew Klein

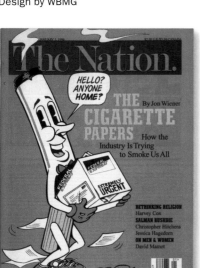

Illustration by Gary Trudeau

Illustration by Ed Sorel

Illustration by Steve Brodner

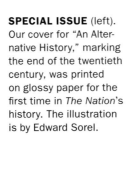

SPECIAL ISSUE (left). Our cover for "An Alternative History," marking the end of the twentieth century, was printed on glossy paper for the first time in *The Nation*'s history. The illustration is by Edward Sorel.

COVERS This selection of covers, including the two on the next pages, represents a small sample of those we designed for *The Nation* throughout the 1990s until 2002.

The Nation.

MARCH 17, 1997

$2.50 U.S./$3.50 CANADA

Mark Crispin Miller

Tom Engelhardt

Celia McGee

David Sarasohn

Todd Gitlin

Janine Jaquet

THE CRUSHING POWER OF BIG PUBLISHING

THE NATIONAL ENTERTAINMENT STATE II

Photograph by Matthew Klein

278

DECEMBER 2, 1996

$2.50 U.S./$3.50 CANADA

The Nation.

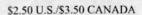

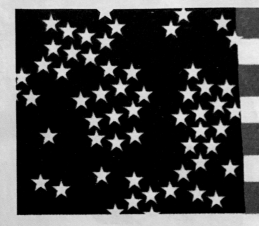

WHERE DO WE GO FROM HERE?

What the Center Doesn't Hold

By Robert L. Borosage and Jeff Faux

47720

Illustration by Mirko Ilić

279

Walter and Milton, 2019.
Photo by Leo Sorel

Magazines we've designed, redesigned, or consulted for:

Adam	Lire
Ad Day	Magazine Week
Adweek	Manhattan Inc.
Alma	Media Week
American Ceramics	Modern Maturity
American Lawyer	Money
The Atlantic	More
Artisinal	Ms.
Audience	Next
Autoweek	The Nation
Business Tokyo	Now
Book World	Newsweek
Biography	New West
Brill's Content	New York
Channels	New York Film Review
Cooking Light	Paris Match
Crain's Business Chicago	PC magazine
ESPN The Magazine	People
Écrivain	Plum
Endless Vacation	Psychology Today
East	Quality
Esquire	Revista Da TV
Events USA	Rio Show
Family Circle	Scandinavian Review
Fortune 1982	Selling
Fortune 1996	Soap Opera Digest
Forbes India	Smart Money
Globe.	The Sophisticated Traveler
Golf Digest	Sunset
Human	Swing
Inspired	Smash
i.e.	Time
India Today	Time Special Issue: Immigration
Inside Sports	Time Special Issue: Asia
Insurance Review	Time Special Issue: Europe
Investment Collector	Time Special Issue: Cyberspace
Jardin des Modes	Today's Homeowner
Journal of Art	U&lc
Knit it!	U.S. News & World Report
Lavanguardia Magazine	USA Weekend
L'Espresso	Var Business
L'Europeo	Windows
L'Expansion	WirtschaftsWoche
L'Express	The Wall Street Journal magazine
L'Express Paris	The Washington Post Magazine
L'Express Science	Wine Spectator
L'Express Style	Winners
L'Express Sports	The Wire
L'Express Votre Argent	Your Company

On May 2, 2013, we received The American Society of Magazine Editors Creative Excellence Award. We were introduced by Michael Kramer (center) our former colleague at *New York* magazine and former chief political correspondent at *Time* magazine.

Photo: Albert Chau/ASME

Acknowledgments

Magazines are a collaborative effort, and so is this book. Our former colleagues generously responded to our many requests, supplying anecdotes and pictures, jogging our memories, and correcting our recollections.

This book exists in large part because of Victor Navasky, who immediately saw its potential and endorsed it to Columbia University Press. Philip Leventhal, senior editor at CUP, guided us from the proposal process to the final edit. Amanda "Binky" Urban, a friend and colleague at *New York* magazine, lent her talents as our unofficial agent, adviser, and advocate.

Steve Heller, Hugo Lindgren, Michael Kramer, and Dan Okrent have contributed their editorial expertise as they looked at every page, offering their suggestions and critiques. Chris Bonanos, city editor of *New York* magazine, graciously supplied us with archival issues and valued information.

Special thanks to Gloria Steinem, who loves magazines, for her thoughts in the foreword.

Most of the black-and-white photographs in the first section were taken by Cosmos Sarchiapone. A studio assistant at Push Pin, Cosmos gave himself the responsibility of documenting the process of making *New York* magazine. We are grateful to his archive for making these photographs available to us.

Our staff for this book worked beautifully as a team—contributing ideas, tracking down old collaborators, and turning up unexpected, useful information. Thanks to Anne Quito, writer and editor; Natalia Olbinski and Fausta Kingué, designers; Bina Bernard, "In the News" editor; Tina Buckman, picture researcher; and Richard J. Litell, contributing editor. They made the whole endeavor a pleasurable experience.

Index

We had fun indeed.

New York magazine, 1974
From left: Byron Dobell (editorial director), Walter Bernard, Milton Glaser; and in foreground,
Jane Maxwell (assistant to the editor). Photo by Cosmos Sarchiapone